AMERICAN SLAVE REVOLTS AND CONSPIRACIES

AMERICAN SLAVE REVOLTS AND CONSPIRACIES

A REFERENCE GUIDE

Kerry Walters

 ABC-CLIO™

An Imprint of ABC-CLIO, LLC
Santa Barbara, California • Denver, Colorado

Library of Congress Cataloging-in-Publication Data

Walters, Kerry S.
   American slave revolts and conspiracies : a reference guide / Kerry Walters.
      pages cm
   Includes bibliographical references and index.
   ISBN 978–1–61069–659–3 (hbk : alk. paper) — ISBN 978–1–61069–660–9 (ebook)
1. Slave insurrections—United States—History—Encyclopedias. 2. Slavery—United States—History—Encyclopedias. 3. Slaves—United States—Social conditions—Encyclopedias. 4. Government, Resistance to—United States—History—Encyclopedias. 5. Conspiracies—United States—History—18th century—Encyclopedias. 6. Conspiracies—United States—History—19th century—Encyclopedias. 7. Abolitionists—United States—Biography. 8. African Americans—History—To 1863—Encyclopedias. I. Title.
E447.W37   2015
306.3′620973—dc23   2015019658

ISBN: 978–1–61069–659–3
EISBN: 978–1–61069–660–9

19 18 17 16 15   1 2 3 4 5

This book is also available on the World Wide Web as an eBook.
Visit www.abc-clio.com for details.

ABC-CLIO
An Imprint of ABC-CLIO, LLC

ABC-CLIO, LLC
130 Cremona Drive, P.O. Box 1911
Santa Barbara, California 93116-1911

This book is printed on acid-free paper ∞

Manufactured in the United States of America

CONTENTS

AUTHOR'S NOTE

M ost slaves were generally called by their given names—if they had surnames, it was their masters'—and I have often followed that convention in this book.

We know very few details about most of the slaves who either led or participated in revolts and conspiracies to revolt. What biographical material we have about them has been described in each chapter. Consequently, the "Biographies" section of this book focuses mainly but not exclusively on white authorities who responded to slave revolts and conspiracies.

CHRONOLOGY OF EVENTS

(Revolts and conspiracies in *italics* are discussed in the text)

1619   The first 20 black slaves in the British North American colonies arrive in Jamestown.

1663   Revolt in Gloucester, Virginia, by indentured white servants and a few black slaves.

1680   Virginia Assembly passes legislature to curtail unauthorized travel of slaves.

1687   *The first all-black slave rebellion conspiracy in Westmoreland County, Virginia.*

1739   *Slaves, at least some of them captured African warriors, lead a revolt that originates near the Stono River Bridge, just a few miles from Charles Town (Charleston), South Carolina.*

1741   *Arsons and alleged slave conspiracy hit New York City during one of the coldest winters on record.*

1791   A revolt of slaves in Saint Dominique (Haiti) erupts. Over the next decade, French colonial army will be defeated and the island, led by Toussaint L'Ouverture, will become a free republic.

1800   *Gabriel Prosser, influenced by Enlightenment ideals of liberty, fraternity, and equality, conspires to seize Richmond, Virginia.*

1808   The international slave trade is outlawed in the United States.

1811	*The German Coast rebellion, probably the largest in sheer numbers in the history of North American slavery.*
1816	*Negro Fort is destroyed by U.S. forces.*
1822	*Denmark Vesey, an ex-slave, plans a revolt in Charleston, South Carolina.*
1829	David Walker, a black man, publishes his *Appeal to the Colored Citizens of the World*, encouraging slaves to revolt.
1831	The first issue of William Lloyd Garrison's antislavery *The Liberator* is published.
	Nat Turner's rebellion erupts in Southampton County, Virginia.
	The New England Anti-Slavery Society is founded.
1833	The American Anti-Slavery Society is founded.
1837	*Slaves in Cheneyville, Louisiana, conspire to flee, but are betrayed by their ringleader.*
1839	Slave rebels capture the slave ship *Amistad*, leading to a legal battle that ends in the U.S. Supreme Court ordering them freed and returned to Africa.
1841	*Domestic slaves in route from Virginia to New Orleans capture the ship* Creole *and sail to the British Bahamas, where they are freed. This is the only unequivocally successful slave rebellion in the history of U.S. slavery.*
1850–1860	The Underground Railroad, a network of abolitionists north of the Mason-Dixon Line who help runaways from the South, flourishes.
1859	John Brown, inspired in part by the 1831 Nat Turner rebellion, tries to launch a slave insurrection by unsuccessfully attacking Harpers Ferry, Virginia.
1861	*Slaves at Second Creek, Mississippi, heartened by the outbreak of the Civil War, conspire to revolt.*
1863	The Emancipation Proclamation frees all slaves in the rebellious states.

1864   The U.S. Congress repeals slave laws.

1865   Thirteenth Amendment abolishes slavery.

1870   The Fifteenth Amendment grants voting privileges to black men.

PANIC IN WESTMORELAND COUNTY

[A] Negro Plott, formed in the Northern Neck for the Distroying and
killing his Maj[esty's] Subjects

—Virginia Council[1]

C aptain John Smith, of Pocahontas fame, was the first European to
see the Northern Neck, the uppermost peninsula of the future
colony of Virginia. That was in 1607. Within 50 years, the Neck
had been divided into three counties, and the area was home to several
tobacco plantations worked by both indentured white servants and black
slaves. Although prosperous, the Northern Neck was relatively isolated
from the other counties in colonial Virginia, separated from them as it
was by the Rappahannock River.

Partly because of their isolation, white planters in Westmoreland
County were fearful of discontent among their many slaves. Anxiety about
the possibility of slave insurrections was not unique to them. In 1680, Virginia's General Assembly passed an act intended to prevent uprisings by severely
limiting the movement of black slaves. The bill forbade slaves from leaving
their master's property without a note of permission, but also from arming
themselves with any kind of weapon ranging from clubs to guns, and from
assaulting "Christians." It warned Virginians that slave burials and weddings
were likely occasions for plotting insurrection, but stopped short of forbidding
them. The fear of unsupervised numbers of slaves gathering together continued to haunt whites, however, because two years later the Assembly passed a
law forbidding slaves from gathering more than four hours on property
belonging to men other than their masters.

Despite these new restrictions, the nightmare that Great Neck white planters and their families dreaded came to pass in Westmoreland County in 1687: a conspiracy on the part of black slaves to revolt. It was the first recorded all-black attempt in British North America to throw off servitude.[2] We know little about the Westmoreland plot, because transcripts of the trials of the accused slaves apparently were not recorded. But from reports made to the Virginia Governor's Council, we can piece together a general idea of what happened.

On October 24, Nicholas Spencer, who first landed in Virginia from England a quarter century earlier, reported to Governor Francis Howard that he had uncovered a slave conspiracy. Slaves, claimed Spencer, had planned to "destroy and kill" His Majesty's subjects in Virginia. But by "God's Providence," their plot had been discovered and "their whole Evill purposes for the present defeated."[3] Spencer further reported that he had taken several of the conspirators into custody and that he was holding them until they could be tried. He urged quick action in order to secure the safety of the colony and reassure frightened whites who had gotten wind of the failed uprising.

Governor Howard and his Council agreed, and a panel of three Westmoreland planters, including Spencer, was quickly appointed to hear the evidence against the captives and to determine their fate. The three men constituted an oyer and terminer court, a special tribunal put together in emergency situations. In subsequent decades, the appointment of such ad hoc courts would become the most common method of trying slaves accused of conspiracy or insurrection. Westmoreland County's may have been the first in Virginia.

We do not know how many slaves were found guilty and executed; we do not even know if any were hanged at all. But given the Council's instructions to the three members of the tribunal, it is reasonable to suspect that at least some of the alleged conspirators went to the gallows. They were instructed "to proceed to Sentence of Condemnacon & Execucon, or to Such other punishments as according to Law they shall be found Guilty off, by such examples of Justice to deterr other Negroes from plotting or Contriveing either the Death wrongs or Injuries of any of this Majesties Subjects."[4]

The Council also took Great Neck planters to task for allowing their slaves too much liberty when it came to gathering together or traveling throughout the three counties. Congregating at burials was especially singled out, as it had been in the 1680 act, as providing key opportunities for slaves to plot. Consequently, the Council sternly reminded Westmoreland planters that they were bound by law to control their slaves, and issued an order "to require and Comand all Masters of families having any Negro Slaves, not to permitt them to hold or make any Solemnity or Funeralls for any deced Negros."[5]

Six months later, a slave named Sam who belonged to Westmoreland planter Richard Metcalfe was tried before another oyer and terminer court and found guilty of conspiring to insurrect. It is not clear if Sam had been implicated in the earlier plot, or if he had embarked on a new one. At any rate, he and several of his comrades were each given 29 lashes, and Sam was also condemned to wear a heavy iron collar for the rest of his life. Should he attempt to remove it, or to leave the confines of his master's plantation, he would forfeit his life.

Neither of these two events escaped the notice of Virginia's General Assembly. Two years after Sam's punishment, a bill was enacted that required the 1680 act to be publicly read every half-year. In the Assembly's next session, a law was passed that gave sheriffs the authority to kill any slave suspected of being a runaway or a conspirator of insurrection, the slave's owner to be compensated in tobacco. For good measure, the bill also prohibited mixed-race marriages.

Nicholas Spencer, the man who first raised the alarm about the Westmoreland uprising, died in 1688, one year after the conspirators were tried. One suspects that he went to his grave satisfied that the likelihood of slave insurrections had been effectively nipped in the bud by the vigilance shown by the Governor's Council, the General Assembly, and himself. Could he have known the future of both Virginia and the rest of the South, he would have died with an uneasy mind. The Westmoreland slave conspiracy was just the first of scores of slave plots and insurrections that would terrify the South until the Civil War finally ended human bondage.

NOTES

1. H. R. McIlwaine (ed.), *Executive Journals of the Council of Colonial Virginia* (Richmond: The Virginia State Library, 1925), 1:86.

2. There had been two earlier revolts in Virginia that, while mostly planned by white indentured servants and tradesmen, may have involved a few black slaves. The first was in Gloucester in 1663 and the second was the better known Bacon's Rebellion of 1676.

3. Ibid.

4. Ibid.

5. Ibid., 1:87.

CHAPTER 1

STATE OF SIEGE

You have seen, it is to be feared, but the beginning of sorrows.
All the blood which has been shed will be required at your hands.
—William Lloyd Garrison[1]

Abolitionist William Lloyd Garrison, who edited the antislavery newspaper *The Liberator* for over three decades, wrote a column in the early fall of 1831 that perfectly expressed the collective anxiety of Southern slaveholders. The occasion for the piece was the Nat Turner revolt in Southampton, Virginia, a bloody spree that had taken place the month before, during which slaves butchered nearly 60 white men, women, and children, sending shock waves of terror throughout the entire South.

Garrison, who had launched his newspaper with the promise that his antislavery message "would be heard!," told his readers that the Turner rebellion was anything but an isolated event. The South was guilty of the unforgivable crime of slavery—as was, in fact, the whole nation for its tolerance of the "peculiar institution"—a crime that would eventually bring about a "war of extermination" between whites and blacks. Then, warned Garrison, the innocent African bloodshed throughout decades of slavery would be "required" from whites.[2]

In writing this, Garrison touched the country's raw nerve, because from the very first years of slavery until the end of the Civil War, slaveholders in both North and South were haunted by the prospect of slave insurrections. One twentieth-century historian estimates that North American slaves either overtly insurrected or conspired to rebel about 250 times until slavery was finally abolished.[3] The first slaves were brought to the colony of Virginia in 1619, and the Thirteenth Amendment legally ended slavery in 1865. That means that there was, on average, at least one insurrection or conspiracy per year during that time span. In fact, because whites were often wary about publicizing slave discontent, it is likely that there were more than 250 efforts to throw off servitude.

William Lloyd Garrison, founder and editor of *The Liberator*, the best-known abolitionist newspaper in the antebellum years, warned that slavery inevitably led to bloody revolt. (National Archives)

The strain the fear of revolt put on whites was palpable. All slaveholding communities endured, as one commentator puts it, the "psychic weathering" induced by their fear of slave insurrection.[4] This anxiety, recorded over and over again in private correspondence, diaries and journals, colonial and state legislation, and newspapers, was never totally absent. It is not too much to say that wherever black slaves were kept in North America, white residents felt, either acutely or subconsciously, as if they lived in a state of siege. In a curious way, the white slave owner was held hostage by the very system of bondage from which he or she also benefited.

This book examines 10 of the most significant slave rebellions and conspiracies. They are, in chronological order, the 1739 Stono revolt, the 1741 New York conspiracy, the 1800 Gabriel Prosser conspiracy, the 1811 German Coast revolt, the 1816 Negro Fort resistance, the 1822

This 1899 cartoon from *Life* magazine entitled "The White Man's Burden" attests to the fact that the American, English, and German Empires were built largely on slave labor. (Library of Congress)

Denmark Vesey conspiracy, Nat Turner's 1831 revolt, the 1837 Cheneyville conspiracy, the 1841 *Creole* revolt, and the 1861 conspiracy at Second Creek. Although scholars sometimes draw distinctions between "revolts," "rebellions," "uprisings," and "insurrections," throughout this book I use the words interchangeably.[5]

TWO MODES OF RESISTANCE

For decades after the American Civil War, historians of America's slavery years tended to portray black slaves as essentially passive and docile. One of the most influential defenders of this point of view was Ulrich B. Phillips, who in his 1918 book *American Negro Slavery* described slaves as slow-witted children who would have been helpless without the paternalistic care of the white people who owned them. Needless, perhaps, to say, Phillips's thesis was based almost exclusively on the points of view, mined from diaries and letters, of plantation owners and their families.[6]

We now know, however, that the picture Phillips painted is mythical. Slaves resisted their bondage and asserted freedom throughout the entire unhappy history of slavery in North America. Sometimes their resistance took the form of flight and at other times of rebellion or conspiracies to rebel. Most often, it was expressed in acts of everyday sabotage. There is no doubt that the institution of slavery intended to and often succeeded in breaking the spirits of people in bondage so as to ensure their obedience. But external obedience does not necessarily equate to interior docility. As abolitionist Frederick Douglass once wrote, many and perhaps most slaves were docile in form but not in fact.[7]

Slaves who resisted their bondage through flight typically headed South if they were located in the Deep South colonies or states, or North, if they happened to belong to masters in border states such as Virginia, Delaware, or Maryland. In the eighteenth century, Deep South slaves made for Spanish-held Florida, lured there by the promise of freedom; in the next century, after Florida had become a part of the United States, Deep South slaves, realizing that making it to free northern states was well-nigh impossible, often headed for the Mexican border. The Underground Railroad, a covert system of safe routes and houses north of the Mason-Dixon Line that assisted runaways, shepherded hundreds of slaves to freedom in the three decades leading up to the Civil War.[8]

Even though the Underground Railroad could offer fugitives assistance once they entered free states, it was still up to individually fleeing slaves to take the initiative and to plan, as best they could, their flight. They had to determine the best opportunities for flight, often on Sundays or holidays such as Christmas; surreptitiously store provisions to take with them; live off the land during their run for freedom; avoid slave patrols on the lookout for fugitive slaves; and somehow guide themselves, often with only the aid of stars, northward. It was an arduous undertaking, and many runaways were either captured in their bid for freedom or, weary and defeated, returned to their masters of their own accord.

The most frequent form of slave resistance occurred day-to-day by slaves who remained on their farms and plantations but found ways to undermine their masters' fortunes and improve their own. Most of the time, the subversion practiced by slaves was covert. Occasionally, however, it exploded

Slave revolts or conspiracies to revolt were relatively rare. More common was flight on the Underground Railroad, as depicted in this 1872 engraving from *The Underground Railroad* by William Still. (Library of Congress)

in obvious disobedience and even physical confrontation. Frederick Douglass recounts in his autobiography a fistfight with a white man, and Gabriel Prosser, mastermind of an 1800 plot for slaves to seize Richmond, likewise fought with and (like Douglass) bested a white man.

Probably the most common kind of daily resistance was telling the masters what they wanted to hear while secretly disobeying, defying, or subverting their orders. Partly out of hubris, but largely because their slaves were good at hiding their true feelings, slave owners frequently found it difficult to believe that their "servants" were disloyal. They distrusted black slaves in general, often thinking of them as either children or savages, but were confident that their own slaves were devoted to them.

Thievery was another way that slaves resisted their bondage. They stole time from their masters by work slowdowns and goldbricking, deliberately damaging tools in order to sabotage harvesting, or simply absconding for a few days of freedom in nearby woods or swamps. Theft of physical items, especially chickens or hogs to supplement their diets, was also common, so much so that most masters were willing to ignore such thefts so long as they did not become too frequent or costly.

Slave owners unwittingly encouraged slave resistance through the practice of hiring their slaves out. Field hands were sometimes "rented" to other white planters, but more often slaves skilled in a craft or trade were hired out to white craftsmen in cities. Sometimes the entire wages paid to the hired-out slaves were handed over to his or her master, but more often slaves were allowed to keep a tiny percentage of the income they earned. This practice actually subverted the institution of slavery because it gave slaves a taste of freedom they otherwise were not likely to get. It also put them in contact with both free blacks who lived in cities and, occasionally, white laborers and craftsmen who disapproved of the institution of slavery. At least one rebel conspirator, Gabriel Prosser, became radicalized through the practice of hiring-out.

THE WORST NIGHTMARE

Whites could tolerate a certain amount of work stoppage and thievery from their slaves as unavoidable consequences of the slave system. Masters took slave flight more seriously, however, first because it constituted a loss of property more valuable than a chicken or hog—any slave who stole himself or herself crossed the boundary of acceptable thievery—but also because they feared that reports of a successful flight on the part of one slave would encourage similar runs by others.

But the form of resistance that was completely unacceptable, and which struck terror into the hearts of whites throughout both North and South during the colonial era and the South in the early republic and antebellum years, was revolt. Lurid visions of muscular blacks slaughtering entire households and sexually assaulting white women haunted slave owners. Mary Boykin Chesnut, the Southern blueblood whose private journal sheds much light on daily life in the slaveholding states, voiced this nightmare. She had just seen a stage play about the great Indian Rebellion of 1857, when native soldiers, or *sepoys*, had revolted against their British colonial masters. Chesnut wrote that "a thrill of terror ran through me as those yellow and black brutes came jumping over the parapets! Their faces were like so many of the same sort at home"—meaning, her own slaves. "How long," she anxiously wondered, "would they resist the seductive and irresistible call, 'only rise, kill, and be free?' "[9]

Just as slaveholders trusted the loyalty of their own slaves and feared the treachery of ones owned by others, they likewise held incompatible views when it came to the possibility of slave insurrections. On the one hand, they tended to assume that slaves were unpredictable savages who at any moment were capable of furious mayhem. On the other hand, however, they also believed that slaves were intellectually incapable of planning elaborate plots to rise up against their masters. Consequently, when confronted with a discovered conspiracy to insurrect, much less an actual rebellion, slave owners often insisted that the slaves must have been working under the direction of, or at least in cooperation with, whites. Foreigners were often suspected of encouraging slaves to revolt; in the colonial era, the Spanish were the primary culprits, and later, after the birth of the republic, the French were frequently blamed. But domestic whites were also suspected, particularly once the abolitionist movement began in the North. So slave owners frequently found themselves fearing two enemies, one within (slaves) and one without (whites, either foreign or domestic).

But why Spain and France specifically? In the eighteenth century, Spain was viewed as a fomenter of discontent among black slaves because of its rivalry with the North American British colonies. During the colonial era, Florida belonged to Spain, and it became a policy for Spain to offer freedom to slaves held in the British colony of South Carolina who could make it to Florida. The obvious motivation for this policy was to undermine Great Britain's toehold in North America, a fact that was not lost on Deep South British colonists. The slaveholding Northern colonies, such as New York, likewise feared Spain because of the intermittent wars between England and Spain. The worry was that Spanish agents would infiltrate New York and, working as a fifth column, incite slaves to riot and revolt, thus diverting England's military attention from Spain.

The fear of France was twofold. The first worry was that the French Revolution's enthusiastic espousal of liberty, fraternity, and equality would come to be known to slaves in the United States, who would be inspired to insurrection. There is an inescapable irony here, since the United States' own founding documents promoted precisely the same human rights. But this worry on the part of slave owners was especially overwrought. Only one slave conspiracy, the one led by Gabriel Prosser in 1800, seems to have been obviously influenced by Enlightenment-based natural rights rhetoric.

The other reason that American slaveholders worried about the influence of France was the successful revolution in the 1790s on the island of Saint Dominique. This was a more realistic threat. A slave rebellion that exploded there in 1791, led by Toussaint L'Ouverture and inspired by the ideals of the French Revolution, within the space of two years wrested most of the island from French colonial control. Many American slaves, especially those located in coastal towns and plantations, soon heard the extraordinary news, conveyed by sailors and other travelers or picked up in whispered conversation among their white masters, that black slaves had succeeded in throwing off their shackles and establishing a black republic. Unlike their slaves, who were thrilled by what they had heard, white slaveholders were so disturbed by the news that many slave states outlawed the importation of black men and women who at one time or another had labored in Saint Dominque.

Southern slave owners came to believe that yet another enemy from without encouraged slave rebellion: Northern abolitionists. After the 1831 Nat Turner revolt, for example, Virginia governor John Floyd insisted that the "spirit of insubordination" that inspired the uprising "had its origin among, and emanated from, the Yankee population." According to Floyd, abolitionist-minded "Yankee peddlers and traders" taught black slaves false religious doctrines—namely, that slavery was an abomination in the eyes of God—and then encouraged them to learn to read. But literate slaves were dangerous, because it was well-nigh impossible to keep them from seditious literature such as Garrison's *The Liberator* or David Walker's *Appeal to the Colored Citizens of the World* (1829).[10] Walker's book was especially threatening. Its author, a black man who was the son of a slave father and a free mother, frankly threatened slave insurrection.

> Remember, [white] Americans, that we must and shall be free and enlightened as you are. Will you wait until we shall, under God, obtain our liberty by the crushing arm of power? Will it not be dreadful for you? I speak Americans for your own good. We must and shall be free I say, in spite of you ... And woe, woe, will be to you if we have to obtain our freedom by fighting.[11]

It is unclear just how much influence Yankee abolitionists such as Garrison and Walker exerted on slaves who plotted rebellion. A much more immediate inspiration was supplied by religion, most often Christianity. In earlier rebellions, like the one in 1739 in Stono, South Carolina, a mixture of African tribal religions also inspired slaves. But in each revolt or conspiracy, a burning desire for freedom from servitude was the ultimate motive.

MEANS AND OUTCOMES

Most documented cases of slave insurrections or conspiracies reveal that the leaders were charismatic men who stood out by virtue of military prowess, religious fervor, independence of spirit, or literacy. The chief of the Stono rebellion, an African named Cato, most likely had been a Konga warrior skilled in the art of war before being sold into slavery. Likewise, the defenders of Negro Fort in 1816 were maroon and Native American warriors who had been trained in the use of musketry and artillery by the British during the War of 1812.

Other slave leaders were either animated by a belief that they were personally called by God to liberate their fellow slaves—Nat Turner is the prime example here—or used religion as a way of recruiting fellow conspirators, as Denmark Vesey did in his plans to conquer Charleston, South Carolina, in 1822. By contrast, some slave rebellions appear to have been motivated by little more than rage and the desire for freedom. The 1811 German Coast uprising and the 1861 Second Creek conspiracy fall into this category.

Some of the leaders were literate—Gabriel Prosser, Denmark Vesey, and Nat Turner, for example—but others, like the conspirators in New York City in 1741 or at Second Creek in 1861, were without lettered learning of any kind. Moreover, even though one slave woman was hanged in the aftermath of Nat Turner's 1831 rebellion, one woman was suspected in Gabriel Prosser conspiracy, and several white women were implicated in the 1741 New York conspiracy, the information we have about slave revolts in the American colonies and states suggests that the participants, and certainly the leaders, were overwhelmingly male.

In most of the conspiracies and plots to rise up, the participants tended to be field hands that had been recruited by leaders who were skilled workers—Prosser, for example, was a blacksmith, Vesey a skilled carpenter (he also had the distinction of being the only free black man to plan a slave revolt), and the putative leaders of the Second Creek conspiracy

were carriage drivers. Domestic or house slaves were approached by conspirators cautiously, the assumption being that slaves who worked closely
with their white masters were more emotionally tied to them than field
hands, and consequently untrustworthy. That suspicion was tragically veri-
fied in several cases; domestic slaves informed authorities about at least two
of the conspiracies explored in this book.

One obvious weakness that hampered any plan to insurrect was the lack
of firearms on the part of the conspirators. Consequently, slaves typically
fashioned makeshift weapons from farm tools. In Gabriel Prosser's plan to
take Richmond, for example, conspirators crafted pikes from mowing
scythes. Other slaves in other conspiracies intended to use rakes, clubs,
axes, and knives in their bids for freedom, hoping to pick up firearms along
the way from the whites they subdued or killed.

Some revolts and conspiracies to revolt were elaborately planned, with
Gabriel Prosser's and Denmark Vesey's being two shining examples. Both
men plotted to divide their forces into three assault waves, to create diver-
sions that would distract the white militia, and to storm arsenals and seize
weapons. But other slave revolts were spontaneous; possibly the Stono
rebellion falls into this category, and certainly the mutiny on the *Creole*
does. Some were so loosely planned by participants—the New York conspiracy, the German Coast rebellion, Nat Turner's revolt, and the Second
Creek conspiracy—as to have no sense of purpose other than fleeing bondage and were only a piecemeal, ad hoc strategy.

The numerous conspiracies and revolts that took place in the colonies and
states attest to the yearning for freedom that animated slaves. Unfortunately,
the nobility of the yearning was not generally rewarded with success. Slaves
in North America were hopelessly out-weaponed, even if, in many parts of
the South, they enjoyed numerical superiority over whites. The 1790s slave
rebellion in Saint Dominique had succeeded in large part because the French
garrison there was tiny in proportion to the island's blacks and because dis-
ease killed off so many of the Europeans that Napoleon gave up retention
of the island as a lost cause. But in North America, ill-fed, overworked, and
underarmed slaves had little hope of pulling off a similar kind of coup.

Consequently, there is only one unqualifiedly successful revolt in the
history of North American slavery: the mutiny aboard the *Creole* in
1841, in which domestic slaves being transported from Virginia to New
Orleans took over the ship and sailed it to the British Bahamas, where they

knew they would be freed and offered asylum.[12] Because records of nearly all slave rebellions and conspiracies are both sketchy and written from the white masters' perspective, it is difficult to know if any individual slaves who participated in a rebellion managed to flee to freedom in the chaotic aftermath of defeat. Some may well have, but they would have been but a tiny minority.

TRIALS AND EXECUTIONS

Conspiracy to revolt, not to mention actual rebellions, on the part of slaves, was a capital offense in every slave-owning colony and state in North America. In most cases, slaves were judged by extralegal tribunals, usually staffed by planters and local businessmen who were likely to own slaves themselves. Although typically the testimony of a slave was impermissible if a white person was on trial, testimony from slaves against other slaves was welcomed in these tribunals as a way of discovering just how far reaching the conspiracy was. Slaves were sometimes offered rewards for informing against their fellows, as in the trials of the Cheneyville conspirators, and sometimes testimony was beaten out of them, as in the Second Creek hearings. Often slave defendants were forbidden legal representation, although sometimes, as in Denmark Vesey's case, they were allowed to question other witnesses.

But just as often as slave rebels were hauled before an extralegal tribunal, they were hunted down by militias and ad hoc posses and executed on the spot, sometimes after being tortured. The leader of the Stono revolt, for example, was maimed before being burned to death. The general mode of legal execution was hanging, but occasionally condemned slaves were shot, beheaded, or even publicly burned. Moreover, in the wake of actual revolts and, to a lesser extent, conspiracies, white militia made little distinction between slaves implicated in plots and innocent ones, and killed indiscriminately. In at least two cases, the German Coast revolt of 1811 and the Cheneyville conspiracy of 1837, white citizens actually asked federal troops to step in to stop the killing—not out of concern for slaves, but out of alarm that valuable human property was being needlessly destroyed by overzealous judges and militiamen. President Thomas Jefferson advised Virginia governor James Monroe to call a halt to the many executions that followed the discovery of Gabriel Prosser's conspiracy, lest the state gain a bad reputation. Colonies and states generally compensated owners for any of their slaves executed or summarily killed, but the compensations were often below market price.

One especially grisly practice often resorted to in the aftermath of revolts was the public display of the heads, and sometimes mutilated bodies, of executed slaves. There is something about beheading that strikes a deep chord of horror and repugnance in the Western mind, and whites relied upon that shock value when they stuck the severed heads of executed slaves on pikes and fence posts. The primary purpose, of course, was to terrify slaves and thus disincline them to contemplate revolt. But the grisly displays also served as visual reassurances to frightened white citizens that rebellious slaves would receive swift and terrible retribution.

AFTERMATHS

Every slaveholding colony and state had "black" laws separate from the codes of justice reserved for white men and women. Intended to ensure that slaves and even freedmen remained subordinate, these laws generally mandated stiff penalties for black misbehavior or crime. Typical provisions included the prohibition of slaves testifying against whites, capital punishment for any number of offenses ranging from striking a master to murder, and restrictions on mobility.

Severe as the black laws already were, each slave revolt or discovered conspiracy tightened them even further. White legislators, panicked by the prospect of slave mayhem, quickly enacted harsher codes that forbade slaves to read or write, to attend church services unless whites were present, to congregate in unsupervised groups larger than three, and so on. After Gabriel Prosser's unsuccessful bid to take Richmond in 1800, several Virginia legislators unsuccessfully tried to outlaw the practice of hiring-out, which they asserted radicalized slaves. Following Nat Turner's bloody 1831 revolt, at least one Virginian publicly uttered the unspeakable: that perhaps Virginia would be better served by freeing all slaves and exporting them instead of keeping them and continuously risking insurrection. But the suggestion came to naught.

Also following Nat Turner's insurrection, according to historian Winthrop Jordan, a new public relations campaign emerged on the part of Southern spokesmen. In previous years, the overall Southern position on slavery had been that it was a necessary evil. Without human bondage, the agricultural South could not have survived. But after 1831, Southerners "began to trumpet the benevolence of slavery and the contentedness of slaves."[13] There were two reasons for this public change of heart. The first was the need to respond to Northern abolitionists who morally condemned slave owners. But the second was to convince themselves that slave rebellions were not the product of slave discontent, but rather of outside agitators inspired by "northern fanaticism." More than one slaveholder must have known that this was a patent falsehood. But the psychic weathering induced by chronic anxiety cried out for relief, and self-deception offered at least some.

The fantastic belief that slaves were contented, born from the strain of living with the fear of slave uprising, was one paradox of the slaveholding South. Another paradox was the South's attitude toward publicizing slave rebellions and conspiracies to revolt. On the one hand, advertising the successful quelling of a planned or actual uprising both bolstered the confidence of whites and deterred future attempts on the part of slaves (or at least such was the hope). But on the other hand, publicizing slave revolts and conspiracies could backfire, increasing white anxiety and black resolve. Moreover, there was Northern public opinion to worry about: every harsh and sometimes savage white response to slave uprisings was morally condemned in the abolitionist press.

As a consequence of this ambivalence about public perception, it was not unusual for newspapers to take little notice of quashed slave actions and little if any transcribed minutes of the trials that might have followed. The documents that we do have, therefore, are nearly all from the perspective of threatened whites. The single extended narrative that comes from a slave defendant is what came to be called *Nat Turner's Confessions*, and even that was edited by a white lawyer in ways that clearly reflected his dislike of Turner and his dismay at Turner's bloodletting.

But hard as they strove to deceive themselves with their fantasies of happy and contented slaves, Southerners never quite managed to forget the state of siege in which they lived. Despite themselves, they knew, as historian Herbert Aptheker put it, "that discontent and rebelliousness were not only exceedingly common, but, indeed, characteristic of American Negro slaves."[14] Terrible and occasionally terrifying to whites as slaves were, the insurrections really should not have come as surprises.

NOTES

1. *The Liberator*, September 3, 1831.

2. Ibid.

3. Herbert Aptheker, *American Negro Slave Revolts*, 50th anniversary edition (New York: International Publishers, 1993).

4. Junius S. Rodriguez (ed.), "Introduction," in *Encyclopedia of Slave Resistance and Rebellion*, vol. 1 (Westport, CT: Greenwood, 2007), xli.

5. In his *Nat Turner's Slave Rebellion* (New York: Humanities Press, 1966), for example, Herbert Aptheker writes, "The aim of an insurrection is not revolutionary; the aim of a rebellion is. A revolt is of less magnitude than a rebellion" (p. 2). His distinctions, therefore, are based on degree. But because eighteenth- and nineteenth-century authors used the terms interchangeably when reporting, I will do the same.

6. Ulrich Bonnell Phillips, *American Negro Slavery* (New York: D. Appleton, 1918).

7. Frederick Douglass, *My Bondage and My Freedom* (New York: Modern Library, 2003), 140. Originally published in 1855.

8. For a history of the Underground Railroad, see Kerry Walters, *The Underground Railroad: A Reference Guide* (Santa Barbara, CA: ABC-CLIO, 2012).

9. Quoted in James Oliver Horton and Lois E. Horton, *Slavery and the Making of America* (New York: Oxford University Press, 2005), 121.

10. Letter from Virginia governor John Floyd to South Carolina governor James Hamilton Jr., in Kenneth S. Greenberg (ed.), *The Confessions of Nat Turner and Related Documents* (Boston: Bedford/St. Martin's, 1996), 110.

11. David Walker, *Appeal to the Colored Citizens of the World*, Peter P. Hinks (ed.) (University Park: Pennsylvania State University Press, 2006), 72–73. Originally published in 1829.

12. Readers might be surprised that a second successful revolt, the one aboard the ship *Amistad* in 1839, is not discussed here. But this book deals with domestic slave rebellions and conspiracies. The slaves aboard the *Amistad* were Africans and had never been domestic slaves in the United States.

13. Winthrop D. Jordan, *Tumult and Silence at Second Creek: An Inquiry into a Civil War Slave Conspiracy* (Baton Rouge: Louisiana State University Press, 1996), 138.

14. Aptheker, *American Negro Slave Revolts*, 374.

CHAPTER 2

THE STONO REVOLT

> Evil brought Home to us within our very Doors awakened the Atten-
> tion of [even] the most Unthinking. Every one that had any Relation,
> any tie of Nature; every one that had a Life to lose were in the most
> sensible Manner shocked at such Danger daily hanging over their
> Heads.
>
> —Official Report of the Stono Revolt[1]

We have only one eyewitness account of the largest and bloodiest slave rebellion in colonial South Carolina, written by no less a figure than Lawrence Bull, the royal province's acting governor. Fifteen months into his office, Bull, a wealthy Carolina Low Country landowner, was returning by way of Pon Pon Road to Charles Town (present-day Charleston) from Granville County, where he had presided at a session of district court. "I was returning ... with four Gentlemen," he wrote, "and met these rebels at Eleven a Clock in the forenoon."[2] It is not clear how many of the "rebels" were in the band Bull ran across. Estimates range from 60 to 100. But the sight sent a shudder of terror through Bull and his companions, for the rebels were a fiercesome sight. Some carried flags or guns and all chanted "Liberty!" in an unsettling rhythmic manner.

Bull vaguely states in his report that he "fortunately deserned [sic] the approaching Danger time enough to avoid it, and to give notice to the Militia." But in all likelihood, his retreat was hasty and undignified. Few things were more alarming to mid-eighteenth-century white South Carolinians than the possibility of a slave uprising. The Stono revolt of 1739, named for the Stono River location where it erupted, was a nightmare come true. By the time it was quelled, 12 plantations had been burnt and 25 whites, men, women, and children, butchered. The revolt had lasted less than a full day. But the horror of it scarred South Carolina's whites and provoked a revised set of slave codes aimed at nipping future uprisings in the bud.

ENEMIES WITHIN AND WITHOUT

The South Carolina colony was part of a much larger holding, the Province of Carolina, that incorporated the modern states of North Carolina, South Carolina, Georgia, Alabama, Tennessee, and Mississippi, and much of modern Florida and Louisiana. Although first claimed by England in 1629, the province went largely undeveloped until Charles II granted proprietorship of it in 1663 to eight men who had aided him in regaining the British throne. For a number of reasons, political as well as economic, the proprietorship was revoked in 1719 and the province returned to the Crown.

A year later, thanks to the introduction of a new variety of seed, rice became the colony's leading crop. The Low Country, sea-level land that bordered the coastline, had proven ideal for cultivating rice, but planters soon extended their plantations inland with the aid of irrigation-flooded fields. By 1740, when it exported 35 million tons of rice, South Carolina was the leading producer of the crop in the entire British Empire, and rice was quickly becoming a staple throughout the Western world. When the American Revolution began in 1776, rice was the third most valuable export of the North American colonies.

But growing this much rice required a huge labor force. For starters, the land had to be carefully prepared and maintained in preparation for sowing. In the Low Country, the landscape had to be refashioned to ensure that just the right amount of freshwater flooded the rice fields. Ditches and drains had to be dug, dams built, and irrigation wheels constructed. Inland ponds, water gates, and canals were essential if a rice planter hoped for success.

Then came the planting, tending, and harvesting. The same sweltering South Carolina climate that bred illness and torpor also allowed for year-round rice cultivation. But the work was backbreaking and nonstop. In the winter, irrigation canals and sluice gates had to be cleared and repaired in preparation for spring planting. After the seedlings were in the ground, the fields had to be flooded, drained, hoed, and reflooded. At harvest time, the rice had to be gathered, sheaved, pounded, and threshed. And when all that was done, it was time to begin tending to canals and sluice gates again.

In the early days of the colony, rice planters had settled the labor problem by enslaving local Indians. White settlers encouraged the various indigenous peoples to war with one another and capture and sell rather than kill their enemies. The strategy worked so well that by the beginning of the eighteenth century, there were at least 1,400 Indian slaves in South Carolina, and costal tribes such as the Kasihta and the Westoe had all but disappeared. Carolina whites bought Indian laborers willingly enough, but never quite trusted them, considering them too independent to be good slaves. So a fair number of the captive Indians were sold to West Indies planters.

One of the local tribes that gladly sold captives to rice planters in exchange for English goods was the Yamasee. But by 1715, worrying that they themselves were in danger of enslavement, the Yamasee allied with the Creeks to attack the white settlers in and around Charles Town. They struck on Good Friday, and for the next two years, South Carolinian planters, town dwellers, and merchants lived in daily fear. By the time the Yamasee were finally defeated in 1717, a full seven percent of the colony's white population had been killed and huge economic losses, in both property and revenue, had been sustained.

The Yamasee War ended the practice of enslaving Indians. South Carolinians forced both Yamasees and Creeks to settle further south, thus freeing up even more land for the cultivation of rice. But the relative peace of mind brought by the expulsion of the Indians was accompanied by a labor shortage that encouraged an acceleration of the importation of African slaves. When the Yamasee War ended, there were fewer than 5,000 African slaves in Carolina, some of whom had fought with whites against the Indians. By the 1730s, slave imports were averaging around 2,500 a year, far more than in any other American colony. When the Stono revolt occurred, there were 40,000 African slaves in South Carolina, outnumbering whites by a ratio of 2.6–1.

Part of the reason for the huge increase in importation was the high death rate of overworked slaves. But part of it was due to the fact that the colony's land-rich but cash-poor plantation owners kept cultivating more and more land to grow rice, which required additional slaves. The trap, of course, was that the more rice that flooded the market, the lower the price fell, which the landowners responded to by growing yet more rice, which required yet more slaves. It was the same vicious cycle that would hit southern cotton planters a century later.

The flood of Africans brought in to replace Indian slaves did little to abate chronic white anxiety about slave insurrections. Beginning in the 1720s, most of the Africans brought to Charles Town were from the west coast of Africa, especially Angola and Konga. By the time of the Stono uprising, probably a full 75 percent of South Carolina's slaves were from that part of Africa. Part of the reason for their desirability as slaves was that rice was grown in Angola and Konga, and so slaves imported from there would have some experience, either first- or secondhand, of cultivating the grain. But another reason was that a number of civil wars had raged in the area for several generations, providing a steady supply of captive soldiers and villagers to be sold to white slavers.

This meant that many of the slaves who worked for white planters and town merchants had been warriors at one time. Like the Indians who were enslaved before them, they were independent by temperament and fierce by training. Moreover, given the history of Catholic missions in their native lands, it is likely that at least some of them were Christian, which would have made them resent even more bitterly their enslavement at the hands of white Christians. Both of these factors, in addition to being outnumbered by black slaves 2.6–1, ratcheted up white anxiety—but not enough to slow down the importation of captured Angolans and Kongalese.

In the months leading up to the Stono revolt, South Carolinians had been frightened by two actual rebellions and a third that was planned but squelched. In 1738, two separate bands of slaves had fled their plantations on different occasions to make their way to Spanish Florida. One of them, passing through Georgia, had killed several white residents. In early 1739, South Carolina was abuzz once more with news of a failed conspiracy on the part of disgruntled slaves. These three incidents were unpleasant reminders not only of the ever-present danger of rebellion from the enemy within—slaves—but also of the eagerness of an enemy without to aid and abet them. That external enemy was Britain's primary competitor for control of the New World: Spain.

Spanish-controlled Florida permitted slavery, although the slaves there generally were treated far more humanely than in the southern British colonies. But in 1733, a royal decree announced that Florida would welcome runaway slaves from the Carolina Province if they could manage to cross the border. Moreover, the slaves would be granted their freedom and, if they chose, trained in firearms so that they could serve as militiamen. As historian Eugene Genovese points out, "The Spanish correctly assumed that self-emancipated black warriors would provide a formidable border army."[3]

Even if runaway slaves opted not to become members of a border army, the promise of freedom given by Spanish officials was a continuous threat to the stability of South Carolina and Georgia, which, of course, is exactly what Spain intended. That the Spanish offer was widely known among slaves, who probably overheard their masters talking about it, is evidenced by the fact that most who absconded headed straight for St. Augustine, about 200 miles south of Charles Town. So far as Spain was concerned, the royal decree was a win-win affair. Either slaves would make it to Florida, which would drain the labor pool of Britain's southern colony, or the mere knowledge that Spain was willing to receive them would stir up rebellion in slave ranks. Both were destabilizers of the economy.

Colonial officials, including South Carolina's Lawrence Bull and Georgia governor James Oglethorpe, were painfully aware that their colonies' slaves, already discontented, were being egged on by Spain. Every disruption of the master-slave status quo, whether minor or large scale, was chalked up to Spanish meddling. This was especially the case in the Stono uprising.

James Oglethorpe, colonial governor of Georgia during the Stono revolt, worried that Spanish Florida incited slaves to revolt in order to undermine British colonies in the New World. Oglethorpe is shown here in council with Native Americans. (Library of Congress)

MURDER AT HUTCHENSON'S STORE

The facts surrounding the outbreak of the Stono uprising—if indeed it actually was an uprising; as we will see later, at least one historian argues that it was not—are far and few between. What is known is that on the night of Saturday, September 8 or the early morning of Sunday, September 9, some 20 slaves broke into a store by the Stono River Bridge, just 20 miles southwest of Charles Town; killed two white men; and stole guns, ammunition, food, and drink. They were led by an Angolan referred to in some records as "Jemmy" and in others as "Cato."

The store was called Hutchenson's and was virtually identical to others that dotted South Carolina's coastline and tidal rivers. These "stores" were actually warehouses, usually single storied, which sold imported goods such as Jamaican rum and English linen that arrived periodically on the trading ships that sailed to the colony. They were often gathering places for locals to sit, have a drink or two, and gossip.

The two white men at Hutchenson's were Robert Bathurst and John Gibbs. Bathurst appears to have been a servant, but Gibbs was a landowner and commissioner of highways, one of whose duties was to supervise the regular clearing of drainage ditches alongside roads. It is not known what the two men were doing at the store. Bathurst may have been the night watchman. But it is possible that the two were asleep—perhaps they had been drinking—with no light showing through the store window. If that is the case, then the slaves, who might have broken into the store solely for the purpose of pilfering, would have been surprised to find the two men there. On the other hand, they may have known that Gibbs and Bathurst were in Hutchenson's and planned from the very start to kill them.

However it happened, the slaves quickly dispatched the two white men. As one contemporary account laconically puts it, "[T]hey surprized [*sic*]a Warehouse belonging to Mr. Hutchenson at a place called Stonehow [*sic*]; they there killed Mr. Robert Bathurst, and Mr. Gibbs, plundered the House and took a pretty many small Arms and Powder."[4] Another account, written by one of Georgia governor Oglethorpe's rangers a week after the incident, is just as laconic but more gruesome. He reports that the slaves "marched to Stono Bridge where they had Murthered two Store-keepers Cut their Heads off and Set them on the Stairs."[5]

What sparked the break-in and murders? And why on that date? There are four possible explanations.

The first is that Charles Town was in the grip of a powerful yellow fever epidemic that killed half a dozen people per day and brought the city's government and commercial district to a standstill. Lieutenant Governor Bull rescheduled the General Assembly's September 12 meeting date because of "the Sickness with which it hath pleased God to visit this Province."[6] The epidemic subsided only with the return of cool, mosquito-killing weather in October, but not before several dignitaries and scores of citizens perished. Given the confusion created by all the sickness and death, the Stono rebels may have judged it a good time to make a move.

Another possible explanation is that the slaves feared that if they waited any longer, their window of opportunity would slam shut. Charles Town newspapers announced in mid-August the passage of a Security Act, which required all white men to carry firearms to church on Sundays. Actually, a long-standing law in the colony required the carrying of guns on Sundays, but it had been generally ignored and seldom enforced. The new Security Act, prompted by growing alarm over the possibility that unsupervised slaves, who generally had Sundays off, might revolt while their white masters and mistresses where in church, mandated stiff penalties for noncompliance. Slaves easily could have heard whites talking about the new law, which went into effect at the end of September.

A third explanation relates to the strained relations between England and Spain. In the same week that the Stono uprising occurred, Charles Town received word that the two nations were in a de facto state of war. The conflict, named years afterward the "War of Jenkins' Ear" by the Scottish essayist Thomas Carlyle, was sparked by the boarding and seizure of British merchant ships by Spanish patrols. (In one of these episodes, the ear of British captain Robert Jenkins was severed.) Historian Peter Wood argues that news of the war might have furnished a "sudden spark" for already discontented slaves to revolt "without hesitation."[7]

A fourth possible explanation of why the slaves struck Hutchenson's store when they did has nothing to do with rebellion, at least not as an initial motive. According to historian Peter Charles Hoffer, the entire Stono uprising may have been a simple burglary that went bad and spiraled out of control.

In the South Carolina Lowland, it was essential to maintain the drainage ditches that paralleled highways; otherwise, roads became soggy and impossible to travel on. Colonial law mandated that the ditches be kept in working order by local slaves. But not wishing to anger slave owners by impressing their human property during the workweek, the law allowed highway commissioners to force slaves to maintain ditches on Sundays, their traditional day off. Slaves deeply resented the practice.

Hoffer argues that it is possible the perpetrators of the Hutchenson break-in were members of a road ditch crew who, angry at being impressed for public work, decided to "reward" themselves by enjoying what food and drink they could steal from the store. Once there, however, they were surprised to find Gibbs and Bathurst. Under colonial law, burglary, when committed by slaves, was a capital crime. So the startled slaves had incentive to kill the two white witnesses. Afterward, horrified by the situation in which they found themselves, they came to the conclusion that force of circumstance demanded they make a break for the Florida border: in for a penny, in for a pound.[8] According to Hoffer, the Stono uprising is one of history's ironies.

THE BATTLE

It is impossible to decide between the conventional interpretation of the Stono revolt and Hoffer's revisionist one. But what is not disputable is what happened after the Hutchenson store break-in: rampage. Some of the slaves involved in the burglary and murder may have slipped off in the darkness to return to their plantations. But most of the band went on a killing spree as they made their way south, presumably headed for Florida.

They struck first at the nearby home of a Mr. Godfrey, killing him and his sleeping wife and two children. Then they headed south down the Pon Pon Road, a highway that ran from South Carolina through Georgia straight to St. Augustine. Around dawn they passed a tavern owned by a Mr. Wallace, whom they spared because they considered him "a good Man and kind to his Slaves."[9] But the next house they came to, on the Lemy spread, was not so lucky. The rebellious slaves slaughtered the entire family and would have done the same to the Rose family at the next house down the road had the Roses not been forewarned by one of their own slaves.

By this time, excited by the blood they had shed and emboldened by liquor taken from Hutchenson's, the band of slaves were "calling out

Liberty, marched on with Colours displayed, and two Drums beating."[10] They urged slaves they met along the way to join them, and many, although not all, did. It was shortly after leaving the Rose place that they ran into the startled Lieutenant Governor Bull and his entourage. Afterward, they ransacked several more homes, killing everyone they could find in them. All told, 23 whites fell at their hands.

The band, which had increased to somewhere between 60 and 100 slaves, halted early in the afternoon after having marched about 10 miles down the Pon Pon Road. They stopped in an open field on the north side of the road, with the Edisto River behind them. Some commentators believe that they halted because they were exhausted or inebriated, if not both. But it is unlikely that field hands used to putting in long days of backbreaking labor would have been done in by a mere 10 miles, even though they undoubtedly were tired, both from the long march and from the killing rampage along the way.

A more likely explanation for the band's halt is that its members, many of whom were warriors from Angola or Konga, were preparing themselves for battle. They could not have failed to realize that after Bull escaped them, he would raise a hue and cry. They knew that it would not be long before they would have to fight not only for their freedom but for their very lives.

That this is most likely the case is suggested by a contemporary description of what the rebellious slaves did after they settled in the field. They "set to dancing, Singing and beating Drums." The author of this account concludes that the hoopla was intended "to draw more Negroes to them," and perhaps that is partly true. But as one historian points out, "military dancing was a part of the African culture of war . . . as much a part of military preparation as drill was in Europe . . . Dancing in preparation for war was so common in Kongo that 'dancing a war dance' (*sangamento*) was often used as a synonym for 'to declare war' in seventeenth-century sources."[11]

The slaves did not have long to wait. One of Bull's companions, a man by the name of Golightly, had made for the nearby Johns Island Presbyterian Church to alert the male worshippers. Among the congregation was Captain John Bee, a prominent landowner and leader of the local militia. He and the men under his command mounted their horses and galloped to the field where the slaves had halted. By around four in the afternoon, armed planters, most of them on horseback, arrived as reinforcements. A contemporaneous account states that the two forces, militia and planters on one side and slaves on the other, were evenly matched with about 100 men each and that most of the African rebels "were . . . drunk with the liquors they found in the stores."[12] The writer of this account apparently took the rebels' dancing as a sign of drunkenness.

The slaves had few arms. Their adversaries were well stocked with muskets, but few of them besides Captain Bee had training in military tactics or experience in actual fighting. In good eighteenth-century battle style, the planters and militia dismounted, formed a more or less straight firing line, and shot a volley into the rebel ranks. Fourteen of the slaves fell, either dead or wounded, and a handful more returned fire at least twice from the weapons they had managed to seize from Hutchenson's and the plundered farmhouses.[13] There may have been a second volley from the militia, after which the rest of the slaves either ran off or were captured. But before their flight, they behaved bravely, as two different contemporary accounts begrudgingly acknowledge. One states that "they behaved boldly" when confronting the militiamen and planters. Another report tells of one of the rebellious slaves recognizing and making a last ditch act of defiance. "One Negroe fellow who came up to his Master[.] his Master asked him if he wanted to kill him[.] the Negroe answered he did at the same time Snapping a Pistoll at him but it mist fire and his Master shot him thro' the Head."[14]

Some of the rebellious slaves fled back to their plantations in the hopes that their participation in the revolt would go unnoticed. But for the most part, they were quickly identified and shot. The slaves that were captured on the field of battle, either because they were wounded or had surrendered, were questioned and similarly dispatched. "Such as were taken in the field were after being examined, shot on the Spot." But the author of this report was proud to announce that "notwithstanding the Provocation they had received from so many Murders, [the militiamen and planters] did not torture one Negroe, but only put them to an easy death." They even pardoned any of the slaves they deemed not to have had a hand in the "Murders & Burnings."[15] Easy death or no, another contemporary account states that the heads of the slain slaves where "Cutt off . . . and set up at every Mile Post" leading into Charles Town, presumably as a deterrent to future rebels.[16]

Despite the battlefield rout of the rebels and the capture and execution of many of those who fled, some of the slaves, including their leader Cato, remained unaccounted for. Within a couple days of the battle, planters and militia "kill'd twenty odd more, and took about 40; who were immediately some shot, some hang'd, and some Gibbeted alive."[17] One of the captured rebels apparently was Cato. But rumors of some 30 rebels still at large panicked the white community for miles around. The area along the Stono River, where the outbreak had originated, went on high alert for the next few weeks as both militia and planters were posted at ferry crossings and along the Pon Pon Road. Even the Charles Town militia, thinned though its ranks were by the yellow fever epidemic, mustered forth those members who were still standing to hunt down the rebels. Indians skilled in the art of tracking were also hired.

Nearly a full week later, the trackers caught up with the band of survivors. They had managed to make their way another 20 miles southward, undoubtedly traveling by night and living off the land. They were "overtaken by the Planters on horseback, fought stoutly for some time and were all killed on the Spot."[18] But even after this second battle, panic remained in the white community, particularly because several of the rebels were still on the loose. (One of them would not be captured and hanged for another three years.) Several planters in the Stono area moved their families to Charles Town, and as late as the following January, the rector of St. Paul Parish, within which the revolt originated, was complaining that if his parishioners kept moving to the safety of Charles Town, he would be left with "but a Small Congregation at Church."[19]

ENEMIES WITHOUT AND WITHIN

A couple of days after Christmas 1739, Charles Town merchant Robert Pringle, reflecting on the Stono uprising, wrote, "We shall Live very Uneasie with our Negroes, while the Spaniards continue to keep Possession of St. Augustine & it is pity our Goverm^t at home did not incourage [*sic*] the disslodging of them from thence."[20]

Pringle captured the mood of white South Carolinians in the wake of the Stono uprising. The common conviction was that the promise of freedom from Spanish Florida was an incentive to resurrection in general and the recent unpleasantness in particular. Enemies without had seduced slaves into becoming enemies within.

The official reports sent to London about the Stono revolt were explicit in their denunciation of Spanish intrigue. In Lieutenant Governor Bull's eyewitness account of what happened—although, in truth, the only "eyewitnessing" that he did occurred during his brief encounter from afar with the rebel band—he informed his superiors that "the Desertion of Our Negroes" was instigated by "a Certain Proclamation published by the King of Spain's Order at St. Augustine declaring Freedom to all Negroes who should desert thither from the British Colonies."[21] The later official report's very title, the "Late Expedition against St. Augustine," squarely indicted Spain, even arguing that a Spanish agent provocateur, instructed to stir up "a general Insurrection of Negroes" in the British Southern colonies, had been discovered and arrested in Georgia. "With Indignation," the report continued, "we looked at St. Augustine that Den of Thieves and Ruffians!," going over "in our Minds" all the efforts of the Spaniards to stir up unrest and disorder among Indians and slaves in South Carolina.[22]

The charge that Spain had deliberately undermined the colony by agitating its slaves persisted for decades. In 1779, the Reverend Alexander Hewatt wrote that Florida officials sent "emissaries" to "secretly tamper" with slaves by encouraging them to revolt.[23] Seventy years later, the antebellum defender of slavery William Gilmore Simms repeated the accusation.[24] It is not clear how much truth there was in it, but given Spain's strategy of undermining the British colonies by tempting their slaves with freedom, the accusation is not implausible. It is certainly the case that South Carolinians believed it true and were rattled by it.

Equally disturbing to whites was the threat of future insurrections by slaves, whom the Charles Town council called "an intestine Enemy the most dreadful of Enemies."[25] So less than a month after the revolt, the South Carolina House of Assembly set about revising the colony's old slave code to guard against uprisings. The "Act for the better ordering and governing of Negroes and other Slaves in this Province" became law early the next spring. It is a curious combination of stick and carrot, and it served as the basis of South Carolina's slave laws until the end of the Civil War.

Legislators were convinced that the mistreatment of black slaves on the parts of their white owners perilously led to discontent and rebellion. So one provision in the Act stipulated that slaves ought not to be overworked, lest they grow "over wrought." Other provisions defined the limits to which owners could go in punishing their slaves. But these and similar mandates were motivated by white self-interest rather than concern for the welfare of slaves, as is plain from the Act's less humane provisions. The assembly of slaves was severely limited. Whenever five or more of them traveled on the roads, at least one white person had to accompany them. Slaves were forbidden to rent accommodations except on behalf of their masters. Anyone who taught slaves to read, sold them liquor or firearms, or harbored runaways headed for Florida was subject to severe penalty. The Act also declared that Indians who tracked down any remaining Stono rebels would be amply rewarded. If the runaways were brought back alive, and depending on age and gender, the rewards ranged from 5 to 50 pounds. But even dead rebels were lucrative: "for every scalp of a grown negro slave, with the two ears, twenty pounds."[26] Presumably the two ears were required to verify that the scalp belonged to a black.

Most notoriously, the Act contained a blanket, retroactive pardon to any and all white persons who might have been overzealous in their response to the Stono uprising by summarily executing slaves suspected of taking part in it. "Be it enacted, that all and every act, matter and thing, had, done, committed and executed, in and about the suppressing and putting all and every the said negro and negroes to death, is and are hereby declared lawful, to all intents and purposes whatsoever, as fully and amply as if such rebellious negroes had undergone a formal trial and condemnation."[27]

This retroactive exoneration revealed better than any other part of the Act just how alarmed both legislators and citizens were by the prospect of another slave insurrection. The message was clear, even if not explicitly stated: suspiciously acting slaves could be handled without fear of the law. It was a tragic but predictable response to the underlying anxiety that the Stono uprising provoked in whites. As one observer wrote in 1740,

> Such dreadful Work, it is to be feared, we may hear more of in Time, in case they come to breaking open stores to find Arms, as they did the last Year; and are able to keep the Field, with Plenty of Corn and Potatoes every where; and above all, if it is considered how vastly disproportionate the Number of white Men is to theirs: So that at best, the Inhabitants cannot live without perpetually guarding their own Safety, now become so precarious.[28]

"WE NOT WHIPPED YET!"

Most of the slave rebellions and conspiracies in the colonies and United States were poorly documented, and it is likely that some have vanished from memory. This is partly because the uprisings were often put down quickly and mercilessly, with niceties such as record-keeping brushed to one side. But as we saw in Chapter 1, it is also the case that whites were not anxious to have word of attempted insurrections reaching other discontented slaves who might be emboldened by the news. So documentation or public notices about such revolts were often deliberately minimalized or suppressed.

Our knowledge of the Stono rebellion is particularly sketchy, more for the first than the second reason. Most intriguing of all the blank spots in the story is the insurrection's alleged leader, Cato. But in a 1937 interview that was part of the Federal Writers' Project, George Cato, who claimed to be a great-great-grandson of the rebellious Cato, offered a few details about his ancestor that had been passed from one generation to the next. His testimony is corroborated in some places by the historical record, and even when there is no corroboration, what he says is worth considering.

According to George Cato, his great-great-grandfather was not physically abused by his master, who in fact taught him to read and write. If this is true, the original Cato could not have been a field hand. Most likely, he was one of the domestic staff who served in the "big house." We know that many of the slave leaders of insurrections, as well as many of the slaves who made their way to freedom on the nineteenth-century Underground Railroad, were relatively educated and rarely worked the fields. So George Cato's description of his ancestor is certainly plausible.

George Cato also said that the original Cato was "elected" as leader by the other slaves because of his obvious talents but that after the break-in at Hutchenson's store and the killing spree that followed, he was unable to control his ragtag army. The reason things got out of hand was drink: the liquor discovered at the store and perhaps at the private houses the rebels ransacked was consumed too quickly and in too great quantities. As a consequence, by the time the militiamen arrived on the scene to do battle with the slaves, most of them were inebriated. The chanting and dancing that historian John Thornton interprets as a war ritual were in fact, claimed George Cato, drunken antics. According to him, the militiamen "found many of de slaves was singin' and dancin' and Cap. Cato and some of de other leaders was cussin' at them sumpin awful. From dat day to dis, no Cato has tasted whiskey, 'less he go 'gainst his daddy's warnin' ... When de militia come in sight of them ... , de drinkin' dancin' Negroes scatter in de brush and only 44 stand deir ground."[29]

George Cato's account of his ancestor also disagrees with historian Peter Charles Hoffer's hypothesis that the Stono rebellion started off as a simple burglary. George admits that even though he asked, none of his older relatives knew exactly how it came to pass that slaves went on a rampage on that September night in 1739. But he was convinced that his ancestor was motivated by a desire for freedom and remarks that the literate Cato had often forged passes for his fellow slaves. The oral tradition in his family held that when surrounded by the militiamen, Cato defiantly cried out, "We surrender but we not whipped yet." Then the elder Cato, and his 43 companions, were hanged, although there is no contemporary record of Cato's execution. "He die," remarked George Cato, "but he die for doin' de right, as he see it."[30]

NOTES

1. "Report of the Committee Appointed to Enquire into the Causes of the Disappointment of Success in the Late Expedition against St. Augustine" (July 1741), in Mark M. Smith (ed.), *Stono: Documenting and Interpreting a Southern Slave Revolt* (Columbia: University of South Carolina Press, 2005), 29.

2. "Lieutenant Governor Bull's Eyewitness Account," in Smith, 17.

3. Eugene Genovese, *From Rebellion to Revolution: Afro-American Slave Revolts in the Making of the Modern World* (Baron Rouge: Louisiana State University Press, 1979), 21.

4. "Account of the Negroe Insurrection in South Carolina" (October 1739), Smith, 14.

5. "A Ranger Details the Insurrection" (September 1739), in Smith, 7. Only the ranger talks about the decapitation of the two white men killed at Hutchenson's.

6. Quoted in Peter H. Wood, *Black Majority: Negroes in Colonial South Carolina from 1670 through the Stono Rebellion* (New York: W.W. Norton, 1974), 313.

7. Ibid., 314.

8. Peter Charles Hoffer, *Cry Liberty: The Great Stono River Slave Rebellion of 1739* (New York: Oxford University Press, 2012).

9. "Account of the Negroe Insurrection," in Smith, 14.

10. Ibid.

11. John K. Thornton, "African Dimensions of the Stono Rebellion," *American Historical Review* 96 (October 1991), 1112.

12. Quoted in Hoffer, *Cry Liberty*, 113.

13. "A Letter from South Carolina, September 28, 1739," *Boston Gazette*, October 29–November 5 issue.

14. "A Ranger Details," in Smith, 7–8.

15. "Account of the Negroe Insurrection," in Smith, 15.

16. "A Ranger Details," in Smith, 8.

17. "A Letter from South Carolina," *Boston Gazette*.

18. "Account of the Negroe Insurrection," in Smith, 15.

19. "Deserting Stono," in Smith, 19.

20. Quoted in Wood, 321.

21. "Lieutenant Governor Bull's Eyewitness Account," in Smith, 16.

22. "Report of the Committee," in Smith, 29.

23. Alexander Hewatt, *An Historical Account of the Rise and Progress of the Colonies of South Carolina and Georgia* (1779), in Smith, 33.

24. Hoffer, 136.

25. Quoted in Wood, 321.

26. "An Act for the Better Ordering of Negroes and Other Slaves in This Province" (May 1740), in Smith, 27.

27. Ibid.

28. Quoted in Wood, 323.

29. "As It Come Down to Me," in Smith, 56.

30. Ibid.

CHAPTER 3

THE 1741 NEW YORK CONSPIRACY

By the course of the evidence, it appears, that a design was conceived to destroy this city by fire, and massacre the inhabitants.

—Daniel Horsmanden[1]

B y the mid-eighteenth century, slaves constituted a full 20 percent of New York City's population. Living in close quarters with their masters, a proximity that later Southern slaveholders would find unimaginable, it was not uncommon for slaves to hobnob with whites of the lowest laboring classes in dramshops, the most disreputable kinds of taverns the city had to offer.

Not surprisingly, those dramshops were frequented by petty criminals who planned their thefts over rum and by prostitutes who entertained and sometimes loved them. Alcohol loosens inhibitions and lips, and occasionally slaves who were in their cups fantasized about robbing and killing their masters and securing their freedom. Less dramatically, slaves and white criminals sometimes cooked up dramshop schemes to burgle New York merchants and residents.

In February 1741, one of the coldest months within living memory, three slaves robbed a small shop on the East River docks and brought their loot to a white dramshop owner who was a known fence. A couple of weeks afterward, Fort George, the citadel at the southern tip of Manhattan, caught fire, and over the next two months several other suspicious fires broke out. By April, following reports that blacks had been seen running from the fires, New York authorities had convinced themselves that a slave revolt of enormous size was in the planning. They began rounding up slaves, including the ones who had robbed the East River establishment, who were immediately labeled as ringleaders. Before long, dozens of blacks, free and enslaved, as well as a handful of whites, found themselves on trial for conspiring to insurrect.

The problem was that either there was no conspiracy or, if there was one, it was loose and informal. A few acts of arson and a handful of petty crimes were blown up by authorities into a nefarious uprising that largely existed only in their imaginations. Fear and hatred of blacks, xenophobia, and anti-Catholicism created a perfect storm of panic in New York City's white population, and the storm abated only after 30-odd people had been executed.

THE "BLOODY CONSPIRACY" OF 1712

Many New Yorkers were primed to believe the accusations of 1741 because they either remembered or had heard about a genuine slave rebellion in Manhattan nearly 30 years earlier. Like slave revolts everywhere throughout the colonies and early republic, this one left a traumatic scar on the collective white psyche.

The Dutch West Indian Company brought the first slaves to New York City in 1625, and by 1712 many of the slaves were warriors from Africa's Gold Coast. Chafing both at their loss of freedom and the degrading nature of the tasks assigned to them—hauling excrement, slaughtering livestock, and so on—some of them conspired with local Indians to rise up and gain their freedom. One historian has suggested that at least some of the Africans rebelled because the ways in which slaves were treated in New York ran counter to the understanding of the master-slave relationship in their home countries.[2]

The rebels chose April 6, a Sunday, to launch the uprising. In the early morning of that day, the rebels congregated in the orchard of one John Crooke, a slave owner and farmer. The orchard was located at the northern rim of the city, more rural farm and forest than urban community, on Maiden Lane. Governor Robert Hunter, who wrote an account of the insurrection, reported that the slaves and Indians, around 23 in number, were provisioned with guns, a few swords, and some knives and axes. The tactic they adopted clearly indicated that they intended to use them to spill blood.

A slave belonging to a resident by the name of John Vantilburgh set fire to one of his master's outbuildings as his fellow insurrectionists crouched in the dark. In the eighteenth century, most of New York City's buildings were built of wood, and fire alarms always brought scores of citizens rushing to the site to keep the blaze from spreading. The rebels counted on the same reaction to the burning of Vantilburgh's barn, and they were not disappointed. As soon as white men arrived on the scene of the blaze, the slaves attacked them, killing nine and wounding five or six others. But the firing of their guns aroused the entire city, and Governor Robert Hunter ordered a detachment of soldiers to march against them. By this time, however, the rebels had retreated into the woods, so the governor ordered the island sealed off and, when dawn broke, sent out search parties. The rebels were eventually found and captured, but not before six of them killed themselves, preferring death to the trial and execution they knew awaited them.

The rebels must have been shocked at the failure of their uprising. When they had gathered in Crooke's orchard, they had slashed themselves with daggers and licked one another's blood, supposedly to bind them together, and a conjuror named Peter had sprinkled them all with a magic powder to protect them from death at the hands of whites. Perhaps despair at the realization that the magic had been ineffective was an additional factor in the six suicides.

During the subsequent trials, a number of alleged conspirators were added to the ones who actually took place in the killing on Maiden Lane. Out of nearly 40 defendants, 13 slaves were acquitted. But 27, including a pregnant woman, were found guilty. All but six of them were executed. (It is not clear if the woman was among those who died. Governor Hunter's report states that her sentence was suspended because of her condition. But whether he meant she had been reprieved or simply that her execution was delayed until she delivered is unknown.) As was usually the case with slaves found guilty of rebellion, the executions were public and grisly in order to deter future rebels. Some were burnt, others hanged, one broken on the wheel, and three others suspended alive in chains to starve to death.

As additional disincentives to rebellion, New York lawmakers tightened up the colony's slave code by severely limiting the number of slaves who could congregate on Sundays, punishing slaves caught with weapons, and giving masters legal sanction to punish disobedient slaves any way they wished, short of killing them. But even with these measures, whites were anxious. Subsequent rumors of new conspiracies in 1721 and 1730, although ultimately shown to be fictitious, nevertheless encouraged a state of siege mentality. As one historian puts it, "Though vigorous cross-examination of various slaves would prove the rumors [of conspiracy] unfounded, the failure to corroborate these plots only fed the anxiety of the authorities."[3]

A RASH OF ARSONS

The winter of 1740–1741 was the most frigid any New Yorker could remember. The Hudson River had frozen over and fireplaces were in such constant use that the city was running out of available firewood. So it was no surprise when a blaze broke out at Fort George on the night of March 18. The wonder was that more fires had not erupted that cold winter.

Built in 1714 and situated on the western tip of Manhattan not far from the Battery, Fort George was a wooden stockade that contained the governor's house and government offices as well as an arsenal full of explosives. Dry as tinder and perpetually vulnerable to fire, the fort was considered a liability by more than one official. New York's lieutenant governor, George Clarke, had complained in 1738 that the fort offered little defense to the city.

The fire that erupted on the night of March 18 confirmed Clarke's fears. It was not clear where the blaze originated, but before long it had spread to the governor's house and the stockade's chapel, and it threatened the arsenal. The office that housed the colony's official documents was completely destroyed, and state papers were saved only because they were dumped by the armful out the windows into the snow. The glow from the fire could be seen from all over the city, and fire brigades rushed to the fort, hoping to quench the blaze before it spread to the rest of the wooden structures in the city. Fortunately, a falling wintry mix eventually kept the fire in check, and by morning tragedy had been averted.

No one would have thought much about the fire except for the fact that 13 equally mysteries ones throughout the city followed. One week to the day after the Fort George fire, the home of one Captain Warren caught fire. On April 1, a storehouse went up. Following that, over the next five days, lofts and kitchens were fired, hot coals were found nestled in straw in stables, and on April 6 no fewer than three fires broke out, one of them of truly monumental proportions at a warehouse owned by a man named Philipse.

The rash of fires that hit the city in less than a month had begun to raise suspicions that the blazes were of nefarious origins, and the fire at the warehouse confirmed those fears. According to a document written by Daniel Horsmanden about the conspiracy, one of New York's supreme court justices who presided at the subsequent trials, "a man who had been on the top of the [ware]house, assisting in extinguishing the fire, saw a negro leap out at the end window of one of them, from thence making over several garden fences in great haste; which occasioned him to cry out, *a negro; a negro;* and that was soon improved into an alarm, that *the negroes were rising.*"[4]

The black man spotted by the firefighter was soon identified as Cuffee Philipse, "a fellow of general ill character," slave to the warehouse owner.[5] After news of his arrest spread, other white residents of the city began reporting that they had overheard suspicious murmuring from other slaves. One woman came forward with the news that she had heard a slave named Quaco Walters laughingly say to two companions, "Fire, fire, scorch, scorch. A little damn it, bye and bye."[6] Before long, the source of the Fort George fire was apprehended, a slave named Quaco Roosevelt. He seems to have set the fire to avenge himself on the lieutenant governor, who had refused to allow Quaco to visit his wife, a cook at the fort. But it soon came out that shortly before his act of arson, he had spoken with other slaves about burning down the entire city. This was enough for the local authorities, who quickly concluded that they had discovered a slave plot to insurrect. On April 11, the city council announced that the spate of fires was due to "some villainous confederacy of latent enemies around us," and offered a reward of 100 pounds to free persons, white or black, coming forward with information.[7] Slaves who brought useful information about a conspiracy were promised manumission.

A WIDENING CIRCLE

As panic over a slave uprising spread throughout the city, authorities began to make connections—or to contrive them—that had been overlooked. A worrying increase in burglaries over the winter of 1740–1741 became associated with the series of arsons. In the eyes of city officials, both burglaries and arsons likely led back to disreputable dramshops, where the dregs of white society socialized with free and enslaved blacks. One of these taverns, located on Crown Street on the Hudson River dock and owned by John Hughson, came under particular scrutiny.

Hughson's establishment was a regular hangout for a criminal gang of slaves known by some as the Geneva Club and by others as the Long Bridge Boys. The leaders were Caesar Varick, who sometimes used the name John Gwin, and his lieutenants Cuffee Philipse, the same man later involved in the warehouse fire, and Prince Auboyneau. Hughson was more than happy to fence the loot that the gang periodically brought in. The authorities had been keeping an eye on the dramshop for some time, and undersheriffs periodically popped in unexpectedly in the hope of catching Hughson red-handed. But he had always been too cagey for them.

That all started to change in February 1741. A white ship's boy by the name of Christopher Wilson appears to have enlisted Caesar and Prince to steal some Spanish coins from the shop of one Robert Hogg, with the intention of having Hughson fence them. Unfortunately for Wilson, however, Mrs. Hogg remembered him as someone who had expressed interest in the coins during a visit to the shop, and after the theft she reported as much to the police, who quickly arrested Wilson. Under questioning, he implicated Caesar and Prince, who were then also arrested. Since both of them had criminal records, they faced the death penalty for this latest offense.

Authorities also questioned Hughson and one of his servants, a 16-year-old girl named Mary Burton. The dramshop owner, realizing that he was in a perilous position, tried to maintain his innocence by first admitting that he had seen some of the stolen coins and then, a few days later, producing a few of them, which he implausibly claimed had been hidden in his tavern without his knowledge. Mary, who was picked up by authorities after boasting that she knew about the robbery, further implicated Caesar, Prince, and Hughson. Additionally, she offered a bit of information that was bound to infuriate her interrogators: Caesar was sleeping with a white prostitute named Peg and had actually sired a son with her the previous fall. On learning of her testimony, Hughson tried to "blacken [Mary's] character ... and declared that she was a vile, good-for-nothing girl."[8] But sensing that Mary was favored by the authorities, he soon changed his tune, declaring her "a very good girl" and a "trusty servant." This abrupt turnabout did nothing to enhance Hughson's credibility, and he and his wife were charged with receiving stolen goods.

When the spate of arsons hit the city the following month, authorities, including Supreme Court Justice Daniel Horsmanden, became convinced of a connection between the slave criminal gang's activities and the fires, especially given the connection between Cuffee Philipse and Caesar. To add to the already alarming prospect of a slave revolt was the fear that the slaves involved in the conspiracy might be in collusion with Spanish sailors and Spanish free blacks who either visited or lived in Manhattan. England had just entered into war with Spain, and the worry was that the Spanish may have covertly planted agents in New York to manipulate slaves and undermine British authority.

The smoking gun testimony that Horsmanden and city authorities needed to establish a conspiracy to insurrect came toward the end of April. Caesar and Prince had maintained stony silence under questioning, probably realizing that they had everything to lose and nothing to gain by speaking. The same went for Cuffee Philipse, who by this time was also under arrest. The witness who clinched the conspiracy case was none other than Mary Burton, Hughson's indentured servant.

After her initial testimony implicated Caesar, Prince, and Hughson in the theft of the coins, authorities, suspecting she knew more than she had said, pressed her for more information. Mary resisted at first, but slipped up when she told her interrogators that she "would say nothing about the fires."[9] This immediately clued them into the possibility that she knew a great deal about them. When they threatened her with jail unless she divulged what she knew, the floodgates opened. Mary testified that she had frequently overheard Cuffee, Caesar, and Prince talk while in their cups about setting the entire city on fire; that John Hughson and his wife, Sarah, had said "they would aid and assist them as much as they could"; that as many as "twenty or thirty" rebellious blacks had met at Hughson's tavern at one time; and that the three leaders of the conspiracy had boasted that after the insurrection, Hughson would be proclaimed king and Caesar governor. For his part, Cuffee was satisfied with the wealth he anticipated falling into his hands after the city's whites had been slaughtered.[10]

Mary's testimony was corroborated by Peg, Caesar's mistress, who had been indicted and convicted in early May along with the Hughsons for receiving stolen goods. Terrified of imprisonment or worse, she hoped for a pardon, or at least a milder punishment, as a reward for her testimony. So on May 7, she signed (with her "mark," since she was illiterate) testimony that Caesar and Cuffee had conspired with 10 other slaves to burn both fort and city, and then to rob and murder as many whites as they could.

The very next day after Peg offered her testimony, Caesar and Prince were found guilty of theft and sentenced to death. At their sentencing, the presiding judge urged them to confess their complicity in the conspiracy to insurrect that Mary and Peg had implicated them in. "I have great reason to believe," he told them, "that the crimes you now stand convicted of, are not the least of those you have been concerned in." But the two slaves went to the gallows without acknowledging guilt. Justice Horsmanden was satisfied that justice had been done. "It was thought proper to execute them for the robbery, and not wait for the [sic] bringing them to a trial for the conspiracy, though the proof against them was strong and clear concerning their guilt as to that also," he said. His hope was that the execution of the two men would frighten other conspirators to come forward and throw themselves on the mercy of the court.[11]

The first two convictions and executions were for simple criminal offenses because there was not enough testimony to convict the men for the plot to insurrect that Horsmanden and the other judges were convinced was behind the fires. But after Caesar and Prince were safely dead, city authorities went into overdrive to establish a conspiracy. More testimony was dragged from Mary and Peg about late-night meetings in both Hughson's dramshop and another one owned by a man named John Romme. More slaves were implicated, as were John and Sarah Hughson, whom Mary accused of accepting money from Caesar—the stolen coins, perhaps—to buy weapons for the insurrection. She then testified that "Hughson afterwards went abroad with his boat . . . and brought back with him seven or eight guns, three pistols and four swords, which were hid away under the boards in the garret floor in Hughson's house."[12] It mattered little that the guns were never found. The mere thought of white men supplying slaves with weapons was alarming enough to take seriously, and the Hughsons, already convicted of the criminal offense of fencing stolen property, now found themselves charged with conspiracy.

The final bit of testimony that nailed the lid on the conspiracy theory in the minds of the authorities came from a teenage slave named Sawney

Niblet. He was one of the first blacks rounded up by the authorities and accused of plotting an insurrection. Niblet, a youth who for the most part was shunned by other slaves, was an unlikely suspect. But he was looking for a way out of the fate hanging over his head, and offering testimony against others seemed the only option left open to him.

Sawney told the court that another slave, Quaco Roosevelt, had tried to enlist him in the plot to fire the city and that he had declined. He further testified, improbably, that despite his refusal to join in their conspiracy, the rebel slaves had freely discussed their plans in front of him. He implicated not only all the whites at Hughson's dramshop, including the hapless Peg, but also several Spanish blacks. The motive for the plot, Sawney testified, was to kill all the whites and take their wives—a possibility that alarmed whites even more than the prospect of armed slaves.

Sawney's testimony led to further arrests, and they in turn led to more accusations as terrified prisoners sought ways to curry favor with city authorities in the hopes of avoiding the noose. The grand jury that heard the testimony was predisposed to take at face value the defendants' accusations against other slaves, even though under normal circumstances slave testimony was always considered suspect, especially if given under duress. But in the minds of the city's white population, a conspiracy had already been proven. All that was needed was to ferret out all those involved. Most likely, the unspoken sentiment was that if it was necessary to sentence a few innocent slaves in order to make sure that the guilty were punished, it was a price worth paying.

THE CONSPIRACY TRIALS

Largely on the strength of Sawney's testimony, Quaco Roosevelt and Cuffee Philipse were tried at the end of May. They were the first defendants to be explicitly convicted of the "vile," "wicked," "monstrous," and "execrable and hellish" scheme of "murder[ing] and destroy[ing] your own masters and benefactors."[13] Their trial took less than a day, and the outcome was as predictable as it was horrific: both were sentenced to be burned to death, a punishment that, given their implication in the arsons, was seen as fitting. There were no eyewitnesses who testified seeing them actually light the fires, but neither Quaco nor Cuffee could provide alibis. Judge Horsmanden, who presided at the trial, told the two condemned men exactly what Caesar and Prince had been told days earlier: confess their guilt and reveal the names of everyone involved in the conspiracy.

Horsmanden's exhortation worked. Probably hoping that their lives would be spared, or at least that they would be given a less-terrible manner of execution, Quaco and Cuffee began talking and did not stop until just before the faggots under their feet were lit. Quaco insisted that the conspiracy was all John Hughson's idea, that he had started the fire at the fort, and that Cuffee Philipse, seen running from the warehouse blaze, had indeed been the arsonist there. Cuffee admitted his presence at the warehouse and echoed Quaco's testimony against Hughson, additionally insisting that he would supply the names of more conspirators if he were allowed to live. The official presiding at the public execution thought about halting it until Cuffee came forth with the promised names, but realized that the crowd that had gathered to watch the bonfire would not tolerate a delay. So the two slaves, who understandably "shewed great terror in their countenances," were burned to death, no doubt to the gratification of onlookers.[14]

The executions occurred on May 30. By that time, a dozen or so slaves were in custody. Quaco and Cuffee had dropped just enough names to add seven more to their number. The conspiracy trials were ready to begin in earnest.

The next defendants in the dock were John and Sarah Hughson and the prostitute Peg, all of whom had already been charged with involvement in the conspiracy. But now the Hughson daughter, also named Sarah, was likewise charged with abetting the plot to burn down the city. One legal historian has speculated that the persecution of Hughson's wife and daughter was a ploy to get a confession out of him.[15] If so, the tactic failed, and the trial began on June 4.

White defendants were a rarity in slave conspiracy trials throughout the colonial and antebellum periods, primarily because participating in the planning of a slave revolt was unthinkable for most whites. The rhetoric that the prosecution threw at John Hughson in court reflected the fury of the city's white citizens at a man who not only consorted with enslaved blacks in his dramshop but also actually colluded with them against his fellow whites. The prosecuting attorney referred to Hughson as a man "sunk below the dignity of human nature" and as "that grand incendiary! That arch rebel against God, his king, and his country! That devil incarnate, and chief agent of the old Abaddon of the infernal pit."[16]

Given the prosecutor's zeal and the general anger of the city's whites, Hughson must have known his prospects were dim. He had already been convicted (although not yet sentenced) of receiving stolen goods, but it was not likely that this conviction would earn him the death penalty. The conspiracy charge, however, was an entirely different matter.

During the trial of the Hughsons and Peg, the last-minute confessions of Quaco and Cuffee, which implicated all four of them, were entered into the record. Mary Burton likewise testified against them. Additionally, and even more damningly, British and Irish soldiers from Fort George who frequented Hughson's dramshop testified that they had often seen there slaves who were already accused of being in the plot. They also claimed, rather fantastically, to have heard the Hughson family openly talking about the plot. At one point during the trial, the Hughson parents broke down and clamored loudly, but judges and jury scornfully dismissed their display as little more than a bid for pity.

The four defendants, to no one's surprise, were found guilty. The judge who sentenced them all to death expressed his shock that white people who called themselves Christians would nonetheless make "negro slaves [not only] their equals, but even their superiors, by waiting upon, keeping with, and entertaining them with meat, drink and lodging, and what is much more amazing, to plot, conspire, consult, abet and encourage these black seed of Cain to burn this city, and to kill and destroy us all."[17]

The Hughsons and Peg were sentenced on June 8, after a trial of only four days. Four days after that, all of them were hanged except for daughter Sarah, who was given a temporary reprieve in the expectation that she would give up more names. She failed to do so, most likely because she had none to divulge, and she was eventually pardoned. Immediately after the four convicted whites were led out of court, six slaves implicated by Quaco and Cuffee were brought before the bar. After a short trial, they were all found guilty of conspiratorial arson and they likewise received the ultimate penalty. But unlike the white defendants who preceded them, only one of the condemned slaves died by hanging. The rest were burned to death. Then the next batch of accused slaves was led before the tribunal.

Over the next two months, more slaves were arrested, questioned, tried, and condemned. But as the city jail became increasingly packed with suspects, and as the executions began to exact an economic cost to the slaves' owners and an emotional cost to a public grown weary of hangings and

The executions of New York colony's slaves found guilty of conspiring to revolt included burning at the stake. More fortunate conspirators were hanged. (Hulton Archive/Getty Images)

burnings, promises were made to all slaves who confessed their roles in the plot that their lives would be spared. Eighty-one arrested slaves gladly obliged. Most of them were spared execution and sold out of the colony, mainly to sugar plantations in the West Indies. But even so, the death toll was high. When the executions finally stopped, 18 slaves had been hanged and 13 had been burned at the stake. Four whites had been hanged as well. Not a single defendant, black or white, was found innocent.

A standout moment in legal proceedings whose outcome had become predictable was the trial of five Spanish-speaking, Roman Catholic slaves whom Mary Burton had implicated in her testimony. She claimed that they had frequented Hughson's dramshop and that she had once heard them boasting about their plans to burn the city and kill its inhabitants.

The Spanish slaves mounted a two-pronged defense. In the first place, they contended, they were not slaves. They had been born as free Spaniards and pointed to the fact that they all had surnames (instead of simply carrying the surnames of their masters, as was the custom with slaves) as evidence of their claim. Consequently, they argued, any slave who testified against them did so illegally, since slaves were forbidden to testify against free men and women. The implication was that Mary Burton, herself an indentured servant, had no right to testify against them. Most likely the Spaniards realized this line of defense was useless, given their predicament, but felt obliged to make it as a matter of principle.

Their second claim was that Mary Burton, who spoke only English, could not possibly have overheard their conversations as she claimed because they spoke Spanish when they visited Hughsons. Mary countered that they spoke in good enough English for her to understand, and the slave Sawney likewise testified that he had heard the Spaniards plotting to burn and kill. The five defendants then tried to argue that their English was so bad that they would not have had the ability to conspire with the other English-speaking slaves and that the cold, which they were unaccustomed to, would have prevented them from taking part in the arsons. But the court was no more convinced by this second set of excuses than by the first and convicted them all. One of them was eventually hanged, and the rest deported.

URY'S TRIAL

In late June, at a time when Judge Horsmanden contemptuously noted that "many Negroes began to squeak"[18] in the hopes of escaping execution, the grand jury that had been handing out indictments with abandon issued one for John Ury. Ury was a white man and a suspected Roman Catholic priest who, according to rumor, had secretly—and in violation of colonial New York's law—heard confessions, offered absolution, and celebrated Mass.

The same fear and dislike of Roman Catholics that had made the conviction of the five Spanish slaves a certainty also fueled the prosecution of Ury. New York authorities had always feared that the French Roman Catholics to their north in Canada were intent on meddling in their affairs, and the recent outbreak of war between Britain and Catholic Spain only intensified worries that fifth-column Catholics would seek to disrupt

civil equilibrium. Horsmanden spoke for the establishment when he
wrote in August 1741, "There is scarce a plot but a priest is at the bottom
of it."[19]

Once again, it was Mary Burton who provided the damning evidence
that brought Ury before the bar. She testified that he had frequently stayed
at Hughson's, and on more than one occasion had listened to the conspirators discuss their plans. She admitted that Ury never spoke on these occasions, but insisted that his silence meant he approved of what he heard.
A couple of slaves and an Irish soldier, known as an unreliable drunkard,
also testified against Ury. Finally, Sarah Hughson Junior, perhaps hoping
to escape the rope (she had not yet received her pardon), insisted that
Ury had told the conspirators that as a Roman Catholic priest he had
the power to forgive the sins of arson and murder they were considering.
She also insisted that Ury was the true leader of the entire plot, a claim
that the judges were happy to take seriously. Otherwise, they were faced
with the unpleasant necessity of admitting that black slaves had the intellectual wherewithal to plan an insurrection on their own.

It is not even clear that Ury was a priest, much less that he was involved
in any conspiracy to launch a slave revolt. He appears to have arrived in
the New World in 1738 and to have scribbled comments in a private journal that might be interpreted as priestcraft. But once the charges were
made, they stuck. The judges convinced themselves that Ury had plotted
with the slaves not because he disapproved of human bondage, but because
he wished to destroy Protestantism in the colony. Ury defended himself as
best he could, contending that it would be irrational to the point of mad-
ness for a fugitive priest to risk his already imperiled safety by conspiring
with blacks to burn down the city. But his argument was to no avail; the
jury returned a guilty verdict after deliberating only a quarter of an hour.
Given an opportunity to make a final statement, Ury denied he was a
priest, proclaimed himself innocent of the conspiracy charge, and warned
accusers, judges, and jurymen that they one day would stand "before the
bar of a God who is consuming fire" and that they would then be hurled
for their dishonesty into a place "where the worm dies not, and the fire is
never to be quenched."[20] Unimpressed, the judges sentenced Ury to be
hanged, and sentence was carried out on August 29, one month to the
day from the beginning of his trial. Ury's execution marked the end of
the New York conspiracy trials.

THE CONSPIRACY THAT MAINLY WASN'T

The New York slave conspiracy of 1741 is a poignant example of the damage that the fear of slave insurrection, especially when coupled with paranoia about foreign secret agents and Catholic priestcraft, could wreak in the slaveholding colonies and, later, in slaveholding states. What began as drunken boasting and petty crimes perpetrated by members of a black gang eventually got blown into a full-scale plot to burn down the city, massacre whites, and rape women. In hindsight, the scenario painted by Judge Horsmanden and his judicial colleagues is ludicrous. But the subsequent executions and deportations were not.

It is almost certainly the case that Hughson's dramshop was the site of angry palavers among slaves and poor whites about taking over the city. The conversation was over drink, and tongues wag loosely in such circumstances without participants necessarily having any intention of actually following through on what they say. It is probably the case that some of the more angry slaves who were regulars at Hughson's actually did set a few fires throughout the city. But there is no evidence that there was an overt conspiracy to do so. The fires seem to have been acts of individual vandalism or personal vengeance, perhaps fueled in part by loose talk at Hughson's but certainly not planned steps toward insurrection.

Even during the trials themselves, some of New York's more reflective citizens suspected that there was much more smoke than fire to the trials and that the accusations were more "a Dream, or a Fiction" than reality. One person actually compared them to the Salem witch trials of 1692.[21] Such doubts about whether there had ever been an actual conspiracy prompted Judge Horsmanden to publish his own account of the trials in 1744. But the case he makes is simply not compelling. Instead, as one historian puts it, what comes across is "a world of prejudice and injustice" that "ensnared the New Yorkers of 1714."[22]

NOTES

1. *Journal of the Proceedings in the Detection of the Conspiracy* (Thursday, September 2, 1741), in Serena R. Zabin (ed.), *The New York Conspiracy Trials of 1741* (Boston, MA: Bedford/St. Martin's, 2004), 149.

2. Thelma Willis Foote, " 'Some Hard usage': The New York City Slave Revolt of 1712," *New York Folklore* 18 (1993), 147–159.

3. Peter Charles Hoffer, *The Great New York Conspiracy of 1741: Slavery, Crime, and Colonial Law* (Lawrence: University Press of Kansas, 2003), 48.

4. Horsmanden, *Journal* (Monday, April 6, 1741), in Zabin, 58.

5. Ibid.

6. Ibid., 56.

7. Quoted in Hoffer, 75.

8. Horsmanden, *Journal* (Wednesday, March 4, 1741), in Zabin, 53.

9. Ibid. (Wednesday, April 22, 1741), 66.

10. Ibid., 67.

11. Ibid. (Friday, May 8, 1741), 73, 74.

12. Ibid. (Thursday, May 14, 1741), 79.

13. Ibid. (Friday, May 29, 1741), 85.

14. Ibid. (Saturday, May 30, 1741), 87.

15. Hoffer, 107.

16. Horsmanden, *Journal* (Thursday, June 4, 1741), in Zabin, 97.

17. Ibid. (Monday, June 8, 1741), 103.

18. Ibid. (Saturday, June 27, 1741), 127.

19. Quoted in Hoffer, 132.

20. Horsmanden, *Journal* (Saturday, August 29, 1741), 148.

21. Jill Lepore, *New York Burning: Liberty, Slavery, and Conspiracy in Eighteenth-Century Manhattan* (New York: Alfred A. Knopf, 2005), xviii.

22. T. J. Davis, *A Rumor of Revolt: The "Great Negro Plot" in Colonial New York* (Amherst: University of Massachusetts Press, 1985), 263.

CHAPTER 4

THE PROSSER CONSPIRACY

The execution of [Gabriel Prosser's] purpose was frustrated only by a heavy fall of rain which made the water courses impassable.

—John Randolph[1]

In October 1799, a burly 23-year-old slave named Gabriel Prosser was brought before a court of oyer and terminer, a kind of county tribunal established by the Virginia legislature over a century earlier to deal specifically with slave offenses. The crime with which he was charged was assaulting and injuring a white man. Under normal circumstances, a slave found guilty of this particular crime faced a death sentence.

The fracas that brought Prosser to the tribunal had occurred the previous month. He and two other slaves had been caught stealing a pig from Absalom Johnson's sty. Pig-stealing by slaves was a common way of supplementing their scanty diet, and it was not uncommon for wealthier planters to turn a blind eye so long as the thievery did not get out of hand. But Johnson was a poor man who did not even own the land he farmed, and he could ill-afford the loss of one of his pigs. So when he caught the slaves in the act, he berated them so fiercely that an enraged Gabriel threw himself on Johnson, thrashing him soundly and biting off a piece of his left ear.

At his trial, Gabriel predictably pled innocence, and just as predictably was found guilty. He might have ended up on the end of a rope except for a rather bizarre loophole in Virginia law known as "benefit of clergy." If sentenced slaves could recite a verse from the Bible, they were spared death when convicted of capital crimes. Although there is no evidence to suggest that he was a particularly religious man, Gabriel belonged to that five percent of Virginia slaves who could read and write. So he was able to produce the required verse and escape the noose. "Therefore," his sentence read, "it is Considered by the Court that the said negro man slave Gabriel be burnt in the left hand."[2] After the branding, he was remanded to jail until his owner, Thomas Henry Prosser, guaranteed Absalom Johnson that he had nothing more to fear from Gabriel.

The immediate provocation of the assault on a white man that could have cost Gabriel his life was Johnson's insults. But as became clear less than a year later, Gabriel's behavior was more deeply fueled by a simmering rage at his own enslavement and the institution of slavery in general. The attack on Johnson was the first act in a drama unique in the history of colonial and early republic slave revolts, for a few months later Gabriel nearly pulled off what could well have been a history-changing conspiracy to capture Richmond, hold Virginia governor James Monroe captive, and kill any and all whites that got in the way. It was the best coordinated of all slave conspiracies, and had it been pulled off, it would have been the largest slave revolt in the United States, even larger than the 1811 German Coast revolt. But Prosser's careful planning was foiled by an unexpected and furious downpour of rain that flooded creeks and rivers, washed away bridges, and made dirt roads impassable. Some of the African-born slaves who had been part of the conspiracy to revolt darkly whispered that the rain came because Gabriel had failed to propitiate the spirits. But others, including Prosser himself, recognized it as simple bad luck.

FROM BROOKFIELD TO RICHMOND

Gabriel and his two brothers, Martin and Solomon, were born on a plantation called Brookfield. Their owner, Thomas Prosser, was a successful tobacco farmer who was also a partner in a Richmond trading firm. Prosser was a man of some wealth. An insurance policy taken out on his mansion in 1802 described it as a two-storied house with five bays and two wings. Surrounding it were the buildings typically found on a nearly-self-sufficient plantation: cook and store houses, smithy, barns, stables, and of course slave quarters. Like all the well-to-do planters in Henrico, the county in which both Brookfield and Richmond were located, Prosser owned several dozen slaves. In fact, only three other planters in the county possessed more.

Truth to tell, Henrico was more black than white. By 1800, the year of the conspiracy, some 5,000 black slaves and freedmen lived in the county's countryside, and over half of Richmond's population was black.

With the exception of Nat Turner, there are no contemporaneous likenesses of slave revolt leaders. This fanciful image of Gabriel Prosser depicts him in an unflattering way. (Historical Marker Database)

Nearly 10 percent of Virginia's black population was free, and the bulk of it resided in the state capital. The presence of so many freedmen contributed to the anxiety many whites felt about the possibility of a slave uprising. The fear was that free blacks would at least offer shelter to rebellious slaves and were likely to join them.

Despite the chronic fear of disgruntled blacks resorting to violence, someone on the Brookfield plantation taught young Gabriel to read and write. It was a strange thing to do, because educated slaves were especially feared by whites. The most likely teacher was Ann Prosser, Thomas's wife. Whether she tutored Gabriel with the knowledge of her husband is unknown. But it is doubtful.

By the time he was 10, a slave boy would have either been put to work in the fields or set to learning a trade. Gabriel and his brother Solomon were placed in the planation smithy to learn the skill that, in all probability, their father had practiced. The eldest brother, Martin, labored in the tobacco fields. We know little about Gabriel's personal life except that he took up with a slave woman on another plantation named Nanny. According to a proclamation published after the conspiracy was discovered, he was over six feet and had a dark complexion with "long visage, gloomy insidious brow, short black knotty hair, some scars on his head."[3] He was also missing his two front teeth, presumably knocked out in one of the fights that also earned him the head scars.

Some time, probably beginning in Gabriel's teens, Prosser began hiring him out to various blacksmiths in and around Richmond. It was a common practice in Virginia to "rent" slaves, sometimes field hands but typically skilled workers, in order to bring in some money to their land-rich but often cash-poor owners. In 1791, for example, Robert Carter, scion of Virginia aristocracy and the state's wealthiest planter, hired out more than two-thirds of his 500 slaves. Originally, planters had directly arranged the terms of the rental, negotiating for specific sums and time periods. But it became increasingly common for slave owners to leave the finding of jobs and negotiating of wages up to their skilled slaves. In return, masters allowed the slaves to keep a small percentage of the wages they earned. In some cases, slaves were even allowed by their owners to rent rooms in Richmond, provided they kept sending a steady stream of cash back to the plantations.

Whether Gabriel was self-hired or contracted out by his master is unknown. But what is certain is that he spent long periods of time in Richmond, both when he belonged to Thomas Prosser and afterward, when he was inherited in 1798 by Prosser's son, Thomas Henry. This not only gave Gabriel a taste of freedom that left him longing for more. It also brought him into contact with white laboring men and skilled workers, some of whom advocated human equality and the abolition of slavery. Virginia authorities were uncomfortably aware that the hiring-out of slaves risked exposing them to such radical notions, and at least one city, Norfolk, unsuccessfully sought to outlaw the practice. But hiring-out was simply too easy a way for planters to make money. Besides, since the practice began, scores of skilled white craftsmen, unable to compete with the cheap labor of slavery, had migrated northward. The practice of hiring-out had created its own niche.

The French Revolution in particular inspired the freedom-seeking Gabriel and the radical whites he met, even as it enraged slaveholding whites. Generally applauded by Jeffersonian Republican-Democrats and deplored by Federalists, the revolution's ideals of liberty, fraternity, and equality were imported into Richmond by Charles Quersey, whom Gabriel met on several occasions. Quersey apparently had arrived in America during the War of Independence and had fought at the siege of Yorktown. Settling for a while in Richmond, he lived a rather shadowy life agitating for emancipation among the white working class and hired-out slaves. One slave later testified that Quersey had "frequently advis'd him & several other Negroes, to rise & kill the White people and said he would help them & shew them how to fight."[4] A second unnamed Frenchman was also implicated. Most likely he was Alexander Beddenhurst, who like Quersey arrived in North America during the war years.

Listening to the incendiary talk of Quersey and perhaps Beddenhurst, and observing the political wrangling in Richmond between Republicans and Federalists, Gabriel grew convinced that white laborers would join in a slave revolt to overthrow their common masters. According to one slave's testimony, Gabriel "expected the poor White people would also join him, and that 2 frenchmen had actually joined."[5] Additionally, any white persons in Richmond, such as Quakers, Methodists, and other French expatriates who had shown themselves friendly to the possibility of freedom for slaves, were to be spared. The implication was that they, too, could be counted on to support Gabriel's bid for freedom.

There is absolutely no reason to suppose that Gabriel's expectations correlated to reality. Both Quersey and Beddenhurst, fearing that they would be implicated in the plot they had encouraged, fled to the north before the day of the uprising. Moreover, Gabriel's conviction that radical white laborers would join hands with Negro rebels was far-fetched. What he did not appreciate was that most people in America who embraced the French Revolution's call for liberty, equality, and fraternity never thought about applying it to enslaved or even free blacks. Nonetheless, what is significant about Gabriel's conspiracy was that it was inspired not by religious zealotry or claims of messiahship on his part, but by the moral conviction that *all* humans were created equal and that slavery was simply immoral.

THE CONSPIRACY

Sunday, August 10, 1800, was an important day for Gabriel Prosser. He had been laying the groundwork for the uprising for months, since at least early spring, recruiting troops, establishing cells, making weapons, and carefully thinking through the actual plan of attack. Now he was finally ready to share the details with his lieutenants. Up to that point, they had been told only as much as they needed to recruit others to the cause.

The occasion was the funeral of a slave child. Slaves from around Henrico received permission from their masters to travel to a place called Sweet Springs to pay their respects to the child's parents. But afterward, Gabriel gathered together the men who were in on the plot and shared with them what he had in mind. Interestingly, he told the assembly that his plan was not to fight just to free the slaves, but for "his Country."[6]

The plan that Gabriel relayed to the men was for a three-pronged attack on Richmond. The rebels would gather in the dead of night near the Brookfield plantation. They would murder Thomas Henry Prosser, Gabriel's master, as well as Absalom Johnson, the farmer with whom Gabriel had fought and been branded and jailed as a consequence. They then would march toward Richmond. Once there, they would split into three columns. The first would take Rockett's warehouse on Twenty Ninth Street down at the docks and set it afire as a diversion. As soon as the alarum was raised, so Gabriel hoped, most of the white townspeople would rush to the docks either to fight or to gawk at the flames. This would clear the way for the second group to take the city's penitentiary, which Governor Monroe had turned into a powder magazine. Simultaneously, the third group, led by Gabriel himself, would march on the capitol building and seize the weapons stored there. One of the rebel slaves later testified to what the rebels hoped would happen next. "If the white people agreed to their [the rebels'] freedom they would then hoist a white flag, and Gabriel would dine and drink with the merchants of the city on the day when it should be agreed to."[7] For their part, Gabriel's rebels would march into Richmond with a banner that read "Death or Liberty."

Some of the men who gathered to hear the plan were uneasy, and one of them, a huge slave named Jack Ditcher, actually challenged Gabriel for leadership. But when a vote was taken, support both for the conspiracy and for Gabriel was overwhelming. The date for the uprising was set for the night of Saturday, August 30. Most of the slaves in Henrico and surrounding counties—and Gabriel had recruited rebels from them all—worked only mornings on Saturdays and had afternoons and evenings free. Whites would not suspect anything amiss if they saw blacks traveling toward the city on Saturday afternoon. It was an ideal time.

The meeting at Sweet Springs came to an abrupt end when a white overseer arrived on the scene and broke up the gathering. Looking back afterward, some of the conspirators might have taken the unexpected termination as a portent of what was to come.

The August 10 meeting in which the date for the insurrection was settled was the culmination of hard and more or less covert work on the part of Gabriel and the handful of men he selected as his lieutenants. When forming his inner circle of conspirators, Gabriel almost immediately selected his brother Solomon, but kept Martin, the eldest of the three brothers, in the dark until the last minute. Apparently he distrusted Martin. In addition to Solomon, Gabriel recruited a number of hired-out slaves he had met while working in Richmond, most of whom were skilled or semi-skilled artisans. Of all the slave revolts and conspiracies to revolt, Gabriel's was the only one that was primarily urban in nature. All the others were agrarian in origin and consisted mainly of disgruntled field workers.

Although Gabriel and his lieutenants were occasionally careless about whom they approached for the purpose of recruiting, for the most part they took care to guard the conspiracy from exposure. The lieutenants kept lists of the men they recruited—a dangerous but necessary thing to do—but no one, not even Gabriel, knew all of their identities. The hope was that if any single lieutenant was discovered and questioned, the uprising as a whole would not be jeopardized.

Slaves who might have access to guns or swords—ones whose masters, for example, served in the local militia—were particularly attractive as recruits. The blacksmiths among the conspirators kept busy making weapons that were crosses between spears and swords; scythes were broken in the middle and the pieces honed to razor sharpness before being secured in wooden handles. Gabriel knew that only a handful of federal troops were stationed permanently in Richmond, and he hoped that most, if not all, of them would join the curious crowds down at the docks when the first group of rebels fired Rockett's warehouse. The few firearms that the slaves could collect, coupled with the fierce stabbing and slashing weapons they fashioned, would be enough to fight through to the powder magazine and capitol building.

As spring progressed into summer, Gabriel extended the scope of his recruiting efforts, sending agents to Petersburg, which had the largest number of freed blacks of any Virginia city; the coastal town of Norfolk, which (unusual in Virginia) had a majority population of whites; and the counties immediately adjacent to Henrico. He also began trying to recruit freedmen to his cause. One he especially courted was Robert Cowley, the aged mulatto son of a Virginia aristocrat who served as the doorkeeper to the capitol building. Gabriel hoped that Cowley, who had the keys to the building, would open the doors to the rebels on the night of the uprising. It was a risk letting Cowley in on the conspiracy, but one Gabriel thought worth taking.

Inevitably, some of the slaves who were approached about joining the conspiracy balked and occasionally threatened to reveal the plot. Typically, they were threatened with swift and deadly retribution if they talked. They were free to join the conspiracy or to walk away from it. But their silence was required. Under the circumstances, threat of sure death was the most that the conspirators could do to protect their secret. But as events proved, it was not enough.

A "MOST TERRIBLE THUNDER STORM"

It started raining about noon on Saturday, the day of the planned insurrection. The rain started quickly and came down fiercely, soon flooding streets, overflowing creek beds, washing away small bridges, and turning roads into trails of mud. James Callender, a journalist who had been imprisoned under the notorious Alien and Sedition Act, laws ramrodded by President John Adams that effectively made it a crime to publicly criticize his administration, was astounded at the downpour. "There came on the most terrible thunder Storm," he wrote, "accompanied with an enormous rain, that I ever witnessed in this State."[8] Nor did the rain abate until late that night or early Sunday morning.

Between Richmond and Prosser's plantation, where the rebellious slaves were to gather, lay Brook Swamp, a small stream and wetlands that ran across the main road to the city and over which there was a bridge. The rain flooded the stream and the surrounding countryside with alarming speed. Sixty years later, a man who had witnessed the torrential downpour remembered that "the entire Brook stream covered the whole flat from hill to hill, some three-quarters of a mile wide," making the area completely unpassable.[9]

This flooding of the route into Richmond spelled doom to Gabriel's plot. Richmond slaves and freedmen who were intended to join slaves gathered at Brookfield for the march on the city could not get across the swollen creeks. Even if they had been able to get out of the city, it is unlikely that either they or their companions could have gotten back. And had they, the blinding rainfall would have severely damaged Gabriel's plans. Rockett's warehouse would have been hard, if not impossible, to fire, thus eliminating the diversion that Gabriel counted on to capture the powder magazine and the capitol.

Moreover, the recruits from Petersburg and Norfolk, as well as those in the adjacent counties of Caroline and Hanover, were unable to make it to Brookfield. It was not long before Gabriel recognized that his plans had been literally washed away. He told the handful of slaves who had managed to make it to the assembly point to disperse and return to their homes. They would try again the following night.

By the time the band of slaves crept off into the sodden night, doubts had begun to assail at least one of them, a 27-year-old man named Pharaoh, the property of Philip Sheppard. He had joined the conspiracy late and was probably never as committed to it as others. Belonging to a man who worked alongside him, Pharaoh, unlike the hired-out slaves who had little personal contact with their owners, had developed loyalties to the white family that owned him. His masters had treated him well, and he must have been conflicted from the very beginning of his involvement in Gabriel's conspiracy.

In his *Black Thunder*, a novel about the failed conspiracy, twentieth-century author Arna Bontemps speculates that the deluge may have taken the spirit out of many of Gabriel's followers because they interpreted it as a sign of disfavor from God or spirits. There is no extant testimony from Gabriel's followers to this effect, but given the deeply religious nature of many slaves, as well as Gabriel's refusal to invoke any religious justifications for his conspiracy, it is not implausible. Perhaps part of Pharaoh's doubts stemmed from this fear.

Whatever his reasons, by the time he arrived back at his master's farm, Pharaoh had decided to betray the plot. Confiding in another Sheppard slave, the two revealed the conspiracy to Mosby Sheppard, brother of Pharaoh's owner. Sheppard immediately galloped to the home of the near-est neighbor, who in turn scurried to the planation of William Austin, a leader in the local militia. Soon, a small posse of whites had been formed to scour the countryside for the rebellious slaves. But the same downpour that foiled the march on Richmond also handicapped the planters in their search for the rebels, and they returned to their homes at dawn soaked through and through.

By then, however, word about a slave conspiracy to take Richmond had spread widely from Richmond to Petersburg. Twenty-four hours after the rain began, Governor Monroe, who a few days earlier had actually received and dismissed rumors of a revolt in the planning, took action. He had all the firearms in the capitol building that Gabriel had hoped to capture removed to the more easily defended penitentiary. But he also insisted that things be done with discretion. He did not want to frighten the public any more than it already was.

At about the same time that Monroe issued his orders, Gabriel got word that the conspiracy had been betrayed and that armed patrols were on the lookout for him and his cohorts. He and his onetime rival Jack Ditcher managed to elude them, although others were not as fortunate. By Monday night, six of Gabriel's followers had been captured and jailed in Richmond. But the authorities only began to appreciate how real the danger had been when a slave named John spilled everything he knew about the plot, including its reach outside of Henrico county. It was at this point, when the planned uprising no longer seemed a local affair, that Monroe decided that safety was more important than secrecy, and he mustered out the state militia. Each county in Virginia had a militia company, products of the South's paranoia about possible slave revolts. The unit called up to protect Richmond would stay mustered throughout the rest of the year.

Calling out militia regiments not only cost Virginia a pretty penny. It also helped to create the very panic that Monroe had hoped to avoid. As more and more guards appeared in Petersburg, Norfolk, Richmond, Williamsburg, and other cities throughout the commonwealth, citizens became convinced that they had narrowly escaped indiscriminate slaugh-ter, and this in turn ratcheted up the level of their chronic anxiety that enslaved and free blacks in Virginia were savages just waiting for an oppor-tunity to rampage. The news of the foiled plot even made its way to

England, prompting one British merchant to write an alarmed letter to his American partner about whether the planned insurrection would be bad for business.[10]

Within 10 days of the plot's discovery, 30 slaves suspected of taking part in it had been rounded up by the militia. Unlike the aftermaths of other slave revolts and conspiracies, there was no indiscriminate slaughter of blacks or extralegal tribunals. Monroe was determined that the suspects would be tried according to the law of the land, and he even ordered that extra blankets and candles be allotted to them as they waited in jail for their day in court. But neither of these gestures meant that Monroe intended to show mercy to the rebels. As he wrote to Thomas Jefferson, he was confident that "the whole, very few excepted, will be condemned."[11]

THE TRIALS

The trials of the arrested slaves began during the second week of September. Gabriel still had not been captured, but Monroe believed it essential to begin the judicial proceedings as soon as possible as a means of reassuring the public that punishment of rebel slaves was swift.

Slave insurrection was a capital offense in Virginia, and the law allowed for no mitigating circumstances such as the "benefit of clergy" clause that had saved Gabriel when he chewed off a piece of Absalom Johnson's ear the previous year. Even though slaves were not allowed to testify against white defendants—the legal justification was that slaves were by nature untrustworthy, but the real reason was that Virginians could not bear the thought of a black accusing a white in court—they could testify against other slaves. So when the trials commenced, the star witnesses for the prosecution were Pharaoh, who had betrayed the conspiracy to his master, and Ben, a young slave belonging to Thomas Prosser who, although a member of the plot, hoped to save his own skin by testifying against his fellow conspirators.

The prisoners knew all too well that there was little to no chance of acquittal, and most of them refused to testify against the others, even though some willingly confessed their role in the conspiracy. One of them surely voiced the hopeless defiance of many of his fellows when he said to the court, "I beg, as a favor, that I may be immediately led to execution. I know that you have pre-determined to shed my blood, why then all this mockery of a trial?"[12] Another was eloquent in his refusal to ask for mercy. "I have nothing more to offer," he told his judges, "than what General Washington would have had to offer, had he been taken by the British and put to trial. I have adventured my life in endeavoring to obtain the liberty of my countrymen, and am a willing sacrifice in their cause."[13]

Some of the prisoners, of course, were terrified and tried desperately to save their lives. Two of them were Gabriel's brothers, Solomon and Martin. Solomon, tried first, kept quiet, perhaps reconciled to his fate, especially given both Ben's and Pharaoh's damning testimony against him. The court quickly sentenced him to death, the sentence to be carried out the following day. But during the night, Solomon became so rattled by death-fear that he petitioned for a stay of execution in order to amend his testimony. He made a full confession to the judges this time, but tried to mitigate his guilt by underscoring Gabriel's leadership: "My Brother Gabriel was the person who influenced me to join him."[14] The tactic did not work, and Solomon was one of the first insurrectionists hanged.

Martin, the illiterate eldest brother whom Gabriel had not wanted to be part of the conspiracy, was tongue-tied with terror when his time in the dock arrived. Hoping, no doubt, that his age would soften the judges' heart, he pled not guilty. But again the testimony of Ben, as well as another slave named John who also hoped to save himself by turning against his co-conspirators, convinced the court of the defendant's guilt. They testified that when Gabriel told Martin he was too old to be useful in the conspiracy, Martin responded by promising to secure bullets. Martin was hanged the day after his trial.

And so it went, day after day, with prisoners being sold out in court by Ben, John, and Pharaoh and typically executed the very next day. During the first week of trials, no fewer than 17 defendants were hanged in Richmond. The first few executions drew large crowds of onlookers, either curious to see men die or anxious for vengeance. But by the third round of hangings, on the morning of September 18, the public had lost interest in viewing them. There was one protest against the executions, but not out of compassion for the prisoners. A few well-bred Richmond ladies complained to the city council about the offensiveness of the hangings and requested that they take place away from their view. The council obliged, and the next five slaves condemned to death were carted out of the city and hanged from a tree. As one historian points out, their deaths would have been much more agonizing than if they had been hanged from a gallows, where a prisoner's neck broke as soon as he dropped through the trap. Strung up on a tree, the condemned man strangled slowly.

All these executions partially reassured the public that Monroe and his militia had things under control. But Gabriel was still on the loose, and this gave citizens cause for continued alarm. Their anxiety came to an end on September 29, when Gabriel was captured in Norfolk after stowing away for a few days in a boat. It is not clear if the white captain of the vessel was aware of his passenger's identity. But one of the man's slaves recognized Gabriel and betrayed him for the $300 bounty on his head.

Gabriel was brought to Richmond in chains. He told his captors that he would speak only to Governor Monroe. Whether Gabriel made this decision because he thought it proper that the commander of a failed rebellion should be interrogated by the commander of the forces that defeated him, or because he wanted to make sure that the governor of the commonwealth was aware of the thirst for liberty, equality, and fraternity that fueled the planned insurrection, is not clear. But Monroe declined interviewing Gabriel, and so the man who had hoped to conquer Richmond remained silent throughout his trial.

Three witnesses testified against Gabriel, all of them playing up the fact that he intended most whites—with the exceptions of Methodists, Quakers, and Frenchmen—to be slaughtered. One of the witnesses outlined in especially gruesome details the plan to kill all whites, "except as before excepted, unless they agreed to the freedom of the Blacks, in which case they would at least cut off one of their Arms."[15] Such bloodthirsty plans whose truth Gabriel neither confirmed nor denied, coupled with the fact that his aborted insurrection was inspired by precisely the desire for liberty that had sparked the American Revolution, outraged the judges. Their sentence of death surprised no one. Gabriel, too much of a celebrity to be quietly hanged in the countryside, swung from the city gallows on October 10. There is no record of his execution upsetting Richmond's ladies.

AFTERMATH

Before the executions finally ended, 27 slaves were hanged. About midway through the executions, Governor Monroe began to feel some uneasiness about all the deaths—an uneasiness probably prompted more by the

$9,000 it cost the state to compensate slave owners for the loss of their property than by compassion for the victims—and wrote his friend and mentor Thomas Jefferson for advice.

Jefferson responded a couple of weeks before Gabriel was hanged. "Where to stay the hand of the executioner is an important question," he wrote. Even in Jefferson's neck of Virginia, "where every thing has been perfectly tranquil, but where a familiarity with slavery, and a possibility of danger from that quarter prepare the general mind for some severities, there is a strong sentiment that there has been hanging enough." Should it continue, "the other states & the world at large will for ever condemn us [for] indulg[ing] a principle of revenge." Jefferson went on to sympathize with the "difficult situation" Monroe was in, acknowledging that the accused slaves could never be "permitted to go at large among us."[16] But the killing had to stop.

Monroe accepted Jefferson's counsel, although only after a few more executions. (The final one fell on October 24.) Thereafter, slaves who were accused of complicity in Gabriel's plot were either acquitted or, if found guilty, transported down South to the rice, sugar, and cotton plantations where life for a field hand was short and harsh. Jack Ditcher, the giant of a slave who had challenged Gabriel's leadership, was one of those transported.

Pharaoh, Ben, and John, the three primary witnesses for the prosecution, fared much better. Despite his willingness to implicate others, Ben was found guilty for his own part in the conspiracy and sentenced to death, a verdict that Governor Monroe overthrew. John likewise was pardoned. Pharaoh, as a reward for being the slave who first betrayed Gabriel's plans, was emancipated and granted $60 per annum by a grateful Virginia legislature.

The terrible irony of Gabriel Prosser's bid for freedom was that he was motivated by the very same republican ideals that inspired James Monroe, Thomas Jefferson, and many of their white fellow citizens. Prosser took seriously the nation's founding document's claim that all men are created equal, and he and his followers willingly risked their all for its sake. Federalist leaders were quick to point out that it was supporters of the French Revolution like their political foes Monroe and Jefferson who had "infused into the minds of the negroes" subversive ideals of liberty and equality. "If any thing will correct & bring to repentance" hotheaded defenders of revolution, one newspaper thundered, "it must be *an insurrection of their slaves.*"[17] But at least one Southern commentator, writing for the Fredericksburg *Virginia Herald,* called for white America to take its own rhetoric seriously. "The question now is a plain one—shall we abolish slavery or shall we emancipate? There is no middle course to it. We must do one thing or t'other."[18]

For their parts, Jefferson and Monroe seemed to appreciate the hypocrisy, but chose to live with it. Jefferson continued to own slaves to the end of his life, and Monroe, whenever asked in later years about the suppression of Gabriel's conspiracy, generally maintained a stony silence.

NOTES

1. John Randolph to Joseph Nicholson (September 26, 1800), in *Gabriel's Conspiracy: A Documentary History,* ed. Philip J. Schwarz (Charlottesville: University of Virginia Press, 2012), 113.

2. Ibid., 5.

3. Ibid., 74.

4. Ibid., 99.

5. Ibid., Trial of Gabriel (October 6, 1800), 152.

6. Quoted in Douglas R. Edgerton, *Gabriel's Rebellion: The Virginia Slave Conspiracies of 1800 and 1802* (Chapel Hill: University of North Carolina Press, 1993), 64.

7. Ibid., 51.

8. James T. Callender to Thomas Jefferson (September 13, 1800), in Schwarz (ed.), *Documentary History,* 54.

9. *Richmond Daily Dispatch,* April 11, 1861.

10. Edgerton, *Gabriel's Rebellion,* 77.

11. James Monroe to Thomas Jefferson (September 9, 1800), in Schwarz (ed.), *Documentary History,* 29.

12. Quoted in Edgerton, *Gabriel's Rebellion,* 82.

13. Ibid., 102.

14. Confession of Solomon (September 11, 1800), in Schwarz (ed.), *Documentary History,* 37.

15. Ibid., Trial of Gabriel (October 6, 1800), 153.

16. Ibid., Thomas Jefferson to James Monroe (September 20, 1800), 89.

17. *Boston Gazette,* October 9, 1800.

18. *Fredericksburg Virginia Herald,* September 23, 1800.

CHAPTER 5

THE GERMAN COAST REVOLT

The heads of the executed shall be cut off and placed atop a pole on the spot where all can see the punishment meted out for such crimes, also as a terrible example to all who would disturb the public tranquility in the future.

—Judicial Proceedings Decree[1]

It was pouring rain in New Orleans on the morning of January 9, 1811, and the road running into the city was quickly transformed into thick mud that sucked in horse hoofs, carriage wheels, and human feet alike. The miserable weather contributed to the traffic jam, stretching as far as nine miles, of frantic planters, along with their families and servants, who were fleeing their plantations for the safety of the city. As one observer described it, the road to New Orleans "for two or three leagues was crowded with carriage and carts full of people, making their escape from the ravages of the banditti—negroes, half naked, up to their knees in mud with large packages on their heads driving along toward the city."[2]

The "banditti" who were the cause of this panicked exodus were slaves who had banded together to throw off their bondage. Many of them were African warriors who had been in Louisiana for only a short while and who chaffed at their chains. They were headed for New Orleans with the rumored intention of taking over the city and killing every white they could get their hands on. William C. Claiborne, governor of the Louisiana Territory, took the rumor seriously. Memory of the all-too-recent slave uprising in Haiti, coupled with the fact that the majority of New Orleans residents were free or enslaved blacks, convinced him that the city and indeed the whole southern tip of the vast territory purchased from France less than a decade earlier were in danger.

Claiborne and the other white residents of New Orleans were right to be alarmed by the slave revolt. Even though they could not have known it at the time, it was the largest armed slave uprising in U.S. history, involving anywhere from 200 to 500 slaves. Despite the large number of participants, the uprising, which came to be called the German Coast revolt after its place of origin, was quickly quashed. But it contributed to an underlying anxiety among whites in and around New Orleans that endured right up to the Civil War.

NEW ORLEANS AND THE GERMAN COAST

The territory that an overextended and cash-strapped Napoleon sold the United States in 1803 stretched from New Orleans north and northwest all the way up to the Canadian border, adding close to a million square miles to the young nation. By far the most settled part of the vast region was the area around New Orleans. The economic importance of the city and its surrounding area was hard to overestimate. New Orleans was the port from which the territory's vast resources sailed to European markets, and the delta land surrounding it was rich from centuries of river overflow. Just to the northwest of the city, along the Mississippi River, the watery route that became the territory's principal highway, was the fruitful and wealthy region called the German Coast.

The German Coast derived its name from the numerous German immigrants who settled there in the early eighteenth century. Once arrived, they intermarried with the French planters who were already established, to the point where the German language gave way after three or four generations to French and Creole. In the intervening years, plantations along the German Coast became ever more opulent, with unparalleled plantation homes and gardens facing the Mississippi River. The wealthy landowners who lived in them constituted the area's aristocracy.

The incredible wealth of the German Coast planters was derived from slave-worked sugarcane fields. The climate of the Lower South was suited to the crop, and the German Coast aristocrats who specialized in it had turned their plantations into efficient sugar factories. Hundreds of slaves planted, grew, harvested, and processed the crop, often in brutally sweltering conditions. They also repaired the levees and dams that held back the tempestuous waters of the Mississippi. The general attitude among the planters was that only blacks were capable of the backbreaking labor required to operate a sugar plantation. As one of them, Jean Noel Destrehan, remarked,

> To the necessity of employing African laborers, which arises from the climate and the species of cultivation pursued in warm latitudes, is added a reason in this country peculiar to itself. The banks raised to restrain the waters of the Mississippi can only be kept in repair by those whose natural constitution and habit of labor enable them to resist the combined effects of deleterious moisture and a degree of heat intolerable to whites.[3]

But even the planters knew that this race-based assumption of blacks' suitability for work in such conditions was a fiction. Once he began working in the sugar fields, the life expectancy of a slave was not much more than five or six years. Fortunately for the planters, there was a seemingly inexhaustible supply of black slaves, both those imported from overseas until the trade was officially banned by the United States in 1808 and those purchased from slave states, especially Virginia, further north. Of the 20,000 African slaves who arrived in New Orleans between 1790 and 1808, at least 10 percent were warriors from Konga with war experience; many of them, in fact, had been captured in battle and sold to white slavers. At least two of them would become leaders in the 1811 uprising.

The market demand for sugar was clamorous, and to meet it—and to keep growing their already vast wealth—German Coast planters cultivated more and more land, which in turn required more and more slaves. By 1810, nearly 90 percent of households in and around New Orleans owned at least one slave, and a whopping 75 percent of the overall population was made up of slaves.

When Thomas Jefferson appointed William Claiborne of Virginia as the territory's first governor, the German Coast aristocracy as well as the institution of slavery was well entrenched. Claiborne, an ardent champion of the American experiment, took up his appointment with the intention of making Louisiana a state as soon as humanly possible. But it soon became apparent to him that he had entered into a culture that he little understood, and which in turn had little interest in cooperating with him.

In the first place, only 10 percent of the residents in the greater New Orleans area were Anglo-American; the rest were French, Spanish, African, and Creole. Most of them were Catholics, and Claiborne was not. Most of them spoke either French or the local French-based patois, and Claiborne spoke only English.

Much more of a threat to his authority, however, was the resistance of the German Coast aristocracy. They had gotten along quite well without outside interference and they bitterly resented being answerable to Claiborne simply because of a transaction between Thomas Jefferson and Napoleon. In quick order they launched a campaign against the governor in the local press, criticizing him for his inability to learn French, for his uncouth manners, and for his obvious preference for Anglo rather than French customs. Claiborne, for his part, blasted the planters as morally wanting—debauched, even—and went so far as to declare in public that they simply were not the kind of stuff from which true Americans were made.

Things came to a head in 1805, when a delegation of planters, led by the same Jean Noel Destrehan who argued that black slaves were well suited to the heat and humidity of the sugarcane fields, traveled to Washington to lay their case before President James Madison. They insisted that Claiborne was unfitted to be governor, that he be immediately removed, and that the true leaders of Louisiana—the French-speaking aristocrats along the German Coast—be recognized. Speaking for them all, Destrehan assured Madison that "we were among the first settlers; and, perhaps, there would be no vanity in asserting that the first establishment of Louisiana might vie with that of any other in America for the respectability and information of those who composed it."[4] Madison was unimpressed, and Claiborne remained in office.

But it was not simply the strange mixed culture and the hostility of the planter aristocracy that Claiborne had to contend with. He also worried nonstop about the presence of Spanish Florida to his east. Like all Americans who defended the institution of slavery, Claiborne fretted over Florida's standing offer of freedom to slaves who could make their way there, fearing that it was a continuous inducement to insubordination and even insurrection. So, with the approval of President Madison, he concocted a rather convoluted scheme in 1810 to seize west Florida, thereby creating a buffer zone between Louisiana and Spanish Florida.

To protect it from being retaken by Spain, in January 1811 Claiborne ordered most of the American troops stationed in New Orleans there. Given what was about to break loose on the German Coast, it could not have been worse timing.

"FREEDOM OR DEATH!"

The ringleaders in the German Coast uprising were an unlikely mix that included Charles Deslondes, a "driver"—a sort of foreman of slaves who himself was a slave; Quamana and Kook, two African field hands stolen from their homeland only five years earlier; and Harry Kenner, a Virginia-born carpenter.

By most accounts, Deslondes was the likely conceiver of the plot to revolt. Born on the German Coast, his light skin and intelligence soon earned him his position as overseer of the slaves belonging to his master, a sugar planter named Manuel Andry. Andry had a reputation for being one of the Coast's harshest slaveholders, and Deslondes must have both seen and been ordered to carry out multiple punishments of the men and women Andry owned. He may have even been ill-treated himself. Whatever his motive, Deslondes began to visit the plantations along the German Coast to incite his fellow slaves to rise up. As a driver, he had a freer rein than most other slaves when it came to travel, and he had a wife on the Trépagnier plantation, several miles away from Andry's, whom he frequently visited. So his comings and goings went relatively unnoticed by whites.

Kook and Quamana, who belonged to planter James Brown, were probably 20 or 21 years of age at the time of the revolt. Both of them were taller than the average slave. Kook towered over six feet. Little is known about them except that they worked in the killing sugarcane fields and that, judging from their names, they could well have been from the warlike Akan nation. As such, they were probably *okofokums*, or soldiers, before being captured and sold into slavery, and they resisted their bondage from the very start. They not only served as Charles Deslondes's liaisons with other Africa-born slaves, but quite possibly were able to offer tactical advice to the rebels.

Harry Kenner, like Charles a light-skinned slave, was a carpenter whose skill rescued him from the drudgery of field work. Twenty-five years old, he lived on a plantation close to New Orleans. Along with his three compatriots, he established cells of resistance up and down the Coast, promising that a well-planned uprising could destroy the hated sugarcane plantations, capture New Orleans, and liberate every slave in Louisiana. After months of careful planning, a 30-mile-long network of slaves awaited the word from Charles. It came on Epiphany Sunday, January 6, 1811: the uprising would begin in two days.

On the night of January 8, in the midst of a steady rain, Charles Deslondes and about 25 companions crept into Manuel Andry's mansion as he and his family lay sleeping. They carried axes, knives, clubs, and any other object they had found that could serve as a weapon. Surprising Manuel and his son Gilbert in their beds, the slaves hacked the younger Andry to pieces, but only managed to inflict three severe but nonlethal blows on Manuel, who broke from his assailants and scampered down toward the Mississippi River, where he had a small boat tied up. Charles decided that chasing after him in the dark would break the momentum of the uprising.

It was a fatal mistake. Despite his wounds, Andry managed to make his way to a neighboring plantation owned by Charles Perret. Horrified by his tale and his wounds, Perret saddled a horse and raced to notify the other plantation owners along the Coast. By morning, all of them had been alerted and were already preparing to quell the uprising.

After butchering Gilbert Andry, the rebellious slaves broke into a storeroom in the mansion and seized muskets, power, bullets, and militia uniforms, all of which had been stockpiled by the two Andry men, who belonged to the local militia. Charles found himself a horse and, mounted, he led his pack of uniformed rebels to the next plantation. The plan was to sack the houses, kill the whites, and recruit slaves as they traveled the 40-odd miles to New Orleans. They expected to make it there within two days, marching to the beat of an African drum and shouting "Freedom or Death!"

They met with mixed success in both the killing and the recruiting, although they did manage to destroy a fair amount of property and along the way were joined by runaway slaves who had made lives for themselves in the swamps. Despite Charles's best efforts over the previous weeks to convince slaves to join him in rebellion, only about a quarter of the German Coast slaves actually did. Many of them warned their masters and mistresses of the approaching storm and secreted them out of plantation houses before Charles and his army could capture or kill them.

When the rebels reached the John Brown plantation, they rejoiced that Kook and Quamana had managed to persuade (or, in some cases, intimidate) about half of Brown's slaves to join the revolt. Numbering some 100 men, they moved on to the estate of Francois Trépagnier, who owned the slave woman who was Charles's wife. Trépagnier sent one of his loyal slaves to warn the planters down the line, but he chose to face the rebellious slaves swarming toward his house. He sent his wife and children into the nearby swamps, but he remained behind on a second-floor landing of his mansion, armed with loaded guns and waiting.

Trépagnier's refusal to flee was probably motivated more by contempt for slaves than courage. Uniformly hated by blacks throughout the German Coast, his cruelty was legendary. It is not clear if the story is true, but it was rumored that "he kept a slave boy named Gustave as a house pet. As Trépagnier ate, he would toss food from the table onto the floor, where Gustave would pick it up and eat it. Other men had dogs, went the story, but Trépagnier had a black child."[5] True or not, the fact that the tale circulated among his contemporaries attests to the reputation for savagery Trépagnier had.

As dawn broke, Charles's army approached the Trépagnier mansion. The planter fired off a couple of shots, convinced that the sound was enough to frighten them away. He was mistaken. Kook broke into the house from the back and killed the hated planter with his ax as other rebels set the mansion on fire. The army was jubilant at the death of Trépagnier. As things turned out, he was the second and last white to die in the revolt.

About the time that Trépagnier's mansion was catching fire, Governor Claiborne, confronted with the long line of refugees pouring into New Orleans, prepared to defend the city from the slave army that his panicked scouts assured him was on the way. With the majority of New Orleans residents black, and with most of the troops normally stationed in the city assigned to West Florida, Claiborne feared chaos. He began hustling women and children to the fortress at Faubourg Marigny and ordered the bridges and roads leading into the city sealed, with instructions to allow "no Negroes to pass or repass the same."[6] Just to be on the safe side, he also shut down the city's taverns and cabarets and imposed a curfew of 6 p.m.

for the city's black inhabitants, regardless of whether they were free or slave.

Claiborne also conferred with General Wade Hampton, whose grandson and namesake would serve as a Confederate general in the Civil War. By chance, Hampton had arrived in the city two days earlier from West Florida, and the governor, grateful for his presence, ordered him to organize a militia and the 30 regular troops left in the city into a force of resistance. Commodore John Shaw, commander of the naval fleet docked in New Orleans, sent 40 of his sailors to shore to lend a hand. By the end of the day, Hampton had managed to put together a motley army of about 100 men. The small force left the city as the sun was setting to meet the insurgents. Some of the planters fleeing to the city they met along the way were either shamed or inspired by the ragtag army and turned around to return to their abandoned plantations to put up a fight. For his part, Governor Claiborne, who doubtless got little sleep that night, turned to prayer. "I pray God that the force sent from this City may soon meet the Brigands and arrest them in their murdering career."[7]

THE BATTLE

During the hours that Governor Claiborne was securing the city and General Hampton was mustering his army, the rebel slaves had advanced steadily toward New Orleans, burning plantations and adding new recruits as they went. As they neared the city, they burned the Meuillion mansion, home to the wealthiest planter on the German Coast, as well as the plantation house belonging to Harry Kenner's master. By nightfall on January 9, they had traveled over 20 miles and decided to rest at the sugar-processing works owned by Jacques Fortier, whose plantation was the last large one before New Orleans.

Hampton's army arrived at Fortier's place about four o'clock the next morning, where his scouts almost literally stumbled on the sleeping slaves. After they reported back to Hampton, he carefully deployed his troops in battle formation. But somehow the slaves discovered what was going on and, under cover of darkness, managed to slip away. When Hampton gave the order to attack just before dawn, there was no enemy to be found.

One historian speculates that the retreat of Charles Deslondes's rebel army was actually a West African military tactic initiated by Kook and

Quamana: tire and confuse the enemy by disappearing suddenly and then popping up elsewhere.[8] Whether or not this was the reason for the slaves' sneaking away in the dark, their departure evidently discombobulated Hampton's bone-weary men who had tramped nonstop throughout the entire night. When the general saw that he had been outwitted, he decided that the smartest thing to do was to give his exhausted militiamen some much-needed rest instead of immediately tracking down the insurgents.

For reasons that remain mysterious, Charles steered his rebel army back along the route it had traveled, moving northwest along the river away from New Orleans. Perhaps he realized that even with the weapons he had secured at the Andry plantation, his men were still outgunned by Hampton's troops. Perhaps he was hoping to draw Hampton's army further away from the city to minimize the possibility of reinforcements. Or he might have backtracked in the hope of picking up more recruits. But whatever his reasons, his rebels retreated about 15 miles, eventually halting at the plantation owned by the Bernard Bernoudy family.

It was there that a posse of around 80 planters discovered them on the morning of January 10. After the badly wounded Andry had made his way to the Perret mansion, male members of the German Coast planter families had assembled to attack the rebel army. Andry, his wounds notwithstanding, and Charles Perret, led them. Charles Deslondes and his companions were taken by surprise; they had not expected another army besides Hampton's to take the field against them, and particularly not from the rear.

Afterward, Perrot estimated that the rebellious slaves numbered about 200, half of them mounted. Other estimates were much higher. But regardless of the actual number of slaves present, two facts are indisputable: there were more of them than of whites, and they were not nearly as well armed as the planters. Battle lines were formed, with men in either army facing one another. Their smooth-bore muskets had an effective range of less than 500 yards.

It is not clear which side let loose the first volley, but the actual back-and-forth shooting ended quickly. In all likelihood the slaves were awkward with the weapons they had, and many may not have had the expertise to reload. The slave line broke, the planters charged, and the killing began. One contemporary wrote, "Fifteen or twenty of [the slaves] were killed and fifty

prisoners were taken including three of their leaders with uniforms and epau-
lets. The rest fled quickly into the woods."[9] Charles Perret put the number of
those slain between 40 and 45. One explanation for the different estimates
might be that the lower estimate counted only those slaves killed outright,
and Perret's included those wounded slaves who were slain where they lay
on the battlefield by the furious planters. None of the planters were killed,
and apparently none suffered any wounds worth reporting.

Other members of the slave army, including Kook, Quamana, and
Harry Kenner, were captured and forced to watch as the planters first fin-
ished off the wounded and then chopped off their heads. The terror of a
slave uprising had turned into rage, and the whites who decimated Charles
Deslondes's army were not satisfied merely with killing the renegades.
They needed to show their disdain for them by mutilating their bodies.
The decapitations created a grisly precedent that would be repeated again
and again in the coming days.

The rest of the slave army had fled into the nearby swamps as soon as
their ranks broke. Among them was their ringleader, the driver Charles
Deslondes, who had initiated the plot. The planters brought out blood-
hounds and Indian scouts to track them, and Charles was one of the first
to be captured. The dogs caught up with him, brought him down, and
mauled him pretty badly before their handlers called them off. He was then
brought back to the cane field where the battle had been fought and
horribly tortured and executed. His two hands were severed, his legs were
broken, he was shot, and then, still alive, he was burned to death.

The largest slave revolt in U.S. history was over. Its prime mover was
dead, and his three lieutenants captured. Now that the immediate panic
was over, terrible reprisals began.

"SCOURING THE COUNTRY IN EVERY DIRECTION"

On the very morning that the battle at Bernoudy plantation was being
fought, federal troops from West Florida arrived in New Orleans to
reinforce the city's defenses. General Hampton posted them in the
German Coast area "to protect and Give Countenance to the Various
Companies of the Citizens that are Scouring the Country in Every direction" for rebels who had fled.[10] Both Claiborne and Hampton were pretty
sure that the immediate danger of revolt was over, but both were also

convinced that the Spanish had encouraged Deslondes and his men to insurrection. So they were on the lookout for further outbreaks of slave violence.

Hampton's "Citizens that are Scouring the Country in Every direction" referred, of course, to the German Coast planters who were busy over the next few days hunting down the rebel slaves. Many of them, once found, were murdered on the spot, and their heads sent to New Orleans. It was not long before over 100 decapitated bodies and severed heads were displayed on poles along a 40-mile stretch extending from the city's center all the way to the German Coast. One planter wrote that the trophies "look like crows sitting on long poles."[11] The purpose of the ghoulish display was twofold: to terrify remaining slaves with horrific examples of the fate that awaited insurrectionists—as Manuel Andry angrily said, to "make a GREAT EXAMPLE"[12]—and to reassure whites of the same thing.

The 20 or so slaves captured during the showdown between the rebels and the planters were chained and marched back to where the revolt was hatched: the plantation of Jean Noel Destrehan, owner of the now dead Charles Deslondes. They were held in a washhouse just back of the big house while a tribunal of five planters was appointed to interrogate them, gather testimony, and hand out sentences. For appearance's sake, a local judge, Pierre Bauchet St. Martin, who had been a member of the hastily raised planter posse and had participated in the Bernoudy battle, agreed to preside over the proceedings, which were held in the parlor of Destrehan's mansion. The captured slaves could have easily been taken to New Orleans to be examined in a proper trial. But the aristocrats of the German Coast, already distrustful of Claiborne and American courts, wanted to make sure that "justice" was sure and swift. As one of the planters said, it was important to arrive at verdicts "with the shortest possible delay" lest other slaves might be inspired to renew the revolt. This was unlikely, however, if "the chiefs and principal accomplices" were "promptly destroyed."[13]

The prisoners were brought before the tribunal one by one and interrogated swiftly over the space of two days. Some of the slaves, terrified at the fate that awaited them and probably hoping that cooperation might bring them a reprieve, denounced both their fellow prisoners and slaves still at large, some of whom may have been perfectly innocent. Other prisoners confessed to participating in the revolt but adamantly refused to implicate anyone else. Harry Kenner, one of Charles's lieutenants, refused to speak at all, thereby demonstrating his contempt of the tribunal to the end. Kook and Quamana proudly confessed to having been leaders in the revolt, and Kook defiantly admitted—even boasted—that he had wielded the ax that killed Francois Trépagnier.

When the verdicts were handed down, there were a few surprises. Eighteen of the 21 captives, including Harry, Kook, and Quamana, were sentenced to death. But some of the slaves denounced by the more frightened prisoners during interrogation were left undisturbed, most probably because their masters resisted having such valuable property destroyed. The condemned prisoners were taken out of the washhouse and shot to death, and afterward, in keeping with the sentence's instructions that "the heads of the executed shall be cut off" and exhibited, they were decapitated, thereby "providing a terrible example to all the malefactors who in the future would seek to disrupt the public tranquility."[14]

Back in New Orleans, more slaves implicated in the revolt were tried at City Hall. As was the case with the Destrehan tribunal, it was pretty much a foregone conclusion that all of the accused would be found guilty. At least seven were executed, and their mutilated bodies put on public display.

AFTERMATH

Governor Claiborne was an ardent supporter of statehood for Louisiana, which was being debated in Congress even as the German Coast revolt erupted. So it suited him to downplay the extent of the uprising by referring to it publicly as a mere criminal act that had been swiftly suppressed. Moreover, like all white Southerners, even transplanted ones, Claiborne knew that it was best not to make much of a slave revolt, lest news of it spread among and encourage emulation on the part of other slaves. Most of the nation was satisfied with Claiborne's account of what happened, although over 20 newspapers in the North published an article decrying the "ferocious sanguinary disposition" displayed by whites in the swift trial, conviction, execution, and mutilation of suspects.[15]

As happened after nearly every major slave revolt in the South, new and harsh laws were quickly enacted to hold slaves in check and discourage future uprisings. The mayor of New Orleans introduced legislation that severely curtailed the movement of slaves in his city. Under his guidance, laws were passed that prohibited slaves from renting rooms or meeting in groups except for worship purposes. The sale of ammunition to blacks, whether free or enslaved, was prohibited. As a kind of finale, the mayor publicly chided the German Coast aristocrats for not keeping a closer watch upon their slaves, thereby placing the city of New Orleans in danger.

For his part, Claiborne set about militarizing New Orleans in the hope of both intimidating other slaves who might be tempted to revolt and warning Spanish Florida to stop encouraging American slaves to flee to freedom. The governor successfully petitioned President Madison to permanently station regular army troops in New Orleans, and he also saw to it that the rather lackadaisical local militia took its duties more seriously. He wanted its volunteers better trained, better equipped, and more dedicated. For this, however, he would need the support of the planters with whom he had been sparring since he assumed office. To his surprise, he got it. Even Destrehan, who had been Claiborne's most vocal critic, backed him on the militia question. The "late unfortunate Insurrection among the slaves," he said, "and the untimely end of some of our fellow Citizens, by the unhallowed hands of the desperadoes, and the loss of property to Individuals ... proves to us the imperious necessity of a prompt organization and discipline of the Militia."[16]

But the planters balked at another one of Claiborne's suggestions: to restrict the importation of new slaves into New Orleans and the surrounding environs. His proposal is evidence that Claiborne was well aware that two of the leaders of the revolt, Kook and Quamana, had been trained warriors from West Africa and that Louisiana was far better off without slaves having this kind of expertise. The importation of slaves into the United States had been abolished in 1808, but this only created a lively black market trade at New Orleans port in African slaves. Given the booming sugar market, and the need of more and more slaves to meet the demand, the German Coast aristocrats looked with extreme disfavor on any effort to curtail the importation of slaves, either domestic or foreign ones.

Although additional rumors of slave revolts in the making were common in and around New Orleans throughout the rest of the winter of 1811, the relationship between black slaves and their white owners settled back into the conventional pattern. Plantation houses were repaired or rebuilt and labor in the sugarcane fields had hardly been disrupted at all by the revolt. At the end of April, the federal government, at the urging of Claiborne, announced that planters would be compensated to the tune of $300 per head for any living property they had lost in the revolt on the battlefield, in the surrounding swamps, or at the hands of the executioners. The *Louisiana Gazette* praised the compensation as a guarantor of social stability. Otherwise, it opined, planters would hesitate to deliver up rebel-lious slaves to the hangman, a hesitance whose "incalculable evil" could shake the foundations of society.

NOTES

1. Glenn R. Conrad, *The German Coast: Abstracts of the Civil Records of St. Charles and St. John the Baptist Parishes, 1804–1812* (Lafayette: Center for Louisiana Studies, 1981), 102.

2. *Louisiana Gazette*, January 17, 1811.

3. Charles Gayarré, *History of Louisiana*, 4 vols (New York: Redfield, 1854–1866), 4:62.

4. Ibid., 4:60

5. Daniel Rasmussen, *American Uprising: The Untold Story of America's Largest Slave Revolt* (New York: Harper Perennial, 2011), 108.

6. Ibid., 118.

7. Ibid., 120.

8. Ibid., 130.

9. Ibid., 140.

10. Quoted in Albert Thrasher, *On to New Orleans! Louisiana's Heroic 1811 Slave Revolt*, 2nd ed. (New Orleans, LA: Cypress Press, 1996), 269.

11. Stanley Engerman, Seymour Drescher, and Robert Paquette, *Slavery* (New York: Oxford University Press, 2001), 326.

12. Thrasher, *On to New Orleans!*, 268.

13. Rasmussen, *American Uprising*, 152.

14. Conrad, *The German Coast*, 102.

15. Rasmussen, *American Uprising*, 161.

16. Ibid., 171.

CHAPTER 6

NEGRO FORT RESISTANCE

If the fort harbors the Negroes of our citizens or holds out induce-
ments to the slaves of our citizens to desert from their owners' service,
this fort must be destroyed.

—General Andrew Jackson[1]

I n the spring of 1816, some five years after the German Coast uprising,
a remarkable correspondence between General Andrew Jackson and
Secretary of War William H. Crawford decided the gruesome fate of
some 300 black men, women, and children.

In mid-March, Crawford sent Jackson, then in Alabama, a letter
expressing concern about a certain "Negro Fort" in which "between two
hundred and fifty and three hundred blacks, who are well armed, clothed
and disciplined," were garrisoned. The fort was on a high bluff overlooking
Spanish Florida's Apalachicola River, about 15 miles from the Gulf of
Mexico.

It was bad enough having a fortress of trained black warriors so close to
the U.S. border. But even worse, the very existence of the fort encouraged
slaves from Georgia to flee captivity. "This is a state of things which cannot fail to produce much injury to the neighboring settlements," warned
Crawford, "and excite irritations which may ultimately endanger the peace
of the nation."[2]

Jackson, ever eager for a fight and having no qualms about invading
another nation's territory if it suited his purposes, immediately interpreted
Crawford's letter as permission to proceed against Negro Fort. Writing to
his subordinate, General Edmund Gaines, Jackson labeled the blacks
holed up there as "pirates," "out-laws," and "banditti" who, because they
were in the business of "stealing and enticing away our Negroes," should

be wiped out and "the stolen Negroes and property" returned to "their rightful owners."[3]

By July, General Gaines was ready to invade foreign soil in order to quash that most frightening of realities to the antebellum Southern mind: fiercely independent and armed blacks, many of whom were fugitive slaves. The campaign against Negro Fort was on.

MAROONS AND ST. AUGUSTINE

The story of how blacks came to occupy Negro Fort is a complicated one that stretches as far back as the colonial era; runs through a savage war between Native Americans, "maroons," and the United States; and reaches boiling point during the War of 1812. The common theme that ties all the chapters of the story together is white fear of renegade black slaves.

As we have seen in earlier chapters, slaves who lived in the Lower South sometimes fled, as did the Stono rebels, toward Florida and freedom. Prior to the American War of Independence, *La Florida*, the "Land of Flowers," was a Spanish possession. As a strategy for weakening the British colonies just to Florida's north as well as strengthening his own colony's labor force and militia, King Charles II of Spain issued a 1693 decree offering liberty to all runaway slaves, men as well as women, who could make it to the Floridian border. The number of slaves who actually escaped British bondage is small. But Florida's offer of freedom was a continuous source of anxiety for Georgians and South Carolinians. The nearly unanimous opinion was that slave unrest, desertion, and even "the most inhuman Murders," as one British colonialist put it, were all attributable to Florida's mischievous promise of freedom.[4]

The Spanish thorn in the Lower South's side was plucked in 1763, when Spain ceded Florida to Britain at the end of the Seven Years' War. By then, there were several communities of free descendants of runaway slaves in the colony, as well as many descendants of fugitives who had sought shelter and intermarried in Creek and Seminole tribes. They were typically called "maroons," from the Spanish *cimarrón*, or "wild horse." Even though Britain-owned Florida was no longer a haven for fleeing slaves, the maroons already there were generally left alone.

Things changed after the American Revolution. Florida, which Britain had divided into two colonies known as East and West Florida, had

declined joining the 13 rebellious colonies. So in 1783, Britain gave up its
20-year hold on the southernmost colony, returning it to Spain. For the
next seven years, slaves in Georgia, Alabama, and South Carolina continued to see Florida as a safe haven. But in 1790, largely through the diplo-
macy of Thomas Jefferson, Spain agreed to rescind King Charles's 1693
edict, and the border was closed, at least theoretically, to runaways.

Recognizing that war-weary Spain was stretched thin in the Americas,
thus leaving Florida vulnerable, and convinced that manifest destiny entitled the United States to the Spanish colony, Congress gave the president
authority in 1811 to begin a covert war of conquest. The act "enable[d] the
president of the United States, under certain contingencies, to take possession of the country lying east of the river Perdido, and south of the State of
Georgia and the Mississippi Territory, and for other purposes."[5] The text of
the act was so intentionally vague that it left the door open for making the
case that anything, including the Spanish presence in Florida, constituted
a legitimate provocation. It was not long before a rough-hewn militia that
self-importantly called itself the "Patriots of East Florida" decided, with
covert federal approval, to "liberate" Florida from Spain. The immediate
target of these adventurers was St. Augustine.

In response to this blatant aggression from his northern neighbor, the
Spanish governor at St. Augustine sent out a call for maroons in his colony
to rally, warning them that they risked enslavement if the Patriots were
successful. Moreover, he let it be known that despite the revocation of
the 1693 edict, slaves who fled from the United States to join in the
defense of Florida would be guaranteed their freedom. He also sent dis-
patches to Havana requesting two companies of black soldiers.

When Georgia governor David Mitchell learned of these measures, he
was outraged, and the anger was clearly born of fear. He insisted that the
promise of freedom had made "most of our male Negroes on the seaboard
restless" to get to St. Augustine, and he was especially alarmed by the
importation of black troops from Cuba. The great Saint Dominique uprising, in which slaves had rebelled against and defeated their French
colonial masters, had sickened most of the slave-holding South with dread.
The thought that Caribbean blacks, some of whom may have actually
fought in the rebellion, were landing in Florida especially alarmed
Mitchell. He actually lodged a formal protest to the Spanish government.
Given the fact of Spain's "certain knowledge" that the southern United

States was heavily populated with slaves, he sputtered, "[O]ne might have supposed" that Spain would have "abstain[ed] from introducing [black warriors] into [Florida], or of organizing such as were already in it."[6]

To make the situation even more frightening, Florida Seminoles, who initially had announced their decision to remain neutral in the looming war between the Spanish colonialists and the Patriots, changed their minds. The apparent cause of their reversal was the preaching of a maroon named Anthony, who eloquently convinced them that a U.S. seizure of Florida would be as bad for them as for free blacks.

The Patriots militia's invasion of Florida from the very beginning was the stuff of which farcical comedy is made. Failing to capture St. Augustine after a long siege, the Patriots decided to turn their attention to eradicating Seminole villages around the city in the hopes of convincing the tribe to abandon black compatriots. But after two weeks in the wilderness, starving and limping from ambushes, the ragtag army emerged utterly defeated and demoralized. It was not long afterward that the siege of St. Augustine was broken, with the Spanish governor giving much of the credit to its black defenders. Attempting to deflect attention away from its inglorious defeat, one of the militia leaders hinted that the Patriots were single-handedly stemming a black flood of revolutionary violence and predicted in hair-raising terms what would transpire if the Patriots received no help:

> [W]e have an army of negroes raked up in this country to contend with. Let us ask, if we are abandoned, what will be the situation of the Southern States, with this body of black men in the neighborhood of St. Augustine, the whole Province will be the refuge of fugitive slaves; and from thence emissaries can, and no doubt will be detached, to bring about a revolt of the black population of the United States. A nation that can stir up the savages round your western frontiers to murder will hesitate but little to introduce the horrors of St. Domingo into your Southern country.[7]

With the hope of conquering Florida put on hold, largely because of the resistance offered by maroons and Seminoles, the humiliated Patriots' only thought was vengeance. Defeat was bad enough, but defeat at the hands of black and red warriors was unbearable. So a detachment of volunteers lead by Thomas Flournoy raided east Florida, burning Seminole villages and crops, slaughtering cattle, and killing many Seminoles as well. After a few weeks of this scorched earth tactic, the Seminoles sued for peace.

But they were told that their request would be taken seriously only if they handed over their black allies. Most of the Seminoles were unwilling to do this, and instead moved into the Florida interior, out of reach (so they thought) of the Americans. By the summer of 1813, nearly two years after the ill-fated Patriots' invasion, many of the maroons also had relocated south and west, with a large number winding up along the Apalachicola River.

But in just a few weeks, white fears of black anger were reignited, this time in a particularly horrific way.

THE FORT MIMS MASSACRE

The harsh treatment of Florida's Seminoles by vengeful American troops was not lost on the Creek nation, which occupied vast regions in what today is eastern Alabama and western Georgia. This was especially so since the Creeks, like the unfortunate Seminoles, were on friendly relations with maroons living in their territory.

At about the same time that Florida's maroons were retreating from the advance of Flournoy's brigands, the Creek Confederacy split apart over the issue of accommodation to the lifestyle of white settlers. One faction was eager to adopt American ways. Another, deeply alarmed by the fate of the Seminoles, preferred to have nothing to do with the whites and, in fact, wanted to see them expelled from Creek territory. They came to be called "Red Sticks" because their war clubs were painted a bright scarlet.

It was not long before the clubs were painted with blood. Red Sticks and Creek accommodationists began raiding one another in the early summer of 1813. The civil war was viewed favorably by Spanish authorities in Florida, who apparently hoped that it would keep southeastern American militia too busy for them to launch another assault on Florida.

The Spanish governor even provisioned the Red Sticks with food and weapons. It was one of the Red Sticks' trips to Florida to pick up Spanish supplies that sparked what came to be known as the Creek War. The Red Sticks had just entered Alabama territory from picking up provisions in Pensacola when they were ambushed by a force of American soldiers from Fort Mims, a frontier stockade about 50 miles north of Mobile. The warriors had stopped to eat their mid-day meal. Taken by surprise, they were quickly scattered, fleeing into the swamps that surrounded their camp ground. But afterward the American troops, too interested in looting the abandoned provisions, were in turn ambushed by the returning Red Sticks. In the fracas, 2 soldiers and 10 or so Creeks were killed before the 180-man strong militia was routed. Each side had drawn blood, and what had previously been a civil war between Creeks now became one between Red Stick Creeks and the United States.

News quickly spread of the Red Stick victory at the Battle of Burnt Corn, as the conflict came to be called, and before long, white settlers, many of whom had married Creek women, and their slaves were leaving their homesteads and seeking shelter at Fort Mims. Accommodationist Creeks also flocked to the stockade for protection. The fort, originally the palisaded home and outbuildings of planter Samuel Mims, had been hastily strengthened and enlarged to accommodate a larger garrison as well as the refugees who flooded in from the surrounding countryside. Located on high ground on the east bank of a lake, it was considered safe haven from the marauding Red Sticks.

The fort's commander was Major Daniel Beasley, who officered a detachment of close to 200 militia volunteers. But in late August, he had dispatched over half of them to other frontier posts that seemed in more danger than Fort Mims, leaving him with only about 70 men. The scarcity of fighting men in the fort was not lost on the Red Sticks, who resolved to gather their scattered forces for an assault.

On August 30, they struck. A force of between 700 and 1,000 Red Sticks and maroon allies surprised the garrison just as everyone was sitting down to their mid-day meal, the timing almost certainly planned to coincide with the surprise assault at the Battle of Burnt Corn. The attackers quickly got inside the walls of the fort. The main entrance's gate was wide open; there are reports that it was so lodged in the sandy soil that it could not be closed. Major Beasley was one of the first to be slain, clubbed to death at the open gate, and his militiamen and the terrified civilians retreated to the fort's blockhouse. A Creek half-blood named Dixon Bailey apparently rallied the men to pour fire upon the assailants. Suffering severe losses, in spite of their leaders' assurances that they were magically protected from bullets, the Red Sticks retreated, ready to give up the fight. But according to George Stiggins, a half-blood who wrote a contemporaneous account of the attack, the maroons urged them to stay the course. "They would not have commenced their attack anew," he wrote, "but the Negroes they had would not cease, urging them on by reciting that they thought it interested them to have the fort destroyed. The Indians were urged on to the charge and renewed the attack."[8]

Emboldened by their black allies, the Red Sticks shot flaming arrows into the blockhouse where the fort's residents had fled. It was soon in flames, and the people inside either died in the fire or were massacred by the Indians when they rushed out. Five hours after the initial attack, the battle was over, with Bailey being one of the final whites to fall. Numbers are uncertain, but most agree that between 250 and 400 men, women, and children were slaughtered by the Red Sticks. Hearing that the British, who had been at war with the United States since June 1812, were paying bounties for white scalps, many of the corpses were mutilated. Judging from the reports of whites who entered the fort after the victorious Indians departed, at least some of the women victims were sexually violated. Most of the black slaves were left unharmed.

The U.S. government and people were shocked and outraged by the massacre at Fort Mims and vowed vengeance on the Red Sticks. General Andrew Jackson, commanding three separate armies, was dispatched to the area with orders to bring the rebellious Creeks to their knees. Throughout the winter of 1813–1814, Jackson fought a series of battles that, although often conducted by the whites in a bungling way, defeated the Indians time and again. Finally, at the Battle of Horseshoe Bend in the closing days of March 1814, Jackson decisively crushed the Red Sticks, killing or wounding 1,000 of them, with his own losses under 200. The Red Sticks surrendered and ceded 20 million acres of their land to the United States.

But a significant number of them remained defiant and fled south to Spanish Florida. They eventually landed in Pensacola, where they and a large number of maroons, some from Alabama and others from Florida, would be recruited by the British to once more fight Americans.

FROM BRITISH POST TO NEGRO FORT

By the early summer of 1814, the United States had been at war with Britain for nearly two years and fighting on two fronts, the Canadian border and the lower South. The British decided to divert American troops from the North by taking advantage of Red Stick and maroon anger in

Seminole and Creek Indians, such as those depicted in this 1816 woodcut, frequently allied with maroons, or runaway slaves. Many of them joined the resistance at Negro Fort. (Corbis)

the South. In May, Lieutenant George Woodbine was commissioned to recruit fugitive Creeks and blacks in Florida. He found dozens willing to fight and soon put them to work building a fort on a crest overlooking the Apalachicola River called Prospect Bluff. The fort was rather unimaginatively called British Post.

At the same time, a Royal Marine officer named Edward Nicolls was also recruiting in Mobile, Alabama. He handed out handbills to the city's black slave population, offering them freedom and land in the West Indies if they joined forces against the Americans. After a few weeks, he traveled to Pensacola, where Lieutenant Woodbine had already visited, to focus his attention on the hundreds of Red Sticks and maroons who had fled there after the Battle of Horseshoe Bend. The Spanish garrison stationed there was too dispirited to resist Nicolls, who brought with him 100 Marines and more than 500 Indians and blacks. Most likely, his overbearing nature quickly cowed the relatively defenseless Spanish governor. Nicolls was a one-eyed, fierce-talking veteran of the Napoleonic Wars who was described by contemporaries as an "impatient blustering Irishman," "brave and cruel," and "a very wild fellow."[9]

Throughout the summer and fall months, Woodbine and Nicolls worked hard at arming their Creek, maroon, and fugitive slave recruits and training them in the techniques of battle. But Andrew Jackson, commanding the Seventh Military District, marched on Pensacola in early November, and once again the war-weary city changed hands. Woodbine, Nicolls, and the Royal Marines set sail up the Apalachicola River for British Post, located about 150 miles east of Pensacola. Nicolls left instructions for the Indians and maroons to follow him. Once arrived at Prospect Bluff, Nicolls strengthened the fort and used it as his base of operations to recruit and train even more Creeks and blacks. All told, he commanded perhaps 3,000 Indians and some 300 blacks, in addition to his Royal Marines.

It is nearly certain that Nicolls had little affection for the Indians and maroons under his command, but it is more than certain that he loathed the Americans. So even after the Treaty of Ghent ended the War of 1812 on Christmas Eve 1814 (Nicolls received word of the peace only in February 1815), he refused to relinquish British Post. The rationale he gave was that the Treaty of Ghent obliged the United States to return the millions of acres that had been seized from the Creeks during the war. Nicolls's stand was legally shaky, since the land had actually been taken before the War of 1812, but he refused to give up. Finally, in May, he left British Post to sail back to London with his Marines and a couple of prominent Red Sticks. He hoped to persuade the authorities there to renounce the Treaty of Ghent, on the grounds that the Americans had broken it by their refusal to return the Indian land. Nicolls was unsuccessful, and he never returned to Florida.

Many of the Creeks and most of the 300-odd black men, women, and children stationed at British Post remained after the departure of Nicolls and his Marines. They knew that if they left the fort, they risked being enslaved by either the Spanish or the Americans. Living inside or close to the stockade, which soon became known as Negro Fort, was a guarantee, they believed, of their freedom.

They had good reason to think this. When the British departed, they left behind a huge blockhouse full of small arms and gunpowder, as well as four pieces of heavy artillery and six light cannons. The fort itself seemed impregnable. Its earthen walls were 15 feet high and 18 feet thick and were surrounded by a 14-foot wide moat whose 4-foot depth was fed by runoff from creeks and swamp. The four heavy guns inherited from the British were located at each of the fort's corners. Moreover, its location was strategically ideal, bounded as it was by swamp and streams on its nonriver sides.

The black soldiers who occupied the fort, each of whom wore the scarlet tunics of a British Royal Marine, were commanded by a 30-year-old ex-slave named Garson. Nothing is known about him except that several sources describe him as a hard and cruel leader. He may have been from Saint Dominique, since his name could have been an adulteration of *garçon*, the French word for "boy." If so, he might have fought in the revolution there. Less dramatically, however, his name might have been given to him by French masters in Louisiana.

The fort was more than a military stronghold. It was also a thriving community of men, women, and children, with a shoemaker named Ambrosio, a caulker named Harry, and an assortment of carpenters, coopers, and bakers. It was not long before a 50-mile stretch along the Apalachicola River had been cultivated with crops. Runaway blacks and maroons grew corn and raised cattle. Some of the runaways knew how to read and write.

THE MASSACRE

The justification for attacking Negro Fort was that it housed "lawless banditti" who presumably raided neighboring farms to steal cattle and crops. But the real thievery, so Andrew Jackson and others believed, was of humans: in running away, slaves had stolen property—namely, themselves—from their masters, the rightful owners. Moreover, the existence of a self-sufficient colony of free blacks was seen as an inspiration to slaves and an incentive for them to flee bondage. Finally, the fact that the blacks were still allied with Red Stick Creeks raised white anxiety level to an unbearable degree. As historian Eugene D. Genovese noted, the thought of a "black-Indian collaboration" terrified whites.[10] So Negro Fort had to go.

Jackson wrote to the Spanish governor of Florida in the spring of 1816 complaining about the outlaws holed up on Prospect Bluff. The governor responded by saying that he too was concerned about Negro Fort, but did not have the manpower to do anything about it. Jackson took this as an invitation to step in—he wrote Governor Mauricio de Zuniga that the presence of the free blacks at Negro Fort would "compel us, in self-defense, to destroy them"—and ordered, as we have seen, General Edmund Gaines to destroy the stronghold, kill the Indians in it, and return the runaways to their owners. Jackson also wrote to Secretary of War Crawford to assure him that there was "no fear of disturbing the good understanding that exists between us and Spain" in attacking the fort.[11] The "good understanding" was that the Spanish governor recognized he was too weak to stop the Americans from doing whatever they wished.

Throughout July, accommodationist Creeks, commanded by American officers, harried the black settlements around Negro Fort, destroying crops and burning houses. In exchange for their alliance, the Creeks were promised all the provisions, including guns and gunpowder, within the fort when it was taken. They were also promised 50 dollars for every ex-slave they captured.[12]

When it came to an assault on the fort itself, Gaines wanted to make sure, as a confirmation of Jackson's condemnation of Garson's men as banditti, that the blacks fired the first shot. The provocation he was looking for occurred on July 17, when Negro Fort men ambushed and killed most of an American patrol in search of freshwater. Lieutenant Colonel Duncan Clinch, in command of the operation, immediately marched his force to the fort and surrounded it as best he could, given the swampland, creeks, and moat. The blacks within the stockade fired cannon at them, frightening off a good number of the Creeks, raised a red battle flag of death, and jeered at the Americans from the safety of their high walls.

Ten days later, American gunboats arrived at the fort after sailing up the Apalachicola, and an artillery duel commenced that produced more smoke and noise than damage on either side. The thick walls of Negro Fort withstood the pounding of the gunboat shells, and the heavy cannons in the fort missed their marks because of the inexperience of the blacks firing them.

This fruitless exchange continued until one of the gunboats' rounds, heated white-hot, hit the fort's gunpowder-packed magazine. The powder ignited and the magazine went up in a terrific explosion that killed most of the people within the stockade. When Clinch's men entered the burning and now silent fort, what they saw was heart-rending. "You cannot conceive, nor I describe the horrors of the scene," wrote one of them.

Lieutenant Colonel Duncan Clinch led the assault on Negro Fort. A lucky shell from one of his gunboats hit the fort's arsenal and sparked an explosion that killed most of the resisting slaves and Indians. (Library of Congress)

> In an instant, hundreds of lifeless bodies were stretched upon the plain, buried in sand and rubbish, or suspended from the tops of the surrounding pines. Here lay an innocent babe, there a helpless mother; on the one side a sturdy warrior, on the other a bleeding squaw. Piles of bodies, large heaps of sand, broken guns, accoutrements, etc. covered the site of the fort.[13]

The soldiers who entered the defeated fort also found about 50 survivors of the explosion, most so severely maimed that they soon died. Garson was still alive, as was an Indian compatriot who had fought by his side. The soldiers turned both of them over to their Creek allies who promptly scalped and then killed the Indian and shot Garson. The corpses of the Negro Fort's defenders and inhabitants, more than 250 of them, were piled up and burned, and the handful of surviving blacks were either returned to their masters or resold on the market. The largest enclave of runaway and maroon slaves in the history of the United States was utterly destroyed.

VENGEANCE

Although nearly everyone within the walls of Negro Fort had been massacred, scores of blacks and Indians who lived in the 50-mile string of settlements adjacent to the fort fled to the swamps and forests and survived. Many of them made their way east to the Suwannee River, where they regrouped and formed alliances with Seminoles and maroons already living there. They also began planning vengeance for the massacre at Prospect Bluff, proclaiming that they wanted to let the Americans know that "they [would have] something more to do than at Appalachicola [sic]" when the fighting resumed.[14] By early 1817, reports of an entire army of blacks training along the Suwannee had reached American ears. Rumor had it that there were some 600 blacks in arms, with at least that many Indian allies. They were led by Bowlegs, a Seminole chief, and a black man named Nero.

The same General Gaines who Jackson had ordered to destroy Negro Fort decided that it was time to nip the growing threat from the Suwannee in the bud. He sent a threatening message to a Seminole chief uninvolved with Bowlegs and Nero, accusing that chief of harboring "a great many of my black people" and warning that things would go badly if they were not returned. The chief tersely responded that runaway slaves were no concern of his, that doing anything about them was a white, not an Indian, affair, and cautioned Gaines to stay off tribal land. A few weeks later, a detachment of Gaines's troops attacked the Seminole village of Fowl Town, killing about 20 of its inhabitants and burning everything to the ground.

The destruction of Fowl Town marked the beginning of what has become known as the First Seminole War, and it is a conflict in which blacks seeking vengeance for Negro Fort fought. Within days, Indians and blacks attacked a large open boat, carrying over 50 people, including women and children, as it made its way down the Apalachicola. Nearly everyone was killed. From then on, Indians and blacks, lined up on either side of the river, harassed American vessels trying to make their way up to Fort Scott, a frontier post that Lieutenant Colonel Clinch had built as he was preparing his assault on Negro Fort. Weary of the blockade, Jackson relieved Gaines in early 1818, assumed command himself, and built a second fort on Prospect Bluff, right on the site of the destroyed Negro Fort. The new outpost was named Fort Gadsden, after the engineer who designed it.

After Gadsden was completed, Jackson took to the field with 3,500 men, 2,000 of whom were Creeks, in pursuit of Bowlegs and Nero. He followed them all the way to the Suwannee. Recognizing that they were outmanned, Bowlegs managed to get most of his people across to the other side of the river. Although frantically ferrying the black women and children accompanying his men, Nero and a few hundred of his troops prepared to meet Jackson's army. They held their own for a few hours, despite being outnumbered and outgunned; the American rifle-barreled muskets had a much longer range than the blacks' smoothbore British ones. But finally, as one black participant in the battle said, Jackson's men "came too hot upon them and they all ran to save their lives," plunging into the Suwannee and swimming to the other side.

Counting the ones who were slain by bullets or who drowned, the Suwannee battle killed an estimated one-fourth to one-half of the black defenders, while Jackson's army suffered nearly no casualties. But as one historian notes, "[D]espite a defeat, Nero's fighting men partly fulfilled their proud boast of a year earlier—to avenge the Negro Fort destruction."[15] They had formed new communities, they had allied with Indians to resist whites, they had stood their own in a pitched battle against a superior force, and at least some of them had survived.

NOTES

1. Quoted in Roger Lyle Brown, "A Stand for Freedom: The Story of Negro Fort," in Y. N. Kly (ed.), *The Invisible War: The African American Anti-Slavery Resistance from the Stono Rebellion through the Seminole Wars* (Atlanta, GA: Clarity Press, 2006), 39.

2. Ibid.

3. Ibid., 39–40.

4. Ibid., 28.

5. Adam Wasserman, *A People's History of Florida 1513-1876: How Africans, Seminoles, Women, and Lower Class Whites Shaped the Sunshine State* (CreateSpace, 2010), 145.

6. Quoted in Jane Landers, *Black Society in Spanish Florida* (Urbana: University of Illinois Press, 1999), 222.

7. Ibid.

8. George Stiggins, *Creek Indian History: A Historical Narrative of the Genealogy, Traditions and Downfall of the Ispocoga or Creek Indian Tribe of Indians* (Birmingham, AL: Birmingham Public Library Press, 1989), 104–105.

9. Quoted in Brown, "A Stand for Freedom," 37.

10. Eugene D. Genovese, *From Rebellion to Revolution: Afro-American Slave Revolts in the Making of the Modern World* (Baton Rouge: Louisiana State University Press, 1979), 69–70.

11. Quoted in Brown, "A Stand for Freedom," 40, 41.

12. Kenneth W. Porter, *The Black Seminoles: History of a Freedom-Seeking People* (Gainesville: University Press of Florida, 1996), 17.

13. Quoted in Brown, "A Stand for Freedom," 42.

14. Porter, *Black Seminoles*, 18.

15. Ibid., 23.

CHAPTER 7

THE VESEY
CONSPIRACY

I have now passed my half-century, and begun to feel lonely among
the men of the present day. I have lived to see what I really never
believed it possible I should see—courts held with closed doors, and
men dying by the score who had never seen the faces nor heard the
voices of their accusers.

—U.S. Supreme Court Justice William Johnson[1]

In the late summer of 1822, officials in the South Carolina coastal city
of Charleston issued a strange ordinance: black persons, slave or
freedmen, seen wearing mourning clothes would be seized and
flogged. Despite the official warning, a few blacks defied the ban and
appeared in public in sackcloth, willing to risk the promised 39 lashes.

Both the ban and its violators were motivated by a series of executions
in the city that began on July 2 and continued for the next five weeks.
In all, 35 black men went to the gallows for their role in a conspiracy to
throw over the harness of slavery. Some historians claim that this plot
was the largest in U.S. history, but the evidence for this is doubtful.
A few other historians insist that there was no plot at all, but only an
excuse on the part of anxious Southerners to put the fear of God in their
slaves by executing a few blacks on trumped-up charges. But while there
is good evidence for the conclusion that the 1741 New York conspiracy
was largely fictional, there is little reason to think that the 1822 Charleston
one was as well.

What makes the Charleston conspiracy noteworthy—and unique—is
that it was conceived and orchestrated not by a slave but by a freedman,
a carpenter and charismatic religious leader named Denmark Vesey who
was known and respected by many of the city's white merchants and political leaders. In fact, shortly after the conspiracy was discovered, many of

them found it hard to believe that Vesey was its ringleader. Even after evidence had demonstrated his guilt, the presiding judge who sentenced him to death could not resist expressing incredulity at his involvement. "It is difficult to imagine what infatuation could have prompted you to attempt an enterprise so wild and visionary," Justice Kennedy exclaimed. "You were a free man; you were comparatively wealthy; and enjoyed every comfort compatible with your situation. You had, therefore, much to risk, and little to gain. From your age and experience, you ought to have known that success was impracticable."[2]

What Kennedy and many other whites either could not or would not recognize is that Vesey willingly risked his life to be free and to help other blacks be free. For in antebellum Charleston, even legally free blacks lived in a state of virtual bondage.

SLAVES AND FREEDMEN IN CHARLESTON

In 1822, Charleston, South Carolina, contained the largest black population of any city in the United States, a population that far outnumbered white residents. As early as the first U.S. census in 1790, there were over four times as many blacks as whites, and that ratio held steady throughout the antebellum years. One of the reasons for the large number of blacks was that Charleston remained a major port of entry for the transatlantic slave trade until Congress put an end to it in 1808. Most of the enslaved blacks were sold to work on rice, sugar, and cotton plantations in the Carolinas and Georgia, but many remained in Charleston as domestic servants. This also meant that the city and its surrounding environs also held the largest concentration of African ethnic groups. By 1822, most of the African-born slaves in the area, many of whom had been warriors in their homelands, were aging. But Vesey managed to recruit a good number of second- and third-generation slaves who had inherited a legacy of fierce independence from their grandparents.

Partly because of the standard Southern anxiety about slave uprisings, and partly as a consequence of the harsh laws enacted after the Stono rebellion, South Carolina in general and Charleston in particular kept a tight legal reign on their slaves. State legislation mandated that it was illegal to teach slaves how to read or write, to sell them liquor without their masters' approval, or to assemble or travel in groups without the presence of a white man. Slaves were forbidden to wear anything but coarse clothing, unless they had been outfitted in livery by their masters, and were expected to honor strict curfews. Moreover, white militia patrols were ordered to stop and interrogate any slave outside of his or her master's property.

Slaves who were accused of malfeasances were to be tried by special tribunals rather than regular courts of law. The state was not obliged to ensure that they were represented by counsel, and any testimony they offered in their own defense, much less any that they made against a white man, was considered untrustworthy. One French visitor, the Duke de la Rochefoucauld-Liancourt, was less than impressed by South Carolina's slave laws. A slave's judges, he reported,

> have the power to condemn him to whatever mode of death they shall think proper. Simple theft by a negro is punished with death. When the crime is not such as to deserve capital punishment, a justice of the peace, with a single freeman, may, in this case, condemn to whatever lighter punishment they shall please to inflict. For the murder of a negro with malicious intent, a white man pays a fine . . . It is easy to see that a white man can seldom be convicted; as negroes are incapable by law of giving evidence; and no white man will readily offer his testimony in favor of a black, against a person of his own color. A negro slaying a white man, in defense of his master, is pardoned. But, if he do the same thing, or even but wound a white man, in defense of his own life, he will eventually be put to death.[3]

Slaves in Charleston were subject to these laws as well as others peculiar to the city. The penalty for a slave breaking a street lamp, for example, was 39 lashes; a white person committing the same crime was only charged a fine. A slave who tried to pass himself or herself off as free within the city precincts was also subject to 39 lashes. And white masters and mistresses were instructed to keep absolutely no more domestic slaves in town than was necessary.

Free blacks in Charleston—and by the time of Vesey's conspiracy, there were many of them—enjoyed more freedom than slaves, but they were still less free than white men and women. They could own property and earn a living, but their income could not exceed one dollar a day. They could not vote or testify against white persons, and they could not serve on juries. They were levied a special poll tax from which whites were exempt. If they were accused of a crime, they were subject to the same kind of extralegal trial mandated for offending slaves. They were forbidden to gather for worship except during daylight hours, and even then the law demanded that most of the congregation had to be white (a regulation, we will soon see, that was not always upheld). Free blacks were not allowed in the city's theaters or in the aptly named peninsular park of White Point after sunset. A white person, even a child, could stop a free black on the street and demand to see his or her papers. And at any time, free blacks were at risk of being kidnapped and sold into slavery under the pretext that they were runaways.

Notwithstanding these restrictions, there were so many free blacks in Charleston by 1822 that more than one white regretted their presence. Polemicist E. C. Holland thundered that "the existence of Free Blacks among us [is] the greatest and most deplorable evil." They were toxic, he said, on two counts: as both laborers and artisans, they deprive white men of employment and hired-out slaves of opportunities to earn their masters an income, and their very presence created restlessness among slaves "when they look around them and see persons of their own color enjoying . . . privileges beyond their own condition." How could they not grow "dissatisfied with their lot"?[4]

It was into this world that Denmark Vesey entered when he was still a teenager. He could not have known it at the time, but in just a few years he would become a freedman who, the city's mayor noted, "was always looked up to with awe and respect"—at least until the conspiracy he hatched was discovered.[5]

FROM SLAVE TO FREEDMAN TO CONSPIRATOR

We know more about Denmark Vesey than most other leaders of a slave revolt or conspiracy to revolt. Even so, many of the details of his life, especially regarding his origins, remain lost or obscure.

Born in 1767 in the Danish Virgin Islands, which may explain how he came to be called Denmark, Vesey was captured at the age of 14 and shipped along with a cargo of nearly 400 other slaves to Saint Dominique. He sailed on a ship commanded by Captain Joseph Vesey, a sailor from the West Indies who specialized in the slave trade. Denmark, who told his captors that his given name was Telemaque (at least that is what it sounded like to English ears), seems to have been a favorite of Vesey's and the crew during the voyage from the Virgin Islands to Saint Dominique. Nonetheless, the slave captain sold him along with the rest of the cargo to a sugar planter, and then departed to pick up another load of slaves.

Upon his return some three months later, the planter to whom Vesey had sold Telemaque tracked the captain down and angrily demanded a refund. The boy he had bought, it seemed, suffered so badly from epileptic fits that he was no use in the sugar fields. Given that there is no subsequent record of fits on Denmark's part, either he was faking them to get out of the backbreaking plantation work or his new and brutal station in life had induced crippling panic attacks. Regardless of the explanation, Vesey took the boy back and made him his valet. For the next two years, Denmark accompanied Vesey on all his ocean voyages, picking up bits and pieces of several languages along the way. He seems to have been particularly comfortable with French, and somewhere along the line he learned to read and write, perhaps taught by Vesey himself.

In 1783, Captain Vesey, then in his mid-thirties, decided that he had accumulated enough wealth to settle down, and the town he chose to reside in was Charleston. For the next 17 years, Denmark, who learned the carpenter's trade after he and the captain sank roots in Charleston, worked as a hired-out slave. Most of his wages went to Vesey. But he was allowed to keep a portion of them, and in December 1799, he used some of the money he had earned to buy himself a lottery ticket bearing the number 1884. Whether Denmark regularly played the lottery or whether this was a one-time shot is unknown. But to his amazement and delight, he discovered in the new year that he held the winning ticket and could claim the prize of $1,500. The windfall was an impressive fortune for either a white or a black man, and Vesey promptly used nearly half of it to buy his freedom from Captain Vesey. He used the rest of the money to start his own carpentry business, either buying or renting a modest house on Bull Street, not far from the private homes of both the state's governor and the city's mayor.

For the next 17 years, Denmark plied his trade, gaining a reputation among free black as well as white communities for industry and honesty. He sired a number of children off of several women during this time. Apparently all of his wives were slaves. After his conspiracy was discovered, the official report stated that he was motivated by his desire to see his children free: "he was satisfied with his own condition, being free; but, as all his children were slaves, he wished to see what he could do for them."[6] Children born to slave women, even if their fathers were free, became the property of their mothers' masters.

Denmark chaffed at the restrictions placed upon him and other Charleston freedmen. As it turned out, he also had to contend with the fact that blacks like him who had very dark complexions were snubbed by the city's free mulatto population who, because of their lighter skin, represented an elite among freedmen. Some of them, including two of Denmark's neighbors on Bull Street, even owned slaves of their own. It was not long before his resentment of both whites and mulattos prompted him to rebel in relatively quiet ways. He ducked the federal census on three separate occasions, for example, and refused to pay the special poll tax demanded from free blacks. He wore fine clothes, defying the expectation that freedmen, like blacks, would dress in ways compatible with their station in life. On one occasion, he rebuked a slave for bowing to a white man who passed them on the street. As for himself, he said, he "would never cringe to the whites, nor ought anyone who had the feelings of a man."[7] At another time, a companion found him reading a book about the "intellectual and moral faculties" of "negroes." Denmark remarked that the climate of Africa, and not inherent inferiority to whites, darkened the skin.[8]

The escalating but undirected anger that had been growing in Denmark eventually got channeled with the opening of an African Methodist Episcopal (AME) Church in Charleston in 1817. The African Methodist Episcopal Church, founded the previous year in Philadelphia, was a denomination for blacks who had come to feel like second-class citizens in the city's mainly white Methodist churches. It is unclear why Charleston authorities allowed the construction of an AME Church in their city. One historian unconvincingly speculates that they wanted to show the North that South Carolingians were enlightened and benevolent masters.[9] Even if that was the motive, the alarming reality of an all-black church in the midst of a culture based on slavery soon hit home. Charleston police raided the church in its first year of operation and again in its second, arresting members both times. They did not, however, shut it down.

The church's minister, Morris Brown, recognized the precarious situation in which he and his congregants found themselves. On the one hand, they all came to the church because they were sick of white ministers who

Although fanciful, this drawing of Denmark Vesey captures the fact that he had been to sea and was a freedman, literate, and relatively well-off, rarities in the antebellum South. (Drawing by Ciana Pullen)

used scripture to defend the practice of slavery and the inferiority of blacks, and Brown needed to respect that by preaching sermons with a contrary message. But on the other hand, he knew that he was no good to anyone if his sermons were so threatening to whites that they arrested him and closed the church. So he tried to walk the fine line between satisfying his black congregants and not riling the white authorities. Given that state law required that whites routinely sat in on his sermons, the challenge to Brown was continuous.

Denmark, who was one of the Charleston church's founding members, was increasingly dissatisfied with Brown's conciliatory approach, and in 1818, he began to lead night sessions at the church, during which no white was present, in which he preached the evils of slavery. He appears to have rarely invoked the name of Jesus or material from the Christian scriptures, focusing instead on the Hebrew scriptures' injunctions against slavery and the Book of Exodus's epic story of the Israelites fleeing Egyptian bondage. At his later trial, the magistrates were impressed by how "readily" he could quote the Bible "to prove that slavery was contrary to the laws of God."

In the antebellum years, Charleston, South Carolina, had the largest ratio of blacks to whites—four to one—of any American city. Slaves lived in quarters like the ones shown in this mid-1800s photograph. (Library of Congress)

White preachers who claimed otherwise, he told his nocturnal audiences, were liars whose motive was to keep blacks from "attempt[ing] their emancipation, however shocking and bloody might be the consequences."[10] Two of his favorite biblical passages, Joshua 6:21 and Zachariah 14:1–2, both focused on the utter destruction of Israel's enemies, a fate that Denmark clearly wanted to see reproduced in Charleston.

Denmark's after-dark sessions, as well as his increasingly frequent visits to slave quarters in and about Charleston, soon won him followers. One of them was Jack Pritchard, an Angolan-born slave commonly known as Gullah Jack because of his knowledge of the patois spoken by Africans and African descendants in the coastal island areas.

Gullah Jack was a colorful character whose eccentricities—he affected oversized side whiskers, for example—were well known around town. Too small in size to be a field hand, he ran errands and did odd jobs for his master. He was known for his medicinal skills—it was rumored that he knew how to poison someone in an undetectably subtle way—and among a large proportion of Charleston's blacks, he was known as a shaman who possessed great magical powers. He had the charisma to reach groups of slaves that might have remained wary of Denmark's style.

Although Denmark and Jack had been quietly encouraging discontent among Charleston's blacks since at least mid-1817, actual preparations for rebellion appear not to have begun until the following summer. In June 1818, the city guard raided the AME Church, doubtlessly on suspicion of some kind of sedition, and arrested 143 of its members. Rev. Brown and four other elders were sentenced to either a month in jail or permanent exile from South Carolina. Eight others were to receive 10 lashes or pay a fine of $5. Although the pertinent record has disappeared, it is likely that Denmark was a member of this second group. The mass arrests infuriated him and prompted his decision to move from words to action.

Over the next four years, Denmark surreptitiously recruited hundreds and perhaps thousands of slaves, either directly or through a handful of trusted lieutenants. He encouraged each of the lieutenants to keep lists of names of the slaves they enlisted, but also warned them against consolidating the lists. That way, if any one of them was arrested, the entire plot would not be jeopardized. Recognizing that the risk of discovery grew with each new recruit, Vesey ordered his lieutenants to exercise extreme caution. Their standard procedure was to tell potential recruits that they were free. When the slaves whom they approached responded in surprise, asking how this was so since they obviously were not free, the lieutenant was instructed to answer with a paraphrase from scripture—"I will show you the man"—and then slowly describe the plot. If the man who was approached was reluctant to join, he was to be warned that certain death awaited him if he betrayed the planned insurrection. Those slaves who did join in were cautioned to obey their masters scrupulously until the rebellion began, giving the whites no reason to suspect that anything was in the air.

One of Denmark's most trusted lieutenants was Gullah Jack, who was especially useful in drawing in African-born slaves. Another was Ned Bennett, who belonged to no less a public figure than Thomas Bennett, the state governor. One of Ned's fellow slaves in the governor's household who also joined the conspiracy vowed to murder the governor and his entire family as soon as the insurrection erupted. He also promised to finish off the city's mayor, James Hamilton.

Denmark was an expert recruiter who knew when to step in himself and when to delegate to his lieutenants. He persuaded AME Church members that they would never enjoy freedom of religion until they won their political and social freedom. He conversed in their own language to the French-speaking slaves brought in to Charleston after the slave rebellion on Saint Dominique, assuring them that the insurrection he planned would be abetted by soldiers from the island. And even though he often traveled to plantations surrounding Charleston to speak to field hands, he wisely let Gullah Jack and Ned Bennett take the lead there. As one of the judges at the subsequent trials observed,

> Every principle which could operate upon the mind of man was artfully employed. Religion, hope, fear, and deception were resorted to as the occasion required. All were told, and many believed, that God approved of their designs; those whose fears would have restrained them, were forced to yield by threats of death; those whom prudence and foresight induced them to pause, were cheered with the assurance that assistance from Santo Domingo and Africa were at hand.[11]

The actual plan of attack was both simple and brilliant. The insurrection would launch on June 16, a Sunday night. That would give the rebels an entire day to fetch the homemade weapons they had hidden and gather at their designated assembly points for the march on Charleston. Slaves within the city would set numerous fires and explosions with black powder they had stolen, and when whites ran out of their homes to quench the fires, they were to be slaughtered in the street. In the midst of the ensuing panic and chaos, three columns of slaves would rush the city from the south, north, and east. One of them would seize the state arsenal and distribute its weapons; another would seize the federal arsenal; and the third would go straight to the city's center, take it, and await the other two columns. Every white person encountered along the way was to be killed. Once the city was ablaze and whites lay dead or dying in the streets, Denmark's plan apparently was to commandeer ships in the harbor along with their crews to sail the rebellious slaves to Santa Domingo and freedom.

One aspect of the plot was the stuff of comic opera. Denmark commissioned a local barber to make several wigs. Wearing these, and with their faces painted white, his hope was that disguised rebels could deceive enough white citizens during the night of the uprising to get to the arsenal without opposition. The wigs would come back to haunt during Denmark's trial.

DISCOVERY AND TRIAL

The risky business of approaching possible recruits finally caught up with Denmark nearly two months before the date on which the insurrection was to take place. On a Saturday afternoon toward the end of May 1822, Peter Prioleau, a slave belonging to a Charleston couple, was approached by a slave who asked him if he had heard news about "something serious" that was in the works. When Peter asked what the slave meant, the reply was unequivocal. "Why, we are determined to shake off our bondage, and for this purpose we stand on a firm foundation. Many have joined, and if you go with me, I will show you the man, who has the list of names, who will take yours down."[12]

Denmark had always warned his lieutenants to be wary of recruiting slaves who served as domestic servants, as Peter Prioleau did, because they generally had more emotional attachment and loyalty to their masters than field slaves. Peter was no exception. He was so upset by his strange encounter that he sought the advice of a free black who was a friend. The friend advised him to inform his master, Colonel John Prioleau, of the plot. The colonel was out of town on business. But when he returned a week later, Peter revealed what he knew.

On hearing Peter's story, the colonel immediately alerted Mayor Hamilton, Governor Bennett, and the Charleston City Council. Following Peter's description of the man who had tried to recruit him, the slave William Paul was hunted down, arrested, and thrown into solitary confinement in the city Work House. He held out under questioning and possible physical abuse for a few hours, but eventually confessed nearly everything he knew about the conspiracy, including that the "indiscriminate massacre of the whites" of Charleston was one of the plotters' goals.[13] He denied knowing who the leaders of the plot were, although he did mention that one of them was a magician whose spells protected him from harm, an obvious reference to Gullah Jack but one that William's jailers did not pick up on. He did not mention Denmark's name, but named as co-conspirators three other slaves: Peter Poyas, Mingo Harth, and Ned Bennett, the governor's slave.

Peter Poyas and Mingo were immediately brought in for questioning, but they cleverly convinced their interrogators that they were innocent. Both of them seem to have played up the simple-minded picayune stereotype to throw off any suspicion that they might have had the wits or the courage to participate in a conspiracy to insurrect. After their release, Ned Bennett preempted his own arrest by showing up at the Work House with the story that he had heard he had been implicated and wished to clear his name. His coolness, as well as the weighty insistence of Governor Bennett that all of his slaves were absolutely trustworthy, convinced the investigators that William Paul's story about a slave conspiracy to take over Charleston was poppycock.

On his release, Bennett went straight to Denmark's home on Bull Street to warn him that suspicions were in the air. Denmark, fearful of discovery, sent out word that the date of the insurrection had been moved forward. But even that proved too late. At about the time Ned Bennett was calming the fears of city authorities, two adolescent boys, one black and the other mulatto, were overheard talking about an impending uprising in which the city's powder magazines would be captured and white citizens murdered. Even though they were whipped for such talk, no one seems to have taken them seriously, notwithstanding Peter Prioleau's and William Paul's earlier testimonies. Then, on June 14, news came in that city officials could not ignore.

Major John Wilson, a Charleston resident and would-be politician, instructed his slave George to cautiously sound out the city's blacks about the rumors of uprising. In just a few hours, George returned with news that an insurrection was indeed in the works, and that he had actually been invited to join by no less a person than Mingo Harth, who just a few days earlier had been questioned and released by Charleston officials. Frighteningly, George also told his master that the uprising was to take place in less than 48 hours later.

The major took this new information without delay to the mayor and governor who, finally recognizing that a plot was indeed under way, called up some 400 state militia to reinforce the city guard on the night of June 16. By the time Sunday arrived, two things had transpired. The first is that news of the planned uprising had gone public, and all of white Charleston anxiously awaited what might happen. The second is that Denmark, realizing that the element of surprise was gone, called off the planned insurrection and advised his lieutenants to burn their lists of recruits. Sunday night came and went without incident, and the arrests began two days later. Denmark, who had fled to one of his wife's homes on June 17 to avoid capture, was apprehended a week later, several days after the trials of his co-conspirators had already begun.

Mayor Hamilton commissioned seven local merchants and lawyers to constitute a *pro tempore* court charged with trying all blacks implicated in the conspiracy. There were no juries, and the verdicts of the court could not be appealed. But the seven judges did allow attorneys to represent the accused blacks and granted them the right to cross-examine and challenge witnesses.

Most of the sentences handed down were based on hearsay because there was little physical evidence to convict the defendants. No lists of recruits, whose numbers were reckoned, almost certainly falsely, to be in the thousands, were presented as evidence. Although there were rumors of cached weapons, only a few were found. But the prosecution did manage to find the wigmaker, complete with one of the wigs Denmark had commissioned.

Several witnesses testified against Denmark, although curiously he maintained his innocence throughout the trial. One witness told of a conversation in which Denmark, challenged by one of the conspirators over the plan to kill women and children, "thought it was for our safety not to spare one white skin alive, for this was the plan they pursued in St. Domingo."[14] Rolla Bennett, one of the governor's slaves, testified that Denmark assured the conspirators that "he expected the St. Domingo people would send troops to help us."[15] Another said that Denmark told him he decided to plan an uprising because he wanted his children, born of slave women, to be free.

Denmark insisted on cross-examining the men who testified against him. No record of the cross-examination was kept, but a possibly unreliable description of his style was provided by one of the judges.

> He at first questioned them in the dictatorial, despotic manner in which he was probably accustomed to address them. But this not producing the desired effect, he questioned them with affected surprise and concern for learning false testimony against him; still failing in his purpose, he then examined them strictly as to dates, but could not make them contradict themselves.[16]

The outcome for Vesey was inevitable. He was sentenced to death by hanging, protesting his innocence to the end, and executed, along with four of his lieutenants, on July 2. Gullah Jack, who during his sentencing was sternly told that "you represented yourself as invulnerable. [But] your boasted charms have not preserved yourself, and of course could not protect others," was hanged along with four others three days later.[17] In all, out of 131 men arrested, 67 were convicted. Thirty-five were hanged, 22 in a single day, and the rest were transported out of the United States to labor and die miserably on Caribbean plantations.

AFTERMATH

In recent years, at least two historians have argued that the vast conspiracy attributed to Denmark was a figment of the paranoid Southern mind. Although the extent of the plot was almost certainly exaggerated at the time, there is little reason to suppose that it was a fiction. But even one contemporary, an associate of the U.S. Supreme Court named William Johnson, expressed public doubts about the scope of Denmark's conspiracy. In an anonymous article published on June 21 in the *Charleston Courier*, he deplored the white panic that could swiftly blow mere innuendo up into unspeakable plans of wholesale murder.

Peter Prioleau, the slave who initially reported the conspiracy to his master Colonel Prioleau, was granted his freedom and a generous monetary reward by a grateful Charleston City Council. He purchased property and made a living as a drayman, enjoying a lifelong exemption from city and state taxes.

The fact that the insurrection had been planned by a free black instead of a slave sent shock waves throughout Charleston's white community, the members of which had always considered the free blacks living in their midst to be a nonthreatening although unwelcome presence. The same year that Denmark and his co-conspirators were hanged, South Carolina passed legislation to clamp down on the freedom of free blacks. The Negro Seaman's Act forbade free black sailors from freely wandering in Charleston or any other of the state's seacoast cities when their ships docked in port. Laws were passed that made it a crime to teach blacks, free or enslaved, to read and write, and heavy restrictions were placed on the practice of hiring out slaves, under the assumption that doing so gave them opportunity to meet with and be corrupted by freedmen. Some legislators even wanted to impose even more severe sartorial restrictions on free blacks by requiring them to wear only rough-cut material.

Mayor Hamilton rode the trials and executions to higher public office. Sharply attacking Governor Bennett, who had made the strategic mistake of showing compassion for the large number of blacks who were executed (including three of his own slaves) or transported, Hamilton won a name for himself as a no-nonsense defender of the South's "peculiar institution" and the man who had suppressed what could have been a bloodbath in the city he led. Within a decade, Hamilton was elected governor of South Carolina and undoubtedly would have been a leading general or statesman in the Confederacy had he not drowned in 1857 and been quickly forgotten. But according to the mid-nineteenth-century free black author Martin Delaney, Denmark Vesey was still remembered by Charleston's slaves and freedmen long after he was hanged.[18]

NOTES

1. Quoted in Donald C. Morgan, *Justice William Johnson: The First Dissenter: The Career and Constitutional Philosophy of a Jeffersonian Judge* (Columbia: University of South Carolina Press, 1954), 138.

2. Lionel H. Kennedy and Thomas Parker, *An Official Report of the Trials of Sundry Negroes, Charged with an Attempt to Raise an Insurrection in the State of South-Carolina* (Charleston: James R. Schenck, 1822), 177.

3. Quoted in John Lofton, *Denmark Vesey's Revolt: The Slave Plot That Lit a Fuse to Fort Sumter* (Kent, OH: Kent State University Press, 1983), 45–46.

4. Quoted in Douglas R. Egerton, *He Shall Go Free: The Lives of Denmark Vesey*, rev. ed. (Lanham, MD: Rowman & Littlefield, 2004), 88.

5. Quoted in ibid., 87.

6. Kennedy and Parker, *Official Report*, 95.

7. Quoted in Egerton, *He Shall Go Free*, 99.

8. Ibid., 98.

9. David Robertson, *Denmark Vesey: The Buried Story of America's Largest Slave Rebellion and the Man Who Led It* (New York: Vintage, 1999).

10. Kennedy and Parker, *Official Report*, 17.

11. Ibid., 21.

12. Quoted in Robertson, *Denmark Vesey*, 70–71.

13. Ibid., 73.
14. Kennedy and Parker, *Official Report*, 82.
15. Ibid., 67.
16. Ibid., 45.
17. Ibid., 179.
18. Robertson, *Denmark Vesey*, 122.

CHAPTER 8

NAT TURNER'S REVOLT

I began to direct my attention to this great object, to fulfil the purpose
for which, by this time, I felt assured I was intended.

—Nat Turner[1]

T homas Ruffin Gray knew an opportunity when he saw it. Immediately following the two-day rampage in August 1831 in which Nat
Turner and his fellow rebellious slaves murdered some 60 whites,
Gray began collecting all the information about the uprising he could get
his hands on. His reason for doing so became clear when the insurrection's
leader was finally captured two months later. He sought and received permission to interview Turner in his jail cell on three separate occasions and
only days after the prisoner's execution published a pamphlet, *The Confessions of Nat Turner*, that sold an astounding 40,000 to 50,000 copies.

Gray, who was born in 1800, the same year as Nat, was badly in need of
the change in fortune his pamphlet brought him. The son of a Southampton County, Virginia, horse breeder, Gray managed to lose most of his fortune, perhaps because of gambling debts, by the time he was in his late
twenties. Concluding that he needed a reliable source of income, he studied law and was admitted to the bar only a year before Nat Turner's uprising. Gray was a likeable fellow, and it was his friendship with the country's
magistrates and judges that gained him access to the most famous prisoner
who ever sat in the county jail.

The pamphlet that Gray published in the wake of the uprising is
remarkable because it is the only document in the entire history of
American slave conspiracies and revolts that allows a slave leader to speak
at some length. It is certainly the case that Gray took some stylistic
liberties in recording his conversations with Nat. Here and there, the
confession is sprinkled with melodramatic flourishes characteristic of
early-nineteenth-century writing that are clear inventions on Gray's part.
Moreover, Gray makes it clear in the pamphlet's "To the Public" introduction that he considered the rebellious slaves "remorseless murderers" and

"savages" whose "flinty bosoms" were impervious to their victims' cries of mercy—Gray referred to Nat Turner as the "great Bandit"—and this judgment on his part likely influenced the questions he asked Nat.[2] But despite the fact that the *Confessions* should not be read uncritically, it does reveal a good deal about Nat Turner, the religious sensibilities that motivated his rebellion, and the details of the terrible night of mayhem that erupted when he and his followers began their "work of death."[3]

And a work of death the rebellion certainly was, resulting in the greatest loss of life of any other slave revolt in North America. By the time it was all over, 200 people, slaves, free blacks, and whites, had died.

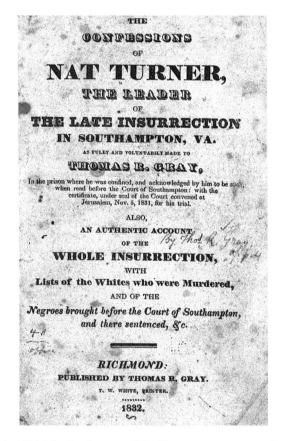

Thomas Gray's 1832 *The Confessions of Nat Turner* was a runaway best seller. Gray transcribed several hours of interviews with Turner as the revolt leader awaited execution, and published a record of them, embellished with his own observations, after Turner's death. (Library of Congress)

A RELIGIOUS VISIONARY

There was nothing distinctive about the southeastern Virginia county that was home to both Nat and Gray. In fact, it was, in the words of one historian, "a relatively isolated, economically stagnant backwater area."[4] There was no industry. The vast majority of the county's inhabitants lived off of mostly self-sufficient farms, despite the fact that much of the land included large areas of uncultivable swampland. What surplus produce the farms generated was generally taken to the county seat, Jerusalem, to be sold at market. Although it was the largest town in the county, Jerusalem boasted a population of only 175 people. There were several other villages scattered throughout the county, but they were little more than crossroads.

In 1831, the year of Nat Turner's revolt, just over 16,000 people resided in Southampton County. But with 7,756 of them slaves, and another 1,745 free blacks, only 40 percent of the population was white, a situation that served as a continuous reminder to white farmers and merchants that their positions were precarious. A third of the county's farmers owned no slaves at all, and the majority of those who did owned fewer than 10. So it is somewhat surprising that the slave population was so large. The nearly 2,000 free blacks who lived in the county were either direct or indirect recipients of manumission.

Nat Turner was born a slave, owned by Benjamin Turner, one of the country's small farmers, and by the time his 31 years were over and done, he had been bondsman to no fewer than five people. When he was 10 years old, Benjamin died, and Nat became the property of Turner's son, Samuel; when he was 21, Samuel died, and Nat was sold to another famer named Thomas Moore. On Moore's death six years later, Nat became the property of Moore's son Putnam. But since the boy was only nine years old, Nat in effect was controlled by Moore's widow. When she remarried, in 1830 to a carriage maker named Joseph Travis, Nat acquired yet another new master. Interestingly, Nat does not refer to this continuously shuffling ownership in his conversations with Gray—or, if he did, Gray chose not to print it. But it surely heightened Turner's sense that, as a slave, his destiny was in the control of others.

From an early age, Nat was marked as someone who was special. When he was three or four years old, he recalled, his mother was startled to hear him prattling on about events that happened before he was born, convincing her that he was "destined for some great purpose."[5] His grandmother, also a slave and a very religious woman, apparently nurtured the young boy's own faith.

In addition to being deeply religious, Nat was also intelligent. He had no recollection of learning the alphabet, but claimed that the moment he first set eyes on a book, he began spelling out the words. This is most likely a bit of mythology that he himself, perhaps, had started to believe. But it is undoubtedly the case that he somehow learned to read and write. He was naturally curious, and his interests soon led him to explore the arts of making paper and gunpowder, childhood experiments that suggested a rebellious nature even at an early age.

But what occupied him more than anything else was his interior life. He prayed and fasted regularly, and soon began having visions. His first revelation occurred one day when he was ploughing. He does not tell us how old he was when it came to him, but he was probably in his teens or early twenties. A "spirit" spoke to him, saying "See ye the kingdom of Heaven and all things shall be added unto you." Nat took this as a sign that he was destined for a grand purpose, although he was not aware, as yet, what it might be. Several years later, despairing of serving under a new and harsh overseer, Nat ran away and remained hidden in the woods for about a month. But the Spirit spoke to him again, telling him to return to bondage and bide his time. Several of his fellow slaves disdainfully "murmured against him" for coming back. But a vision he had around this time, in which he saw "white spirits and black spirits engaged in battle, and the sun darkened—the thunder rolled in the Heavens, and blood flowed in streams,"[6] suggested that his return was not due to a subservient spirit.

This revelation occurred in 1825, and after it, Nat devoted himself increasingly to prayer in preparation for new ones. On one occasion he saw a vision of Christ's outstretched arms in the sky. Another time he discovered what he thought were drops of blood on corn and strange "hieroglyphic characters" on leaves, both of which he interpreted as Christ's blood presaging a swiftly approaching Day of Judgment. Nat was not shy about communicating his visions to both blacks and whites, and he actually converted and baptized one white man. When white congregants refused to allow the baptism to take place in their church, Nat took his disciple down to a nearby river and baptized him there.

It is not clear when it occurred to Nat that the Day of Judgment he believed was on its way was also a call for him to rise up, throw off his bondage, and slay whites. But as the conviction of his personal destiny grew, so did the ferocity of his visions. In May 1828, he "heard a loud noise in the heavens, and the Spirit instantly appeared to me and said the Serpent was loosened, and Christ had laid down the yoke ... and that I should take it on and fight against the Serpent"—which in Nat's mind was slavery.[7] But the time was not yet ripe for overt rebellion, and Nat was told to await further signs.

In February 1831, an eclipse of the sun convinced Nat that the time had come to "arise and prepare myself, and slay my enemies with their own weapons." After informing four trusted compatriots that the "work of death" would commence on July 4—a day obviously chosen for its association with independence—Nat fell ill, almost certainly from anxiety, and the plan had to be postponed. But it was arranged that the five men, along with others whom they had taken into their confidence, would meet secretly in the woods on a mid-August Saturday night to share a meal and make new plans. One of the slaves stole a pig, another some brandy. Perhaps because of the alcohol, events moved more swiftly than even Nat had anticipated.

THE RAMPAGE

There was probably no overall plan of action decided at the late-night gathering. Nat and his followers seemed to have no more ambition than to march on Jerusalem, killing all the white people they encountered along the way. As an apocalyptic visionary, perhaps he decided that he needed no other plan than cooperation with providence's punishment of slave owners.

Around two o'clock on the morning of August 22, Nat led the rebels to his master's house. He later acknowledged that Joseph Travis was a "kind master" and that he "had no reason to complain of his treatment of me."[8] But Travis was nonetheless targeted as the first victim. After breaking into the farm's cider press and fortifying themselves with even more alcohol (Turner appears not to have touched spirits either at the forest gathering or at the cider press), the men crept up to the farmhouse where Travis and his family slept. Nat used a ladder to climb to a second-story window, crept downstairs, and unbolted the front door.

Partly in keeping with his vision of destruction, but mostly to live up to his reputation as an avenging prophet, Nat realized he had to shed the first blood. So armed with a hatchet and accompanied by another slave, he entered Travis's bedroom and took a swing at him. However, "it being dark, I could not give a death blow, the hatchet glanced from his head, he sprang from the bed and called his wife, it was his last word, Will [one of Nat's accomplices] laid him dead, with a blow of his ax, and Mrs. Travis shared the same fate, as she lay in bed. The murder of this family, five in number, was the work of a moment."[9] It was only after the rebels had seized all of the guns they could find and left the house that Turner remembered that Travis had an infant child, and two of his companions returned to the house to butcher the child.

It is significant that Nat actually killed only one person in the deadly spree that he instigated and led. The wayward blow he directed at Travis was not the only one he delivered that night, but by his own confession, only one of them was mortal. At the Whitehead residence, he admitted to killing one of the daughters, a girl named Margaret, by bashing her head in with a fence rail. But even then it appears that Nat's murder of her was a spontaneous act of mercy, since the poor girl had been slashed numerous times with a sword.

Although Nat dreamed of an apocalyptic shedding of white blood, it is probable that he flinched once the killing started. Despite his biblical sense of destiny as the scourge of Southampton County's slave owners, he simply did not seem to have the stomach for the violence. The mere thought of it had sickened him back in July. Still, in his *Confession*, he tried to play the man. "I sometimes got in sight in time to see the work of death completed, viewed the mangled bodies as they lay, in silent satisfaction, and immediately started in quest of other victims."[10]

Nat's own personal aversion was of little consequence, however, because his followers seemed perfectly willing to take on the killing. After they left the Travis's place, they proceeded to the next farm, and then several others, breaking down doors, chopping sleeping whites to pieces, shooting others, and showing mercy to none. At the Waller household, for example, Nat's rebels slaughtered 10 children. At the home of William Williams, they killed Mr. Williams and his two sons. Mrs. Williams had managed to run from the mayhem. But she was quickly caught and dragged back to the corpses of her family and taunted. Forced to lie down beside her husband, she was shot to death with one of the captured guns.

The killing continued through the night and on to the next day. By the afternoon of August 22, Nat's army, which now numbered between 50 and

60 slaves, "all mounted and armed with guns, axes, swords and clubs,"[11] had traveled some 20 miles and murdered nearly 60 men, women, and children. Nat steered the rebels toward Jerusalem, only three miles distant. But some of his men wanted to pause at the farm of James Parker because they had relatives who were slaves there. Turner reluctantly agreed, and it was during this pause that a posse of nearly 20 whites who had been tracking the rebels' route caught up with him.

Nat rallied his men, forming them into a battle line, at which point a member of the posse fired on them. A good half of the rebels fled, but the rest stood their ground, fired off a volley, and then charged the whites, who quickly retreated up a small hill. As luck had it, a second party of white vigilantes arrived on the scene just as the men in the first one were reloading. They all charged down the hill toward the rebels, who quickly scattered. This time, Nat's efforts to rally his men for a counterattack were futile. All but about 20 of them "were dispersed in every direction."[12] Over the next few hours he managed to collect 20 more of his army, but as they rested in preparation for what Nat hoped would be a march on Jerusalem, they were alarmed by a sentinel who gave a false alarm, and half of them scattered. After trying without success over the next two days to muster his forces, Nat finally decided that the revolt had failed and that it must be every man for himself. So, "on Thursday night [August 25] after having supplied myself with provisions, I scratched a hole under a pile of fence rails in a field, where I concealed myself for six weeks, never leaving my hiding place but for a few minutes in the dead of night to get water."[13]

The disappearance of Nat Turner immediately provoked a $500 bounty for his capture, and a physical description of him appeared in newspapers throughout the commonwealth.

> Nat is between 30 & 35 [years old]—5 feet 6 or 8 inches high—weighs between 150 and 160 rather bright complexion, but not a mulatto—broad-shouldered—large flat nose—large eyes—broad flat feet rather knock kneed—walk brisk and active—hair on the top of the head very thin—no beard except on the upper lip and the tip of the chin. A scar on one of his temples produced by the kick of a mule—also one on the back of his neck by a bite—a large knot on one of the bones of his right arm near the wrist produced by a blow.[14]

In the meantime, Virginia was preparing for war. On the very night of the rebellion, word was dispatched to Petersburg and Norfolk, and then to Governor John Floyd in Richmond, that Southampton slaves were armed and on the march. Norfolk's response was a panicked determination not to allow the rebellion to spread. Volunteers and militiamen were mustered, and the city's mayor contacted the commander of nearby Fortress Monroe, urging him to assemble federal troops. For his part, Governor Floyd ordered six companies of Richmond, Norfolk, and Portsmouth militia, including one each of cavalry and artillery, to move on Southampton. Moreover, a militia company as far away as North Carolina was mustered. Nearly 3,000 troops converged on Jerusalem in the days immediately following the revolt, even though by that time the danger was well over.

The combination of all these militiamen, commanded by General Richard Eppes, and Southampton vigilantes, many of whom had lost family and friends to Nat's army, created a situation in which retaliation was both brutal and indiscriminate. The number of slaves and freedmen who were killed in the aftermath of the revolt is probably somewhere around 120, while the actual number of men who joined Nat's ranks is likely half that. But the panic caused by the rebels' killing spree was so intense that the general sentiment was that it was better to be safe than sorry when it came to identifying and punishing suspects. That the rebels had butchered their victims so savagely both alarmed the country's whites and made them, and the militia that joined them, merciless in their response.

By Saturday, six days after the revolt and two since Nat disappeared, nearly 40 slaves had been killed and another 50 jailed in Jerusalem. One farmer by the name of Nathaniel Francis boasted that he had personally killed 15 rebellious slaves. Many of the captured slaves were tied to trees and shot outright by enraged locals. One of the captured rebels, whom the whites considered to be one of Nat's "generals," was tortured before he was finally beheaded. His hamstrings were severed, his ears and nose cut off, and his skin was burned with red hot pokers. Afterward, his headless body was "spiked to a whipping post for a spectacle to other negroes."[15]

As was generally the case in the aftermath of a slave revolt or conspiracy, the corpses of the slaves who were murdered in retaliation were often displayed as grisly warnings to others. The North Carolina militia company was particularly bloodthirsty, beheading some 15 captured slaves and placing their heads atop poles along the roadway. The killing was so

Although crudely drawn, this period illustration of Nat Turner's revolt and the subsequent pursuit of the rebels captures some of the horror experienced by white Virginians. (Library of Congress)

indiscriminate, and the butchering so loathsome, that some whites objected. One of them protested that even though the conduct of Nat's rebels was "outrageous, that of the whites was most Barbarous." Another lamented that slaves were seized and killed "without judge or jury," so that only the "victims and God knew if they were guilty or innocent."[16]

Ironically, the 50 or so slaves and free blacks who were jailed in Jerusalem had a better chance of survival than slaves who were captured by the militias and posses. They were eventually tried by a panel of 12 local farmers. Eighteen of them were hanged, another 14 transported out of the state, and the rest acquitted. One of the condemned was Lucy Barrow, the only woman implicated in the uprising. Lucy, about 20 years old, was the property of John T. Barrow, one of the insurrection's victims. Witnesses claimed she had attempted to prevent her mistress from escaping Nat's army and that afterward she had been discovered with money belonging to the Barrow family.

Horrified as Southern whites were by the uprising, some Northerners, although publicly condemning the bloodshed, could hardly suppress their satisfaction at what they took to be a justified rebellion against the horrendous institution of slavery. Abolitionist William Lloyd Garrison, editor of *The Liberator*, the famous antislavery newspaper then only a few months old, called Nat Turner's revolt "the first step of the earthquake which is

ultimately to shake down the fabric of oppression." The uprising, he predicted, was but the "beginning of sorrows" for the entire nation. Every
white, Northern or Southern, was guilty of the "crime of oppression" for
tolerating human bondage. In case any whites were sanctimonious enough
to condemn the bloodshed by Nat and his men, Garrison reminded them
of the catalogue of wrongs done to slaves, "dripping with warm blood fresh
from their lacerated bodies."[17]

Garrison also devoted some space in his rather purple editorial to
defending himself against Southern charges that he and his fellow abolitionists had instigated the revolt, or at least encouraged it by their continuous denunciations of slavery. He said he was "horror-struck at the late
tidings," insisting that he had always "preached to the slaves the pacific
precepts of Jesus Christ." Besides, the slaves "need no incentives at our
hands. They will find them in their stripes." So to those Southerners who
accused him of urging Nat Turner on, Garrison shouted: "Take back the
charge as a foul slander!"[18]

Most Southerners were unimpressed by Garrison's protests of innocence, and one of them was Governor Floyd. Writing a couple of months
after the rebellion, he insisted that the "spirit of insubordination" among
his state's slaves could be chalked up to the insidious influence of the
"Yankee population." First, the Yankees told slaves that "God was no
respecter of persons [and] that the black man was as good as the white."
Then they compounded their crime by assuring slaves that all men "were
born free and equal." Given the "incendiary publications" of agitators
such as Garrison, bloodthirsty uprisings like Nat's were as predictable as
the seasons.[19]

NAT TURNER'S CAPTURE

White patrols, both civilian and militia, roamed the countryside searching
for Nat even as trials and hangings of his fellow slaves, guilty as well as
innocent, were going on. Although many people believed he had fled
the county and even the state, he in fact was holed up on the farm of his
slain master Joseph Travis. The question remains as to why he stayed in
the vicinity of the uprising. Nat himself later said that he was forced to
do so because the area was too well patrolled for him to venture very far.
But it may also be the case that he remained because it was easy for him

to steal provisions from the number of deserted farms in the area whose owners had either been slain during the uprising or had fled in panic.

After a month and a half of concealment in the hole he dug under the fence rails, Nat was discovered by a couple of slaves who were drawn to his hiding place by the barking of a dog. Realizing that the slaves would notify the authorities, Nat managed to elude capture for another couple of weeks until Benjamin Phipps, a local farmer, discovered him hiding in a hole under a fallen tree. Armed with only a sword and without coat or shoes in the freezing late October weather, Nat surrendered. He was taken to Jerusalem on October 31 and jailed under strong guard, as much to protect him against angry locals as to prevent his escape.

That same day, Nat was interviewed by two magistrates. One of them later reported that the captured rebel leader displayed cogency and intelligence in answering the questions set him and that furthermore he confessed that he had been led astray by religious zeal. But at least one onlooker came to a quite different conclusion, saying that Nat was vague in his responses and seemed under the spell of superstition.

The next day, November 1—All Saints Day—attorney Thomas R. Gray, who may have been present at the previous day's interrogation, walked into Nat's jail cell and asked to interview him. Nat seemed willing enough, probably because he wanted to get his side of the story before the public. Over the next three or four days, Gray posed his questions and took notes on Nat's responses.

On November 5, Nat's trial began. He was provided with a lawyer, to whom the county paid $10 for representing the rebel leader. Nat pled not guilty, probably on the advice of his lawyer. Extra guards were stationed in the courtroom to prevent any extralegal harm coming to the defendant. Nat's attorney, probably realizing the futility of representing a man whose guilty verdict was inevitable, called no witnesses. When asked if he had any words to speak before the pronouncement of sentence, Nat replied that he had said all there was to say in his confession to Thomas Gray. Then the solemn words that spelled death by hanging were spoken:

> You have been arraigned and tried before this court, and convicted of one of the highest crimes in our criminal code. You have been convicted of plotting in cold blood, the indiscriminate destruction of men, of helpless women, and of infant children. The evidence before us leaves not a shadow

of doubt, but that your hands were often imbrued in the blood of the innocent ... Borne down by this load of guild, your only justification is, that you were led away by fanaticism.[20]

Nat was sentenced to hang on the next Friday, November 11. He went to his death silently and displayed incredible will power. After the noose was placed around his neck and the trap sprung, he astounded the assembled crowd by refusing to struggle as he died. In his newspaper, Garrison marveled that "not a limb nor a muscle was observed to move."[21] It is not clear what happened to his corpse. One account said it was dissected by medical students, who doubtlessly sought for some physical evidence of Nat's fanaticism when they had him open. Another reported that Nat's body was skinned, and grease made from his flesh.

A SMOTHERED VOLCANO

Nat Turner's revolt struck fear into the hearts of Southerners as no rebellion or conspiracy before or afterward did. For months anxiety ran throughout Virginia and, indeed, the other slave states. One woman aptly described the tension. "It is like a smothered volcano," she wrote. "We know not when, or where, the flame will burst forth but we know that death in the most horrid forms threaten us. Women have died, others have become deranged from apprehension since the affair."[22]

To forestall future uprisings, Maryland, North Carolina, and Alabama quickly passed legislation to restrict the activities of both enslaved and free blacks within their borders. For his part, Virginia governor John Floyd was determined that a repetition of insurrection would never occur. In his annual message to the commonwealth's legislature, he recommended that laws be passed "[t]o confine the Slaves to the estates of their masters—prohibit negroes from preaching—absolutely to drive from this State all free negroes—and to substitute the surplus revenue in our Treasury annually for slaves, to work for a time upon our Rail Roads etc etc and these sent out of the country, preparatory, or rather as the first step to emancipation."[23] Floyd's final point was revealing. Nat Turner's revolt had so rattled the people of Virginia that they were willing to consider what in other circumstances seemed unthinkable: the elimination of slavery in the state. When the new legislative session opened in January 1832, just weeks after

Nat's execution, Thomas Jefferson Randolph, a grandson of Thomas Jefferson, actually proposed a referendum to end slavery by gradual steps in Virginia. His thinking was clear: if there were no slaves, there would be no threat of white citizens having their throats cut as they slept by rebellious slaves.

Commonwealth legislators debated Randolph's proposal for two months, prompting a sympathetic Richmond newspaper editor to marvel that "Nat Turner, and the blood of his innocent victims, have conquered the silence of fifty years."[24] In the end, though, custom and economic interests proved too powerful, and the legislators declined to abolish slavery, the institution upon which so many of their fortunes rested, and of which they were so frightened.

NOTES

1. Kenneth S. Greenberg (ed.), *The Confessions of Nat Turner, and Related Documents* (Boston, MA: Bedford/St. Martin's, 1996), 46.

2. Ibid., 41, 42.

3. Ibid., 48.

4. "The Confessions of Nat Turner: Text and Context," in ibid., 6.

5. *Confessions*, 44.

6. Ibid., 46.

7. Ibid., 47.

8. Ibid., 48.

9. Ibid., 49.

10. Ibid., 51

11. Ibid.

12. Ibid., 52.

13. Ibid., 53.

14. Henry Irving Tragle (ed.), *The Southampton Slave Revolt of 1831: A Compilation of Source Material* (New York: Vintage, 1973), 420–421.

15. Thomas C. Parramore, "Covenant in Jerusalem," in Kenneth S. Greenberg (ed.), *Nat Turner: A Slave Rebellion in History and Memory* (New York: Oxford University Press, 2003), 69.

16. Ibid., 70, 71.

17. *The Liberator*, September 3, 1831.

18. Ibid.

19. Tragle, *The Southampton Slave Revolt*, 275.

20. *Confessions*, 56–57.

21. Parramore, "Covenant in Jerusalem," 73.

22. Quoted in Herbert Aptheker, *American Negro Slave Revolts* (New York: International Publishers, 1993), 306–307.

23. Tragle, *The Southampton Slave Revolt*, 276.

24. Eric Foner, *Nat Turner* (Trenton, NJ: Prentice Hall, 1972), 8.

CHAPTER 9

THE CHENEYVILLE CONSPIRACY

A concerted movement among a number of slaves on Bayou
Boeuf . . . has become a subject of general and unfailing interest in
every slave-hut on the bayou, and will doubtless go down to succeeding generations as their chief tradition.

—Solomon Northup[1]

Slave conspiracies were sometimes betrayed by uninvolved slaves
who got wind of the plot and, out of loyalty or fear, told their masters and the authorities. Gabriel Prosser's planned 1800 revolt and
Denmark Vesey's 1822 conspiracy were both foiled in this way. But the
1837 Cheneyville conspiracy is unique in the history of slave revolts in
that it was betrayed by the very man, Lew Cheney, who organized it. It is
a poignant example of how the ever-present threat of punishment for
rebellion was so feared by slaves that some were willing to sacrifice their
fellows to avoid it. Just how Cheney managed to pull off his deception
remains unclear. But that he did is uncontested.

The Cheneyville conspiracy is also noteworthy for the scope and
extremity of extralegal vigilante "justice," born of white panic, that was
meted out indiscriminately to guilty and innocent alike. Things got so
bad that some of the white residents eventually called in federal troops
for protection—not from slaves, but from noose-happy whites.

A WHITE MINORITY

In the 1830s, the interior of Louisiana was still pretty much frontier. Commerce was primarily situated in the south of the state at the port city of
New Orleans. The state's only other sizeable antebellum city, Shreveport,
was not founded until 1837, the year of the Cheneyville conspiracy.

Cheneyville itself, a tiny outpost named after its founder, was in Rapides Parish, located in the center of the state and situated on the Red River. Alexandria, the closest town of any size to Cheneyville, was about 40 miles away.

The economy of the parish and of Cheneyville was built on cotton. At one time, sugarcane had been a staple crop. But a lowering of the tariffs placed on imports of sugar crippled the domestic market, at least in Rapides, and planters began turning to cotton. Like sugar, cotton demanded a strong labor force to plant, cultivate, and harvest, and so large numbers of slaves were needed for the often land-rich but cash-poor planters to keep their heads above water. In 1837, the population of Rapides Parish was probably just over 10,000; the 1840 federal census would record it at just barely 14,000. But a full 70 percent of the parish's inhabitants were slaves. Planters and their families felt like a tiny white island in a black ocean, and their anxiety level was correspondingly high. They regularly petitioned the state legislature for funds to pay for policing the parish's black population, and were just as regularly turned down due to the paucity of state revenue. The white residents of Rapides were so alarmed after the 1831 Nat Turner insurrection that they actually begged the federal Department of War to send troops to protect them. This request, too, was refused.

Being surrounded by black slaves was cause enough for anxiety. But the fact that only one parish separated Rapides from the Mexican border was downright alarming. Mexico had abolished slavery within its borders in 1829, and ever since then, the free nation had been a constant temptation for slaves in the Deep South and a constant source of worry for their masters. Granted, the part of Mexico on Louisiana's western border had been claimed by the breakaway Republic of Texas in 1836, and Texas was a slaveholding country. But both whites and enslaved blacks still believed that freedom lay westward.

If slaves did make a run for the border or, even worse, if they banded together in insurrection, the only real force capable of systematically dealing with them were the troops garrisoned at Fort Jesup, situated about 60 miles northwest of Alexandria. The fort, established by General Zachary Taylor in 1822, was situated on what was once known as the "Neutral Strip," a slice of land on the U.S.-Mexico border claimed by both nations until an agreement was finally reached in 1819. By 1837, the Department of War was considering abandoning Fort Jesup. But the post's commandant, Colonel James B. Many, argued for its preservation on the grounds that its location was "well calculated to protect the planters and others on the Red River against their slaves."[2] What Many could not have anticipated was that his troops would wind up protecting Red River slaves against whites.

THE REAL CONSPIRACY AND THE MYTHICAL ONE

Details about the Cheneyville conspiracy are so scarce as to be nearly non-existent. But what the available records tell us is this. Sometime in 1837, Lewis or "Lew" Cheney, a slave belonging to planter David Cheney, descendant of the man after whom the town was named, began making surreptitious rounds to five different plantations along the Red River to encourage slaves to join him in a flight to the western border. He told them that he was angry at his master for demoting him from house service to field work. If true, it suggests that Cheney could well have been at least semi-literate and that his visits to plantations must have been under cover of darkness, since he would have been working the cotton fields during daylight hours. He also told them that even though the Republic of Texas recognized slavery, there were Mexican nationals just across the border eager to help runaways.

Cheney made no bones about the fact that any slaves who joined him might have to fight their way to the border, and he encouraged them to steal and store not only foodstuff but also weapons of any kind they could lay hands on. Apparently the pilfered cache was hidden in a storehouse in a swamp on a sugarcane plantation owned by a man named Hawkins. According to Solomon Northup, the free black man and author of *Twelve Years a Slave* who was kidnapped and sold into slavery in Rapides Parish, the supplies were accidentally discovered just as "the expedition" was about to get under way. It was at that point that the real conspiracy to flee mutated into a fictional conspiracy to murder. As Northup tells it,

> Lew Cheney, becoming convinced of the ultimate failure of his project, in order to curry favor with his master, and avoid the consequences which he foresaw would follow, deliberately determined to sacrifice all his companions. Departing secretly from the encampment, he proclaimed among the

planters the number collected in the swamp, and, instead of stating truly the object they had in view, asserted their intention was to emerge from their seclusion the first favorable opportunity, and murder every white person along the bayou.[3]

It comes as no surprise that Cheney turned informant to save his own skin. It was a moral failing, perhaps, but hardly an unpredictable move for someone in his circumstances. What is surprising is why he thought it necessary to inflate a simple plan to flee bondage into one of bloody insurrection. Was he possessed of an excitable temperament that drove him, when confronted with the terror of discovery, into blood-curdling exaggeration? Did he secretly plan all along for his followers to massacre local whites, but refrained from telling them lest he frighten off the more timid ones? Or was his motive more sinister? Did he deliberately exaggerate the threat in order to frighten whites into a retribution so swift that it would minimalize the risk of Cheney's central role coming to light during interrogation?

Just as puzzling is exactly what part whites believed Cheney actually played in the plot he disclosed to them. The record is completely silent on this. We know that the Louisiana legislature emancipated Cheney as a reward for his betrayal, awarded his master the compensatory sum of $1,500, and paid Cheney $500 to enable him to leave the state, presumably to protect him from vengeance on the part of Rapides Parish slaves. But his emancipation and monetary award could be grudging as easily as genuine gratitude, depending on what the white community believed Cheney to be.

Did he portray himself as accidentally stumbling across the conspiracy? Did he pretend to have been approached by the conspirators in an effort to recruit him? Did he confess to being part of a plan to flee to freedom, but that he had a change of heart when the conspirators switched their intentions from flight to murder? Each of these, of course, would be a self-serving lie. The question is which one, if any, Cheney chose to go with, and how it happened that he was not found out. Surely at least some of the arrested and executed conspirators must have told their captors of Cheney's role in the conspiracy. Was their testimony dismissed as desperate last attempts at avenging themselves on the slave who had discovered and revealed their plot?

There is also the possibility that whites were well aware of Cheney's involvement and even his leadership in the conspiracy. But if this is so, why would Cheney have increased his own personal danger by dressing up a simple plan of flight into one of carnage? Moreover, despite the $500 bounty intended to help Cheney resettle elsewhere, he appears to have hung around Rapides Parish at least on and off for four years after the conspiracy was revealed. Solomon Northup claims to have actually met him, and Northup did not arrive in the parish until around 1842. (In his memoir, Northup inaccurately states that the conspiracy occurred the year before his arrival.) Surely whites would not have allowed the planner of an insurrection to remain in their midst. Northup's testimony confuses the issue even more. He harshly describes Cheney as "a shrewd, cunning negro, more intelligent than the generality of his race, but unscrupulous and full of treachery,"[4] suggesting that everyone in the parish, whites as well as enslaved blacks, knew that Cheney had been the instigator of the conspiracy he subsequently betrayed.

Whatever his motives, and whatever whites thought of his role in the conspiracy, Cheney's sell-out of the slaves he himself recruited sparked a general panic throughout the entire parish. By the time the dust settled, at least 15 persons, some of them possibly innocent of conspiracy, were dead.

RETRIBUTION

Cheney's betrayal of the slave plot occurred in early October. Within a week, the panicky planters of Rapides Parish, meeting in Alexandria's courthouse, had established a "Committee of Vigilance" to root out, interrogate, and punish participants. Additionally, on October 6, they sent an urgent dispatch to Fort Jesup requesting that troops be ordered to the parish to protect whites. On that same day, the first executions occurred. Two slaves whom Cheney had fingered were hanged, even though there appears to have been no formal trial for either of them. Their deaths, like all the deaths to follow, were extralegal judgments. Moreover, their executions followed so quickly on their capture that they could not have been thoroughly interrogated—a circumstance that must have relieved Cheney.

Subsequent interrogations of suspects conveyed some information that, when coupled with Cheney's hair-raising insistence that the conspirators had debated among themselves whether to slaughter only white males or women and children as well, stirred up a perfect frenzy in the parish. It is impossible to know how much of what the slaves told the Committee of Vigilance was actually true, and how much of it was fiction coerced by actual or threatened physical torture. But they implicated several local whites suspected of abolitionist sympathies as well as a Spaniard, and one of the parish's planters, a man named Fuzilin, was apparently so enraged by this race treason that he shot and killed one of the alleged abolitionists. Free blacks in the area also came under suspicion. Some were arrested, and a sizeable percentage of whites wanted the rest driven out of Cheneyville.

One piece of hard evidence was discovered that was authentic: a letter from Boston businessman Arthur Tappan. Tappan was a well-known and active abolitionist who in the early 1830s collaborated with William Lloyd Garrison, future editor of the abolitionist newspaper *The Liberator*, to found the American Anti-Slavery Society. Along with his brothers Benjamin and Lewis, he was a tireless opponent of slavery who was hated and reviled in the South. That one of the arrested slaves had been in contact with him convinced Rapides authorities that the plot to murder them in their sleep had been carefully crafted and financed by Northerners bent on destroying the institution of slavery. It was not long before a large number of suspects had been rounded up and 12 of them, nine slaves and three freedmen, hanged. The alarm whipped up by Cheney's lurid story generally led to hasty arrests, summary trials that completely ignored due process, and quick executions. One local observer noted in a remarkable understatement that the trials were "without the form and contrary to law,"[5] but the majority of Rapides Parish whites were unconcerned with such niceties. All they wanted was not to be murdered in their beds, and the more people arrested, the safer they felt.

The panic traveled outside of Rapides when a couple of gallows "confessions" suggested that the conspiracy extended far beyond Cheneyville to include Natchitoches to the northwest and New Orleans to the southeast. The state legislature reacted to this news by designating the Cheneyville conspiracy a full-fledged insurrection. Alarm grew so heated that in late December, three months after Cheney betrayed the conspiracy, troops from Fort Jesup moved into Natchitoches to forestall a feared but utterly fictional slave revolt there.

Soldiers from Fort Jesup had arrived in Alexandria much earlier. On October 10, four days after the first executions took place, about

100 men from Companies D and K of the 3rd Infantry marched into the parish with orders to restore order. But unlike the mission of the force that went to Natchitoches at the end of the year, the troops in Rapides were dispatched to discourage a spirit of anarchy that had infected the white community. The first two things the commander of the troops did were to order that the jerry-rigged gallows be torn down and to release most of the dozens of slaves crammed into Alexandria's jail. About 30 prisoners were retained, extralegal seizures of slaves were halted, and law and order established. This satisfied many of the white residents who had begun to worry that the witch hunt would affect their pockets by sweeping up their human property. But diehard vigilantes were outraged that cooler heads had prevailed. One of them defiantly proclaimed, "[W]hen laws can not be made to preserve society, give it up and let each preserve himself."[6]

Giving up laws is exactly what happened for a few days of violence in Cheneyville, Alexandria, and other parts of Rapides Parish. Although order was quickly restored, lives had been lost; white distrust and dislike of all blacks, free or enslaved, were raised to a new level; and the fear of white outrage that was the perpetual burden of slaves was deepened. As Solomon Northup noted, the Cheneyville conspiracy became the "chief tradition" of local blacks and whites. The irony is that the conspiracy was totally fabricated by the one person who seems genuinely to have profited from the tragedy.

NOTES

1. Solomon Northup, *Twelve Years a Slave,* Sue Eakin and Joseph Logsdon (ed.) (Baton Rouge: Louisiana State University, 2010), 188.

2. Junius P. Rodriguez, "Complicity and Deceit: Lewis Cheney's Plot and Its Bloody Consequences," in Michael A. Bellesiles (ed.), *Lethal Imagination: Violence and Brutality in American History* (New York: New York University Press, 1999), 141.

3. Northup, *Twelve Years,* 189.

4. Ibid., 188.

5. Rodriguez, "Complicity and Deceit," 143.

6. Ibid., 145.

CHAPTER 10

THE *CREOLE* REVOLT

The slaves of the *Creole* were not a whit the less men because "mutiny had changed their course on the ocean. They stood up at the port of Nassau with all the attributes of men, and the government would not without wrong have denied their character and corresponding claims.

—William Ellery Channing[1]

S lave revolts and conspiracies to revolt in the American colonies and states rarely ended any way except tragically. As we have seen in previous chapters, most perpetrators, as well as scores of innocent blacks, both enslaved and free, were quickly captured and killed. Occasionally, as in the Stono revolt, the German Coast revolt, and Nat Turner's rebellion, white lives and property were also lost.

There is, however, one slave insurrection that was unequivocally successful: the 1841 mutiny on the domestic slave ship *Creole*, in which Virginia-born slaves who were being transported to a New Orleans slave market revolted, took command of the vessel, re-routed it to the British Bahamas, and gained their freedom. The *Creole* incident challenged the slave states' claim that enslaved human beings were mere transferable property, thereby enraging Southerners while delighting abolitionists. It also threatened to torpedo a treaty intended to establish once and for all the border between the United States and Canada.

SLAVE SHIP UPRISINGS

Revolts of captured Africans aboard slave ships were not uncommon. Uprisings occurred on about one-tenth of the ships involved in the transatlantic slave trade. Over half of them took place when the vessel was still within sight of the African coast, but many also erupted on the long Middle Passage voyage. The majority of them occurred in the eighteenth century.

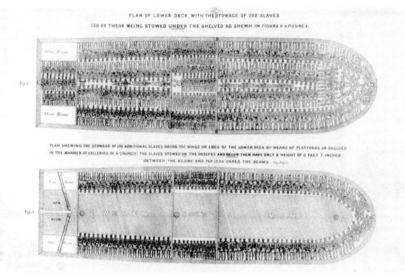

PLAN OF LOWER DECK WITH THE STOWAGE OF 292 SLAVES

130 OF THESE BEING STOWED UNDER THE SHELVES AS SHEWN IN FIGURE 5 & FIGURE 1

PLAN SHEWING THE STOWAGE OF 130 ADDITIONAL SLAVES ROUND THE WINGS OR SIDES OF THE LOWER DECK BY MEANS OF PLATFORMS OR SHELVES IN THE MANNER OF GALLERIES IN A CHURCH. THE SLAVES STOWED ON THE SHELVES AND BELOW THEM HAVE ONLY A HEIGHT OF 2 FEET 7 INCHES BETWEEN THE BEAMS AND FAR LESS UNDER THE BEAMS.

Whether transported from Africa to North America on the Middle Passage or sailed from northern to southern slave markets in the United States, slaves were frequently packed closely together in ships' holds. (Library of Congress)

The importation of African slaves into the United States was banned in 1808. After that, the regular exchange of slaves between the Upper South states and the Lower South ones replaced the older transatlantic trafficking of slaves. States like Virginia had a surplus of black persons in bondage, which rice and cotton planters of South Carolina, Alabama, Georgia, and Louisiana were eager to buy. One of the worst fears of an Upper South slave was the prospect of being "sold south." Working conditions there were harsh, and the life expectancy for field hands was unpromising. So it is not surprising that the nineteenth century saw an uptick in revolts on American vessels transporting slaves from upper slave states to lower ones.

The domestic ship revolts, with the exception of the *Creole*, were all unsuccessful. Perhaps the most notorious one before 1841 was also one of the earliest: the uprising aboard the *Decatur* in 1826. She left Baltimore loaded with 29 slaves owned by Austin Woolfolk, one of the city's leading slave merchants. Five days out, the slaves revolted, tossed the captain and first mate overboard, and tried to make it to Haiti. The *Decatur* was overtaken by a couple of ships, however, and the mutinous slaves were hauled back to New York City—where, incredibly, all but one of them, named

William, managed to escape. The hapless William was tried, convicted of murder, and sentenced to hang. Woolfolk attended his hanging, and when William publicly forgave him from the gallows, Woolfolk is said to have mocked and cursed him.

The story did not end there. Abolitionist Benjamin Lundy, who edited a virulent antislavery newspaper entitled *The Genius of Universal Emancipation*, excoriated Woolfolk after William's execution, calling him a "soul seller" and a "monster in human shape" whose "barbarous, inhuman and unchristian" trafficking in human flesh was responsible for the death of not only the unfortunate William but also the *Decatur's* captain and first mate. Woolfolk, incensed at what he took to be Lundy's slander, confronted him on a Baltimore street and severely pummeled him. Lundy was so badly injured that he was confined to bed for a week. Lundy subsequently brought suit against Woolfolk. The presiding judge had no choice but to find Woolfolk guilty, but fined him a mere one dollar, announcing from the bench that Lundy "had received no more than a merited chastisement for his abuse of the traverser."[2]

Lundy was dead a bit over a year when the *Creole* revolt took place. The news of it would have gladdened his heart.

THE MUTINY

On October 25, 1841, the *Creole*, a ship only about a year old, left Richmond bound for New Orleans. She was loaded with slaves and tobacco, both of which were to be sold in Louisiana. Along the way, the ship's captain, Robert Ensor, stopped twice to pick up more blacks. Eventually, the ship carried approximately 135 slaves. The count is uncertain; the ship's log and the later legal case brought against the insurance company by the slave owners record different tallies. In addition to the slaves, the *Creole* carried a crew of 10, 4 passengers, a few black servants, and Ensor's wife, daughter, and niece.

The slaves were kept below decks, men on the forward side, women on the aft, with the tobacco freight separating them. They apparently were unchained, and First Mate Zephaniah Gifford later testified that both men and women "were allowed to come on deck day and night if they wished."[3] The only restriction was that the male slaves were not allowed in the female slaves" compartment at night.

One of the slaves bound for the New Orleans market was a man named Madison Washington. Reliable facts about Madison are few, even though both Frederick Douglass and William Wells Brown, ex-slaves themselves, wrote about him: Douglass in a novella entitled "The Heroic Slave" (1853) and Brown in a hagiographical history entitled *The Negro in the American Rebellion* (1867). We know that he was in his early twenties at the time of the *Creole* revolt, that he was born in Virginia and had been a slave there all his life, that he married another slave, and that he escaped sometime in late 1839 or early 1840, following the Underground Railroad to Canada. A year later, pining for his wife, he returned to Virginia in the hope of secreting her away. But he was quickly captured and sold to a slave trader named Thomas McCargo, who in turn intended to sell him down south with the other slaves on the *Creole*. (One of Brown's many inaccuracies is his claim that Madison's wife was on board the ship and that the revolt reunited them. It is a charming but improbable tale.)

Described as a strong and powerful man, Madison may have also known how to read. He was called "Doctor" by the *Creole*'s crew members, an ironic title whites often gave to any slave who displayed intelligence. He was appointed cook for the other slaves on board, and so had lots of opportunity to speak with all of them. From his surreptitious conversations, he identified 18 men who were willing and eager to cooperate with him in a mutinous bid for freedom. By all accounts, he was the revolt's leader.

According to testimony later given by Captain Ensor and his crew, the slaves on board the *Creole* were "perfectly obedient and quiet, and showed no mutiny or disturbance," until the evening of November 7.[4] After the ship laid to for the night, all the crew except for First Mate Gifford, who was on watch, went to bed. Sometime afterward, Elijah Morris, one of the slave conspirators, shouted from below decks that a male slave had snuck into the aft where the women slept. Gifford called for William Henry Merritt, a man who had been promised free passage in exchange for guarding the slaves, and the two of them lit a lantern and went to investigate. When they reached the aft, they discovered Madison. Merritt expressed surprise that a man like Madison would be up to hijinks with the women slaves—"Doctor, you are the last man I would have expected to find here, and that would disobey the orders of the ship"[5]—whereupon Madison leapt past him toward the hatchway to climb up on deck. The two men tried to hold him back, but the burly slave shook them off.

The slaves who revolted aboard the *Creole* in 1841 broke out of the below-deck hold in which they were kept to commandeer the vessel and sail it to the British Bahamas and freedom. (Time Life Pictures/Getty Images)

Just then, Elijah Morris pulled a pistol—it is not known how or when he acquired it—and fired at the two white men, grazing the back of Gifford's head. Washington shouted from the deck for the other conspirators to act, threatening to kill them and throw them overboard himself if they hesitated.

Gifford, despite his wound, ran to Ensor's cabin to rouse him, although the report from Elijah's pistol had probably already done that, and Merritt fled to his own cabin. In the meantime, all of the conspirators rushed to the deck, clamoring for the death of every white person aboard the *Creole*. They were particularly anxious to locate John R. Hewell, the overseer in charge of all the slaves, including Madison, owned by Thomas McCargo. Given his subsequent fate, it is reasonable to suppose that he was a harsh man when it came to the treatment of the slaves in his care. At any rate, when Hewell, roused by the commotion on deck, stepped out of his cabin armed with a handspike, he was immediately stabbed by one of the mutineers, almost certainly a blacksmith named Ben. Either Ben cut Hewell multiple times, or other slaves also stabbed him. Hewell collapsed in his berth, groaning that "I am a dead man. The damned negroes have killed me,"[6] and soon died. After they gained control of the ship, the rebels took his body, tried to decapitate it with a knife, and finally tossed him overboard. It was a frightening act of retribution. But as events turned out, Hewell was the only white man aboard the *Creole* to lose his life.

Ensor, seeing the attack on Hewell, dashed to his aid. But he was assailed by angry blacks and himself stabbed several times. Realizing that he was unable to save Hewell and that his own wounds incapacitated him for further battle, he painfully climbed the rigging on the main mast and hid in the darkness. Gifford, seeing the captain's wounds, also climbed up and tied Ensor to the rigging lest he faint from loss of blood and fall.

Merritt had scrambled under the bedclothes in his berth and made two slave women servants sit on top of him to conceal him. But when the mutineers rushed into the cabin, the women fled and Merritt was discovered. "He is here," one of the rebels shouted. "Kill the son-of-a-bitch, don't spare him; and kill every white person on board, don't spare one."[7] The same man who killed Hewell brandished his bowie knife at Merritt, clearly wanting to kill him as well. But Merritt, who had some previous sailing experience, shouted that he could navigate the ship for the slaves, and Madison, assuming that both Ensor and Gifford were dead and knowing that neither he nor his men knew how to navigate, intervened.

The slaves soon found Mrs. Ensor and the children, and left them, along with Thomas McCargo's young son, who was also aboard the *Creole*, in charge of one of the women servants. Then they went looking for Second Mate Lucius Stevens, who had also climbed into the ship's rigging. When someone finally spotted him at about 4:30 that morning, one of the slaves shouted, "Damn you, come down and receive your message."[8] Stevens thought his "message" was a sentence of death, but in fact it was an order to help Merritt sail the ship. The revolt on the *Creole* was over by about 1:00 in the morning of November 8, with the slaves thoroughly in command of the vessel. They then sat down in the captain's cabin to decide their next move. Madison urged them to set course for Liberia, but Merritt finally convinced him that the ship lacked provisions for such a long journey. Ben, the man who slew Hewell, suggested that they go instead to the Bahamas. He knew of the fate of the *Hermosa*, another slave ship that had wrecked near the islands the previous year. The crew and passengers had been rescued by the British, who promptly freed the slaves. Britain had emancipated its slaves nearly a decade earlier, and now considered any slave that stepped on the shore of any of its vast global holdings to be emancipated.

Merritt and Stevens set a course for the Bahamas. The rebels told them they had three days to get there, or risk being thrown overboard. Captain Ensor was retrieved from the ship's rigging and handed over to his wife for nursing. The captured crew was closely guarded on the off-chance that they might try to take back the ship. The following day, November 9, the *Creole* arrived at Nassau. The slaves aboard her undoubtedly gave a shout of victory. They were confident that their days in bondage were over.

A FAILED "RESCUE"

As soon as land was sighted on the morning of November 9, Madison ordered all weapons to be brought on deck and, except for a single musket and pistol, dropped overboard. He clearly did not want to give the British the impression that he and his rebels were brigands. As the *Creole* entered Nassau harbor, a pilot boat, captained by a black man, came alongside her. First Mate Gifford managed to break away from his captors. He jumped into the boat and demanded to be taken to the American consul, John Bacon. He also requested that none of the blacks aboard the *Creole* be allowed to follow him to shore, well aware that once they were on British soil, they would declare themselves free men.

On hearing Gifford's report, Bacon immediately contacted the island's royal governor, Sir Francis Cockburn, and repeated Gifford's request that the slaves aboard the *Creole* not be allowed to disembark. Cockburn was not at all sure that he had any jurisdiction in the matter, but was willing to grant Bacon's request until he had the opportunity to consult with his council. He dispatched a squad of black soldiers, commanded by a white officer, to take command of the *Creole*.

After deliberations with his advisors, Cockburn recalled Bacon and gave the American counsel bad news. The 19 mutineers implicated by association in the murder of Hewell would be detained, pending instructions from London about how to proceed. But in keeping with British law, the rest of the slaves on board were to be allowed their freedom if they wanted it.

Cockburn set up an investigative panel to depose Captain Ensor, whose fragile condition forced him to cut short his testimony, and the rest of the crew. But even as the depositions were being taken, Bacon was conspiring with the commanders of two American ships docked at Nassau, the *Louisa* and the *Congress*, to "rescue the brig from the British officers then in command, and conduct her to Indian Key, where there was a United States vessel of war."[9] The plan was to row out to the *Creole*, board her, force off the Bahaman squad, and sail away before any of the slaves on the ship could escape. Gifford and Bacon went in search of weapons to carry out their plan, but were rebuffed by every Bahaman they approached. Gifford later indignantly complained that people in Nassau all recognized him as "one of those damned pirates and slavers," and wanted nothing to do with him.[10]

At last recognizing that they would have to make do with the weapons on hand—three muskets, as many swords, and a pair of pistols—Gifford and the rescue party rowed to the *Creole* on the morning of November 12. Whether the Bahaman soldiers on board the vessel had gotten word of the impending attempt to recapture the ship, or were alerted only when they saw the boat approaching, is unknown. But what is certain is that the British officer in charge of the squad stood firmly, warning that his men would fire on the boat if it did not depart. So the attempt to "rescue" the *Creole* from the British was a dismal failure.

It is not clear if the British authorities knew of the attempt to seize the *Creole*, although it is unlikely that they did not. Apparently the ship had been surrounded by numerous boats during the abortive operation, owned by Bahamans offering to take the slaves to shore, so there were plenty of witnesses to the ignominious conclusion of Gifford's folly. As soon as he heard that the attempt to retake the *Creole* had failed, Bacon scurried to Cockburn to complain that the locals were trying to board the vessel by force. This incredible charge was apparently an effort on Bacon's part to divert attention away from his own foiled plot.

By this point, Governor Cockburn had grown weary of Bacon's shenanigans, and he informed the American consul that he was sending the island's attorney general and provost marshal to the *Creole*. Once there, the men would take the 19 mutineers into custody until the Crown determined their fate, and also make sure that all the other slaves on board who wished to be free were safely escorted off the ship and onto dry land.

Bacon was furious, insisting that the freeing of the slaves was actually nothing less than thievery. The slaves on board the *Creole*, like the tobacco, were cargo, pure and simply. Whether on land or sea, British or American soil, Bacon insisted, slaves were chattel, and offering them freedom was a violation of their owners' property rights. The claim that slaves remained property regardless of their geographical location would be deliberated by the Supreme Court years later in the landmark 1857 *Dred Scott v. Sandford* case. Writing for the majority, Chief Justice Roger Tawney declared in favor of the defendant. Slaves, he wrote, were moveable property.

As a final sorry bit of retaliation, First Mate Gifford, taking over for the wounded Captain Ensor as the *Creole*'s master, refused to release the blankets and clothes that the slaves had used on board ship, claiming that because they were personal property themselves, they had no right to own personal property. The British authorities were unimpressed with this spiteful argument and commandeered all items that had been used by the slaves.

PROTESTS, DIPLOMATIC AND OTHERWISE

The *Creole* set sail for home without her human cargo toward the end of November, arriving in New Orleans on December 2. As soon as Gifford and the other crew members let it be known what had happened, an intensely anti-British storm erupted. Southern newspaper editors opined that Britain had overstepped her authority by confiscating American property. The *Charleston Mercury* called it an outrage, the *New Orleans Bulletin* announced that the entire city was aflame with indignation, and even some Northern papers unsympathetic to slavery fretted that Britain had gone too far.

Injury was added to insult when word came in January that the Crown had ordered the release of the 17 slaves held in Nassau under suspicion of murder and piracy. (Out of the original 19, two had died, one from injuries sustained during the uprising and one from natural causes.) The official British position was that piracy had not occurred because the slaves were simply seeking their freedom; that Britain had not confiscated American property at all, since the slaves had voluntarily come to the Bahamas; that there was no reason to hand over the 17 slaves to the United States; and that they were to be released from jail and emancipated from slavery.

Secretary of State Daniel Webster immediately ordered Edward Everett, the American ambassador to England, to file a formal protest of the way

Britain handled the *Creole* incident. So far as Webster was concerned, the arrival of slaves in Nassau had not been voluntary at all, since the men who were authorized to command and sail the *Creole* had been forced there against their will. Everett was instructed to inform Her Majesty's government that, at the very least, the owners of the slaves should be indemnified.

Opinions about the propriety of what the British had done in the *Creole* affair continued to fly fast and furious throughout the first months of 1842. Southern statesmen like John Calhoun deplored what they called British aggression, while many Northern statesmen applauded the decision to free the slaves. Ohio senator Joshua Giddings spoke so strongly in favor of the Crown's ruling that the Senate voted to censure him. Giddings promptly resigned his seat, returned to Ohio, and was enthusiastically reelected by his constituents. South Carolina senator William Preston, on the other hand, sputtered that the mutineers aboard the *Creole* were "slaves and not persons."[11] Unitarian minister William Ellery Channing wrote an entire essay on the *Creole* affair in which, contrary to Preston, he acknowledged the full humanity of the slaves and applauded the British decision, insisting that the laws of one country properly had no jurisdiction in other nations.

Controversy over the *Creole* also threatened to derail the diplomatic negotiations that finally culminated in the August 1842 Webster-Ashburton Treaty. The United States and Great Britain had been wrangling over the borders between Northern states and territories and Canada since the War of 1812. Alexander Baring, Baron Ashburton, past Master of the Mint, was dispatched to Washington, D.C., in early 1842 to work out a settlement with Secretary of State Webster. Webster kept dragging protests about the British freeing of the *Creole* slaves into the discussions, and Ashburton kept insisting that they were irrelevant. The British statesman finally managed to get the matter off the bargaining table by agreeing that colonial governors would be instructed not to indulge in future "officious interference" with any American slave ship that might be driven onto their shores by accident or mutiny.[12]

For their parts, the owners of the slaves who had been bound for the New Orleans slave market before they revolted demanded compensation. Beginning in March, no fewer than eight law suits were filed against the insurance companies covering the value of the slaves who had escaped to the Bahamas. The owners wanted indemnification because, they claimed, the slaves had been stolen by the British. The insurance companies countered by insisting that the slaves had insurrected, an event that none of the policies covered. The slave owners eventually lost six of the eight suits, the courts ruling in the unsuccessful ones that the slaves had indeed been lost through insurrection.

One of the ironies (or, perhaps, hypocrisies) of the lawsuits is that the insurance companies were represented by Judah Benjamin, future attorney general, secretary of war, and secretary of state for the Confederate States of America. In arguing that the defendants were not entitled to indemnification because the slaves had revolted, he made an eloquent case for their humanity—which, of course, the law denied by insisting that they were property. "What is a slave?" asked Benjamin, deliberately or unconsciously echoing Shylock's famous speech in *The Merchant of Venice*. "He is a human being. He has feeling and passions and intellect. His heart, like the white man's, swells with love, burns with jealousy, aches with sorrow, pines under restraint and discomfort, boils with revenge and ever cherishes the desire for liberty."[13] So of course, Benjamin concluded, slaves would rebel against their chains at every opportunity, and this was exactly what happened aboard the *Creole*.

Some 12 years after the insurrection, the Anglo-American Claims Commission, following extensive petitioning by the U.S. government, finally agreed to pay slightly more than $100,000 in indemnity claims to the owners. As for the slaves aboard the *Creole* who mutinied and won their freedom, nothing definite is known about their fate. But it is likely that they, along with their leader Madison Washington, settled in Nassau.

NOTES

1. William Ellery Channing, "The Duty of the Free States; or, Remarks Suggested by the Case of the *Creole*," *Works* (Boston: American Unitarian Association, 1887), 862–863.

2. Merton L. Dillon, *Benjamin Lundy and the Struggle for Negro Freedom* (Urbana: University of Illinois Press, 1966), 118–120.

3. "Edward Lockett v. The Merchants Insurance Company of New Orleans," *Louisiana Annual Reports* X (March 1845), 206.

4. *Senate Documents,* 27 Cong., 2 Sess., No 51: "Message from the President of the United States" (Serial 396, Washington, 1842), 37.

5. Ibid., 24.

6. Ibid., 38.

7. Ibid., 30.

8. Ibid., 32.

9. Ibid., 44.

10. "Edward Lockett v. The Merchants Insurance Company of New Orleans," 213.

11. Quoted in George Hendrick and Willene Hendrick, *The Creole Mutiny: A Tale of Revolt Aboard a Slave Ship* (Chicago: Ivan R. Dee, 2003), 113.

12. Quoted in Edward D. Jervey and C. Harold Huber, "The Creole Affair," *The Journal of Negro History* 65 (Summer 1980), 208.

13. Hendricks and Hendricks, *The Creole Mutiny,* 119.

CHAPTER 11

THE SECOND CREEK CONSPIRACY

If the black folks were turned loose with hoes and axes they would whip the country.

—Edmund, a slave[1]

In 1937, as part of the Federal Writers' Project, authors interviewed elderly blacks who remembered the years before and during the Civil War. One of the ex-slaves was an old man named Charlie Davenport. As a boy, he had belonged to a wealthy farmer, Gabriel Shields, whose plantation was on the outskirts of Natchez, Mississippi, in a region called Second Creek, named after the stream that ran through it. In recalling scenes from his childhood, Davenport mentioned a slave conspiracy to insurrect. His recollection put the conspiracy before the Civil War, but in fact it took place in the spring and summer of 1861, weeks after the opening salvo fired at Fort Sumter thrust the nation into conflict.

> When I wuz a little boy they wuz a slave uprising planned . . . De slaves had hit all worked out how dey wuz goin to march on Natchez aftah slayin all dare own white folks. Us folks wouldn't jine 'em kaise what we want to kill Ole Marse fur? One night a strange nigger come en he harangued de ole folks but dey wouldn't budge . . . My granny tole me next day dat [a sheriff's posse] kotch him hidin in a bayou en hung him on a limb. Dey didn't need no trial kaise he was kotch rilin de folks to murder.[2]

Mississippians, like all Southerners in the slaveholding states, were constantly worried about the possibility of slave uprisings. The bloody revolt led by Nat Turner in 1831 ratcheted up the anxiety level for everyone south of the Mason-Dixon Line, and a panic four years later in western Mississippi, when rumors of a planned slave insurrection led to a witch hunt that hanged over 20 slaves and white men, raised it even higher.

John Brown's abortive uprising in 1859 struck even more terror in the hearts of slave owners.

Planters who worked their acreage with slave labor were frequently ambivalent about news of slave revolts and conspiracies to revolt going public. On the one hand, they wanted to deter future insurrections by meting out swift and harsh punishment to suspects, and this required publicity. But on the other hand, they feared that news of slave conspiracies and revolts would encourage other slaves to similar actions, and so they also wanted to shun publicity. As the nation drew closer to Civil War in the 1850s, Southerners had yet another reason to be secretive about slave discontent: news of it, they feared, only provided more ammunition for Northern abolitionists to condemn the South.

That ambiguity ended in Second Creek, which is the primary reason why knowledge of the conspiracy there was virtually unknown, except for Davenport's testimony, for an entire century. With the outbreak of Civil War, the plantation owners at Second Creek feared that news of a slave conspiracy would incite other slaves to revolt in the hope of joining forces with the Union Army. Enemies without and within was a double-fronted prospect that alarmed the white residents of Second Creek and Natchez, and so word of what had happened there in the late spring of 1861 was hushed up. No newspaper accounts publicized it, and only a cursory and incomplete record of the trials of suspects was kept.

It was not merely the thought that word of the Second Creek conspiracy would incite other slaves to revolt that scared whites. Equally anxiety-provoking was the realization that white women and children were left relatively unprotected by the enlistment of so many husbands and fathers in the Confederate Army. A daughter of former Mississippi governor John Quitman worried that the Home Guard was not strong enough to ensure her safety. "It is indeed unsafe and dangerous to be so let alone as we are," she complained in a letter to her husband, who was a Confederate captain.[3]

"THE PLAN"

Second Creek is located in Adams County, a southwestern area of the state that borders on Louisiana. It has the distinction of being the oldest county in the state and the only one in the entire South named after

We know very little about the Second Creek slave conspiracy to revolt, which occurred in the opening months of the Civil War. The ringleaders were from Mississippi plantations like the slaves in this period photograph. (Miller, Francis Trevelyan and Robert Sampson Lanier, *The Photographic History of the Civil War*, Vol. 9, 1911.)

Massachusetts-born John Adams. In the opening decades of the nineteenth century, the county was Mississippi's top cotton producer, but by the time of the conspiracy, the land had been leached by continuous planting and cotton harvesting was down.

About one-third of the county's population lived in Natchez, the county seat, and was predominately white, despite the fact that the overall population of Adams was overwhelmingly black, as were most Deep South agricultural areas that relied upon slave labor. The county also had a sizeable population of free blacks, most of whom lived in Natchez, not only because they were skilled workers but also because white planters owned all the farmland in the area. Apparently Natchez was a violent town; even attorneys sometimes resorted to fisticuffs in the courtroom. Given the volatile atmosphere, the town's free blacks must have felt especially vulnerable, despite the fact that they were not legally enslaved.

By contrast, most of the slaves in the county lived outside of Natchez. They were field hands engaged in planting, tending, and harvesting cotton as well as other cash crops on several plantations owned by Second Creek aristocratic planter families—the Surgets, Mosbys, Scotts, Dunbars, Metcalfes, and Mitchells—each of which owned more than 50 slaves.

After the conspiracy to insurrect came to the attention of Second Creek whites, a Vigilance or Judicial or Examining Committee (it went by all three names), manned by planters who had not left to join the Confederate Army, was established to try suspects. The president of the committee, one Lemuel Connor, kept a sketchy record of some of the testimony offered by interrogated slaves that provides what details we have of what came to be called "The Plan."

The assault on Fort Sumter in Charleston Harbor that launched the Civil War took place on April 12, and news of it began circulating among Second Creek slaves, 700 miles away, a week later. Apparently the news was initially spread by slave carriage drivers who, because of their jobs, had better access to information about what was going on in the wider world than most other slaves. Before long, several of the drivers were speaking to field hands, telling them that the time was ripe for revolt and for joining forces with "Marse" Lincoln's bluecoats. There is no evidence that slave house servants were involved in the plot. As we have seen in earlier chapters, domestic servants had closer emotional ties to their masters than field hands and accordingly were often looked at by other slaves with distrust. If Davenport's memory can be trusted, it also appears as if some slaves who knew about the plot refused to join.

The Plan, which one defendant reported was hatched while several slaves were fishing in Second Creek, appears to have been pretty vague. It is not clear who the leaders were, although at their trials, several of the suspects gave themselves impressively highfalutin titles like general, captain, lieutenant, governor, and president. Moreover, it is not clear what The Plan's goal was other than to overthrow the Second Creek planters and join up with Union forces.

Nor was it clear what course of action the rebels would pursue. Several of the slave defendants testified that most of the conspirators planned to make their move just as soon as "Genl Scott" captured New Orleans, although some thought it better to wait until Scott moved inland to take Natchez. The Genl Scott referred to was, of course, Winfield Scott, the aged and Washington-bound commander of the Union forces. Slaves confused him with Benjamin Butler, the Union general who in fact would not take New Orleans for another year. At least two other slaves testified that they believed "Mr. Lincoln" was coming down south with an army. The slaves knew that the planters were Mr. Lincoln's enemies, and according to Connor, they "had the idea in their heads that Capt. Lincoln was to set them free."[4] William Minor, a white Second Creek resident, recorded in his diary that any planned slave uprising "seems to be dependent on the 'whipping' of the Southern people by the people of the North, when [slaves] thought they would be free, then they were to rise and kill their masters etc."[5] Ironically, one of the slave defendants mentioned that he was prepared to fight "abolitionists," clearly misunderstanding what the word designated.[6]

Several earlier slave insurrections and plans to revolt had been motivated by religion; Denmark Vesey's plot and Nat Turner's uprising fall into this category. One planned rebellion, Gabriel Prosser's, seems to have been inspired at least in part by Enlightenment-based human rights rhetoric. Judging from Lemuel Connor's fragmentary transcript of the trials, the Second Creek conspirators were motivated purely and simply by a desire to kill their white masters and, nearly unique in slave rebellions, to ravish white women. (The only other alleged conspiracy that might have contained a sexual motive was the 1741 New York conspiracy.) According to Connor, "Some [slaves] talked of killing with such weapons as they could collect," and "others thought of firing the houses at night and burning the sleepers to death before they could get out."[7] Another slave defied his interrogators by proclaiming that "if the black folks were turned loose with hoes and axes they would whip the country."[8] A third, named Simon, "said he hoped to see the day when he would blow down a white man who called him a damn rascal."[9]

Connor's record of slave testimony returns again and again, almost obsessively, to lurid claims that rebellious blacks intended to take white women as their own after their husbands, fathers, and sons were slaughtered. One slave is recorded as having said that he would "kill master and ride Mrs." Another boasted that he would "kill old master and ride the ladies." Still another expressed special attraction to the young daughter of one of the targeted planters.[10] Miscegenation, especially if it came as the consequence of an armed slave revolt, was a chronic nightmare in the South. It is impossible to determine whether the conspiring Second Creek slaves actually had intentions of rape, or if Connor inflated his record to reflect deep-seated white male anxieties. In all probability, the truth lay somewhere in between.

Another feature of the Second Creek conspiracy that came to light during the trials was the possibility that one or more white men had encouraged the slaves to revolt, similar to alleged white encouragement in the 1741 New York and the 1800 Gabriel Prosser conspiracies. A couple of slaves indicated that they had talked to a white man—generally referred to in Connor's transcript as "WM"—who had told them that the "second planters" in the area, the local designation for small-time nonaristocratic farmers, would join them in revolt. The white man was described by one slave as a rawboned, beardless, and "not tall" Irishman. Another slave suggested that there were two white men, one of whom stayed in the shadows of a tree. He described the one who spoke to him as a "Dutchman or Irishman." There was some speculation as to whether the other "white man" in fact was either a light-skinned mulatto or a black who had painted his face. Still others reported that at least one of the white men was dressed nattily in wool hat, linen clothes, and nice shoes.[11] It is impossible to determine whether the testimony about the involvement of white men was accurate, although it seems likely. But it is also what the members of the Vigilance Committee needed to hear to bolster their convictions that slaves lacked both the intelligence and the gumption to plan a revolt on their own.

TRIALS AND EXECUTIONS

In retrospect, there is probably little chance that The Plan would have actually moved from talk to action. Even if it had, it was too vague and too leaderless to have gotten very far. But when whites along Second Creek got wind of it—apparently the son of one of the planter's overseers heard slaves talking about it—they reacted with predictable ferocity. Conspiracy to revolt was a capital offense in Mississippi, as it was in all other slave states, and the fact that the South was now at war with the North convinced local whites that they had to act quickly. So an Examining or Vigilance Committee was established, and some 20 slaves belonging to seven or eight Second Creek masters, some of whom were away at war, were arrested and questioned.

The extralegal tribunal held court first at Cherry Grove, a plantation owned by Jacob Surget, then moved to a local racetrack that was also used as a holding pen for prisoners. Slave testimony satisfied the committee's members that a plot to insurrect was indeed in the wind and that it extended all the way to Natchez, some 10 miles away. The Natchez rebels were supposedly led by a black man named Bill Postlethwaite, who was said to have promised his followers that insurrection would be "an easy job now as so many [white] men had gone away."[12]

The trials began in the summer of 1861 and lasted until early November. Dozens of slaves were interrogated. They were permitted no legal counsel, and the decisions of the tribunal were final. Angry and frightened, the members of the Examining Committee did not hesitate to use physical abuse in order to coerce confessions. One of the black men "questioned" was James Carter, the slave of the local druggist. He was held at the racetrack for three weeks, but was finally released after a final beating failed to break his insistence that he was innocent of conspiracy. As Carter described it,

> The final day they carried me out[,] then they whipped me terribly. Several of them were whipping me at once. The object in whipping me was to make me confess to something. They questioned me first, and I told them I knew nothing about it, which was the truth. They said they would make me know, and then they whipped me. They would whip until I fainted and then stop and whip again. Dr. Harper sat by and would feel my pulse and tell them when to stop and when to go on.[13]

Carter was one of the lucky ones. Before the tribunal wrapped up its work, between 30 and 40 slaves were executed. Some were hanged at Cherry Grove, others at a place called Brighton Woods, and still others at the impromptu racetrack prison. Surprisingly, their masters waived their right to appeal to the state of Mississippi for compensation. Perhaps they did so out of patriotic loyalty to the fledgling Confederacy. But it is also possible that they refrained from demanding compensation because doing so would have inevitably spread the word about the Second Creek conspiracy.

FINALE

Natchez was taken by Union forces in the early summer of 1862, and blue-coated soldiers were stationed there until the end of the war. One of them, an officer from Wisconsin named Van Bennett, heard about the conspiracy and recorded a conversation he had with one of the locals, a Mrs. Henry, in a diary entry dated January 1864. Apparently the woman sought either to downplay the violence meted out to suspected slaves at Second Creek or to exonerate herself and others by claiming that the killing was done by ignorant backwoods rednecks. Bennett did not buy any of it and let his fury and disgust fly in his diary.

> The outrages committed on the poor, unfortunate Negroes who were suspected of evil designs surpass any thing I ever heard or read of. The cruelty of the chivalrous gentry of Natchez would put to blush the warmest advocates of the Spanish Inquisition as practiced in the dark ages of popery ... the usual cry of "educational prejudice" has no force whatever. We can never know half the evil.[14]

The tragedy is that the judgment Bennett pronounced on the people of Second Creek and Natchez equally applied to the white prosecutors and bystanders in other slave conspiracies and revolts, both the ones discussed in this book and the scores of others attempted during the years in which the British colonies and the United States allowed slavery. As we have seen, some of the uprisings, such as Gabriel Prosser's and Denmark Vesey's, were meticulously planned; others, like the ones at Second Creek and New York, much less so. And at least one, the Stono uprising, may have been a spontaneous eruption.

But what tied all of them together was a burning desire for freedom on the part of men, and sometimes women, who were tired of being treated like chattel. That the conspiracies and revolts took place is a tribute to the human spirit, just as the ugly fact of slavery is a tragedy whose burden the people of the United States still carry.

NOTES

1. Winthrop D. Jordan, *Tumult and Science at Second Creek: An Inquiry into a Civil War Slave Conspiracy*, rev. ed. (Baton Rouge: Louisiana State University Press, 1995), 273. Jordan's book is groundbreaking. After years of combing through archives, he pieced together the facts about the Second Creek uprising.

2. Quoted in ibid., 131.

3. Ibid., 242.

4. Ibid., 240.

5. Ibid., 239.

6. Ibid., 223.
7. Ibid., 240.
8. Ibid., 127.
9. Ibid., 203.
10. Ibid., 166.
11. Ibid., 142, 144.
12. Ibid., 240.
13. Ibid., 257.
14. Ibid., 325.

BIOGRAPHIES

THOMAS BENNETT (1781–1865)

Governor of South Carolina during the Denmark Vesey conspiracy, Bennett's criticism of the extralegal prosecution of implicated slaves damaged his political career. After his term expired in 1822, he would not hold elective office for another 15 years.

Born and raised in Charleston, South Carolina, Bennett was a tradesman and banker before winning a seat in the state assembly in 1804, a position he would fill, with a few gaps, for nearly a decade before becoming governor.

As governor, Bennett took the unprecedented step of calling for an end to the interstate slave trade. He was unsuccessful. Later, during the trials of the Vesey conspirators, Bennett expressed alarm at both the swiftness of the proceedings and the number of defendants who were jailed without thorough investigations of their complicity. His perceived sympathy with the slave conspirators, his publicly stated doubts that the conspiracy was as widespread as prosecutors claimed, and the fact that several slaves from his own household were implicated were used by Charleston's mayor, James Hamilton, as leverage for his own political rise. Hamilton publicly disagreed with Bennett by arguing that the prosecution of conspirators had rescued Charleston from a bloodbath. Within a year, the publicity that Hamilton generated for himself earned him a seat in the South Carolina Assembly, where he served until becoming governor in 1830.

After stepping down as governor, Bennett lived as a private citizen in Charleston except for another short stint in the state assembly, 1837 to 1839. Unlike his rival Hamilton, Bennett lived to see the Civil War, dying three months before Confederate General Robert E. Lee's surrender effectively ended the conflict.

WILLIAM BULL (1683–1755)

Lieutenant governor and acting governor of the colony of South Carolina during the 1739 Stono uprising, William Bull was the son of one of the earliest settlers of Charles Town (Charleston). Beginning when he was 23, he was elected to South Carolina House of Assembly on three separate occasions and served on the province's Executive Council from 1721 to 1737. Elected acting governor in 1737 and appointed lieutenant governor the following year, nearly all of Bull's adult life was spent in public service.

Less than a year after he became lieutenant governor, the Stono rebellion broke out. By a bizarre coincidence, Bull nearly ran into the army of drumming and chanting rebels. He and four companions were returning to Charles Town from a session of the district court when they encountered the insurgents. Since the white men were on horses, they were able to outrun the slaves. One of Bull's companions, a Mr. Golightly, rode fast and furiously to a nearby town and alerted militiamen who were at worship in a Presbyterian church. Because South Carolina law required militia members to carry weapons with them at all times, even in church, a posse was quickly formed and it attacked the rebels later on in the day.

Bull's official report of the Stono rebellion was terse, perhaps partly because he was embarrassed by his own flight at the sight of the rebels and partly because he, like all slaveholders, wanted to downplay slave revolts. He did, however, make clear that he believed the rebellion was instigated by agents from Spanish Florida. Fear of covert Spanish encouragement of slave revolts would be a continuous theme for the next few years in other slave revolts or conspiracies to revolt.

Bull's term as acting governor ended in late 1743, with the arrival of a Crown-appointed governor. But he continued to serve as lieutenant governor until his death in 1755.

WILLIAM CLAIBORNE (c. 1772–1817)

Governor of the Territory of Orleans (Louisiana) during the 1811 German Coast uprising, William Claiborne was a career politician. Although born in Virginia, he traveled extensively throughout the South. While still in his twenties, he was appointed to Tennessee's Supreme Court. After serving one year, he resigned to run, successfully, for the U.S. Congress. At the end of his term he was appointed governor of the Mississippi territory, remaining there until 1803, when he was appointed governor of the recently acquired Louisiana territory.

Claiborne's arrival in New Orleans stirred up unrest among the aristocratic French-speaking planters along the German Coast. Claiborne knew no French and rarely consulted the planters on public policy, which led to strained relations. Moreover, he mustered a militia of freedmen, a move that proved to be unpopular with white Louisianans. Eventually a delegation of planters went to Washington to protest his appointment.

During the German Coast uprising, Claiborne acted with cool swiftness to protect New Orleans. He posted guards on the roads leading into the city, imposed a curfew, and recalled federal troops from Florida.

A year after the rebellion, when Louisiana was admitted to the union, Claiborne served as the state's first governor. When his term expired in 1816, he won a seat in the U.S. Senate, but served less than a year before his untimely death.

SIR FRANCIS COCKBURN (1780–1868)

Governor of the British Bahamas from 1837 to 1841, Francis Cockburn resisted diplomatic pressure from the United States to return the mutinous slaves aboard the *Creole*. The ship was seized by Virginia slaves, led by Madison Washington, who were being transported to New Orleans markets. The slaves knew that Britain had outlawed slavery 10 years earlier and that American slaves who could make it to British-controlled land, either in Canada or in the Caribbean, would be welcomed as free men and women. So the slaves aboard the *Creole* forced the white crew to sail them to the Bahamas.

As soon as the *Creole* docked in Nassau, John Bacon, the American consul in the Bahamas, insisted that the slaves were private property and ought to be treated as such. Cockburn refused to acknowledge Bacon's argument, although he did agree to jail a few of the mutineers accused of killing one of the white passengers. He played for time by insisting that he required instructions from London, but the outcome was foregone.

The slaves were given their freedom, and the jailed slaves were released, under the presumption that their slaying of the white passenger had been justified self-defense. Bacon was furious, but had no choice but to bow to Cockburn's decision. In all likelihood, the *Creole* slaves, including Madison, settled in the Bahamas.

The *Creole* crisis occurred during Cockburn's final year as governor of the Bahamas. A soldier by training and inclination, he served in the War of 1812 and as a colonial administrator in Canada. By the time of his death, he had attained the rank of general.

WILLIAM LLOYD GARRISON (1805–1879)

Abolitionist and editor for 35 years of *The Liberator*, the leading antislavery newspaper in the United States, Garrison championed immediate and uncompensated freedom for slaves. Although a pacifist who favored "moral suasion" rather than violence as a strategy to end slavery, his editorial on the heels of Nat Turner's 1831 revolt suggested that white blood would continue to be "required" at the hands of rebellious slaves. Moreover, he argued that the entire nation was guilty of the sin of slavery, the South for trading in human lives and the North for tolerating it. As a consequence, he was considered a vicious outside agitator by slaveholders in the South and a fanatic by many people in the North.

Garrison launched *The Liberator* with the promise to readers that he would neither equivocate nor retreat in his campaign against slavery, and he remained true to his word. One year after the newspaper began publication, he founded the New England Anti-Slavery Society and a year later co-founded the American Anti-Slavery Society. His opposition to slavery continued until 1865, when he published the final issue, number 1,820, of his newspaper. After the war, he devoted himself to the struggle for civil rights for blacks and women.

THOMAS RUFFIN GRAY (1800–?)

The most extensive contemporaneous profile of a slave rebellion leader was written by Thomas Gray, a Virginia planter-turned-lawyer. When published, *The Confessions of Nat Turner* sold thousands of copies.

Born in Southampton County in the same year as Nat Turner, Gray was in dire financial straits by the time he was in his late twenties, most likely because of gambling debts. In 1829, he owned nearly 1,000 acres in land and 21 slaves. Just two years later he would sold most of his land and all but one slave to pay off debts. Moreover, his father had cut him out of his will. So Gray turned to the law as a way of supporting himself.

After Turner's rebellion ended, Gray was appointed by the county to defend five of the captured slaves. When Turner himself was finally captured on October 30, nine weeks after the revolt, Gray asked permission to interview the rebel leader in his jail cell. Over three days, Gray asked Turner questions and jotted down his replies, publishing the whole as a 24-page pamphlet shortly after Turner's execution.

The accuracy of Gray's account has been debated, but the consensus is that it manages to capture Turner's voice more often than not. It is clear from the pamphlet's prefatory "To the Public" that Gray, like most whites, was horrified by the brutality of the rebellion, and he did not hesitate to refer to Turner and his followers as "remorseless murderers" whose "flinty bosoms" were immune to cries for mercy. But the body of the *Confessions*, despite some nineteenth-century rhetorical flourishes, remains more or less true to what Turner told Gray. In fact, Turner approved the document when Gray read it back to him.

Sales of the document reached upward of 50,000, including a second printing in 1832. Ironically, some Southern communities refused to allow its sale, under the fear that it would incite further unrest among slaves. Gray undoubtedly received some financial benefit from the pamphlet. But whether it was enough to repair his bad fortune is unknown.

JAMES HAMILTON (1786–1857)

The mayor or "intendant" of Charleston, South Carolina, during the 1822 Denmark Vesey conspiracy, James Hamilton rode his denunciations of the defendants to a seat in Congress and then the governorship of his state. His public skirmish with Thomas Bennett, the state governor during the conspiracy, showed Hamilton to be a stalwart defender of slavery.

Born in Charleston but educated in New England schools, Hamilton studied law and married well; his wife brought him over 200 slaves. He entered politics in 1818, successfully running for a seat in the state assembly, where he remained until elected mayor of Charleston.

Claiming that the city was in crisis when news of Denmark's conspiracy broke, Hamilton insisted that the trials be conducted swiftly and secretly.

To ensure a steady stream of defendants, he gave the city militia free rein to round up suspects on the flimsiest of evidence.

Hamilton was publicly criticized for his disregard of due process as well as inciting public panic by both Governor Bennett and a U.S. Supreme Court justice. But Hamilton insisted that any measures he took were in the interests of public safety, and his response won the day.

Hamilton's loyalty to South Carolina and the institution of slavery became even more pronounced after his term as mayor. He was governor during the 1832 Nullification Crisis, in which South Carolina legislators tried unsuccessfully to insist that they had the constitutional right to ignore or "nullify" any federal law that they deemed contrary to the interests of the state. Hamilton was a champion of nullification, and when his term as governor ended in the midst of the debate, he had himself appointed a general in the state militia, thereby displaying a readiness to battle federal troops that President Andrew Jackson threatened to dispatch to South Carolina.

Toward the end of his life, Hamilton relocated to the newly acquired state of Texas. On a return journey there from Washington, D.C., he perished when the steamboat on which he was traveling caught fire and sank.

DANIEL HORSMANDEN (1691–1778)

Chief justice in the colony of New York, member of the governor's Executive Council, and recorder for the city of New York, Daniel Horsmanden also served as one of the judges in the 1741 trials of the alleged slave conspirators. He afterward published *A Journal of the Proceedings in the Detection of the Conspiracy*, a running summary, with occasional verbatim quotations from testimony, of the proceedings.

Born in England, Horsmanden immigrated to the British colonies as a young man and became involved in New York politics. Although he fell out of political favor for a few years in the late 1740s, he was eventually reinstated and exerted considerable influence in New York until the outbreak of the Revolutionary War. He also served as a founding trustee of King's College, later renamed Columbia.

More than any other person, Horsmanden is responsible for pushing the thesis that a slave conspiracy to revolt lay behind a couple of petty thefts committed by blacks in New York during the winter of 1841. His *Journal* was published, he said, in order to convince skeptics that there had indeed been a conspiracy and that the executions he ordered were justified. Historians are still divided as to whether, and to what extent, there was a conspiracy.

Shortly after the publication of his *Journal*, Horsmanden fell on bad times. His book did not bring him the income he had anticipated; four years after its appearance, it was remaindered at a cut-rate price. Moreover, his reputation was harmed by critics of the 1741 trials as well as by factional political disputes. So Horsmanden turned his hand to political journalism and continued writing a steady stream of essays on New York politics that brought him an income as well as a good deal of public notice. By the time of his death, he had managed to rehabilitate his good name and reestablish his fortune.

JAMES MONROE (1758–1832)

The fifth president of the United States and the 12th and 16th governor of the state of Virginia, Monroe was the leader of Virginia when Gabriel Prosser conspired to conquer Richmond in 1800. Although Prosser, after his arrest, asked to speak to Monroe, as one "general" to another, Monroe refused.

Born in Virginia, Monroe dropped out of William and Mary College at the age of 17 to join the Continental Army. Wounded in the Battle of Trenton on Christmas Day, 1776, he returned to Virginia to recuperate and, later, to serve in the Virginia militia.

After the war, he studied law under Thomas Jefferson, who became his lifelong mentor. Elected to the Virginia House of Delegates in 1782, he won a seat in the U.S. Congress the following year and served one term before moving to the Senate in 1790. Four years later, President George Washington appointed him minister to France. He returned to the United States in 1796 after managing to arrange the release of American prisoners, including Thomas Paine, held in French prisoners. Four years later he became governor of his home state for the first time.

Monroe's initial reaction when he received word of Gabriel Prosser's conspiracy was that it was a local plot and could be easily handled by Richmond authorities. But as it became clear that the conspiracy had spread to counties other than Henrico, where Richmond was located,

Monroe mustered the state militia. He insisted that the slaves who were rounded up be treated humanely and in accordance with the law, even ordering extra blankets and candles to be given them in their jail cells. But he was disinclined to show mercy to any of them and predicted to his friend Thomas Jefferson that most of the slaves accused of conspiracy would be condemned.

After nearly 30 slaves were hanged, Monroe began to be uneasy about the ongoing trials, motivated perhaps by pity but certainly by economics: both the cost of keeping the militia active and the compensations paid to slave owners ran up an enormous bill. Moreover, Monroe was influenced by Jefferson's warning that if the hangings continue much longer, the world would morally censure Virginia.

Monroe enjoyed a successful career after his first term as Virginia's governor, going on to serve as minister to Great Britain, another stint as governor, secretary of state and war, and finally president. He also accumulated vast wealth as a plantation owner who owned numerous slaves. But to the end of his days, he disliked speaking about the 1800 Prosser conspiracy and generally replied tersely when questioned about it.

SOLOMON NORTHUP (1808–c. 1863)

In his memoir *Twelve Years a Slave*, published in 1853, Solomon Northup mentions the 1837 Cheneyville conspiracy and its turncoat leader, Lew Cheney.

Born a free man, Northup, a musician, was lured to Washington, D.C., with the promise of employment. Once there, he was accused of being a runaway slave, seized, and sold into bondage, eventually winding up in Louisiana's Red River region, not far from Cheneyville. After more than a decade as a field hand, he was finally able to secure his freedom, thanks to the intervention of New York governor Lawrence Hunt.

Lew Cheney (his surname indicates the master whom he served) conspired to lead slaves to the Texas Republic, under the mistaken assumption that doing so would liberate them. (The Republic allowed slavery.) But when the plot was discovered, Lew turned his conspirators in and denied any participation in it. Even worse, he blew the plot up into a lurid tale of planned murder and arson. On his testimony, several slaves were executed and even more murdered, while Lew was rewarded with his freedom and a monetary reward. Northup most certainly spoke for the slaves in the region when he described Lew as "a shrewd, cunning negro, more intelligent than the generality of his race, but unscrupulous and full of treachery."

After his release from slavery, Northup toured in the North for a few years as an abolitionist speaker before dropping out of public sight.

Primary Documents

Stono Revolt (1739)

The official report of the Stono rebellion, dated July 1, 1741, interprets it as an act of domestic violence instigated by foreign aggression. Toward the end of the report, in unintended irony, lament is made that the institution of slavery, which should be the means of the good life, has been used as a weapon against slaveholders.

In September 1739, our Slaves made an Insurrection at Stono in the Heart of our Settlements not twenty miles from Charles Town, in which they massacred twenty-three Whites after the most cruel and barbarous Manner to be conceived and having got Arms and Ammunition out of Store they bent their Course to the Southward burning all the Houses on the Road. But they marched so slow, in full Confident of their own Strength from the first Success, that they gave Time to a Party of our Militia to come up with them. The Number was in a Manner equal on both Sides and an Engagement ensued such as may be supposed in such a Case wherein one fought for Liberty and Life, the other for their Country and every Thing that was dear to them. But by the Blessing of God the Negroes were defeated, the greatest Part being killed on the Spot or taken, and those that then escaped were so closely pursued and hunted Day after Day that in the End all but two of them were taken and executed. That the Negroes would not have made this Insurrection had they not depended on St. Augustine for a Place of Reception afterwards was very certain; and that the Spaniards had a Hand in prompting them to this particular Action there was but little Room to doubt, for in July preceding Don

Piedro, Captain of the Horse at St. Augustine, came to Charles Town in a Launch with twenty or thirty men (one of which was a Negro that spoke English very well) under Pretence [sic] of delivering a Letter to General Oglethorpe although he could not possibly be ignorant that the General resided in Frederica not Half the Distance from St. Augustine and in his Return he was seen at Times to put into every one of our Inlets on the Coast. And in the very Month in which the above Insurrection was made the General acquainted our Lieutenant Governour [sic] by Letter that the Magistrates of Georgia had seized a Spaniard whom he took to be a Priest, and that they thought from what they had discovered that he was employed by the Spaniards to procure a general Insurrection of the Negroes.

On this Occasion every Breast was filled with Concern. Evil brought Home to us within or very Doors awakened the Attention of the most Unthinking. Every one that had any Relation, any tie of Nature; every one that had a Life to lose were in the most sensible Manner shocked at such Danger daily hanging over their Heads. With Regret we bewailed our peculiar Case, that we could not enjoy the Benefits of Peace like the rest of Mankind and that our own Industry should be the Means of taking from us all the Sweets of Life and of rendering us liable to the Loss of our Lives and Fortunes. With Indignation we looked at St. Augustine that Den of Thieves and Ruffians! Receptacle of Debtors, Servants and Slaves! Bane of Industry and Society! And revolved in our Minds all the Injuries this Province had received from thence ever since its first Settlement, that they had from first to last, in Times of profoundest Peace, both publickly [sic] and privately, by themselves and Indians and Negroes, in every Shape molested us not without some instances of uncommon Cruelty.

Source: J. H. Easterby et al. (eds). *Journal of the Commons House of Assembly*, July 1, 1741. (Columbia: Historical Commission of South Carolina, 1953), 83–84.

> *In the wake of the Stono revolt, South Carolina legislators enacted a slave code that remained law, with a few amendments over time, until slavery was abolished in 1865. It also served as a model for slave laws in other colonies and antebellum states. The incredible detail with which the act regulates every aspect of a slave's life, including even his or her clothes, reflects just how shaken South Carolina whites were by what the act calls the "barbarous murders at Stono."*

WHEREAS, IN HIS MAJESTY'S PLANTATIONS IN AMERICA, SLAVERY HAS BEEN INTRODUCED AND ALLOWED, AND THE PEOPLE COMMONLY CALLED NEGROES, INDIANS, MULAT-TOES AND MUSTIZOES, HAVE BEEN DEEMED ABSOLUTE SLAVES, AND THE SUBJECTS OF PROPERTY IN THE HANDS OF THE PARTICULAR PERSONS, THE EXTEND OF WHOSE POWER OVER SUCH SLAVES OUGHT TO BE SETTLED AND LIMITED BY POSITIVE LAWS, SO THAT THE SLAVE MAY BE KEPT IN DUE SUBJECTION AND OBEDIENCE, AND THE OWN-ERS AND OTHER PERSONS HAVING THE CARE AND GOVERNMENT OF SLAVES MAY BE RESTRAINED FROM EXER-CISING TOO GREAT RIGOUR AND CRUELTY OVER THEM, AND THAT THE PUBLIC PEACE AND ORDER OF THIS PROV-INCE MAY BE PRESERVED:

WE PRAY YOUR MOST SACRED MAJESTY THAT IT MAY BE ENACTED:

... **3.** And for the better keeping slaves in due order and subjection, be it further enacted by the authority aforesaid, that no person whatsoever shall permit or suffer any slave under his or their care or management, and who lives or is employed in Charlestown, or any other town in this Province, to go out of the limits of the said town, or any such slave who lives in the country, to go out of the plantation to which such slave belongs, or in which plantation such slave is usually employed, without a letter super-scribed and directed, or a ticket in the words following:

Permit this slave to be absent from Charlestown, (or any other town, or if he lives in the country, from Mr. X plantation, X parish,) for X days or hours; dated the X day of X.

Or, to that purpose or effect; which ticket shall be signed by the master or other person having the care or charge of such slave, or by some other by his or their order, directions and consent; and every slave who shall be found out of Charlestown, or any other town (if such slave lives or is usually employed there,) or out of the plantation to which such slave belongs, or in which slave is usually employed, or if such slave lives in the country, without such letter or ticket as aforesaid, or without a white person in his company, shall be punished with whipping on the bare back, not exceeding twenty lashes.

4. And be it further enacted by the authority aforesaid, that if any person shall presume to give a ticket or license to any slave who is the property or under the care of charge of another, without the consent or against the will of the owner or other person having charge of such slave, shall forfeit to the owner the sum of twenty pounds, current money.

5. And it shall be further enacted by the authority aforesaid, that if any slave who shall be out of the house or plantation where such slave shall live, or shall be usually employed, or without some whiter person in company with such slave, shall refuse to submit or undergo the examination of any white person, it shall be lawful for any such white person to pursue, apprehend, and moderately correct such slave; and if any such slave shall assault and strike such white person, such slave may be lawfully killed.

6. Provided always, and be it further enacted by the authority aforesaid, that if any Negro or other slave, who shall be employed in the lawful business or service of his master, owner, overseer, or other person having charge of such slave, shall be beaten, bruised, maimed or disabled by any person or persons not having sufficient cause or lawful authority for so doing, (of which cause the justices of the peace, respectively, may judge,) every person and persons so offending, shall, for every such offence, forfeit and pay the sum of forty shillings, current money, over and besides the damages hereinafter mentioned, to the use of the poor of that parish in which such offence shall be committed;

And if such slave or slaves shall be maimed or disabled by such beating, from performing his or her work, such person and persons so offending, shall also forfeit and pay to the owner or owners of such slaves, the sum of fifteen shillings, current money, per diem, for every day of his lost time, and also the charge of the cure of such slave; and if the said damages, in whole, shall not exceed the sum of twenty pounds, current money, the same shall, upon lawful proof thereof made, be recoverable before any one of his Majesty's justices of the peace, in the save way and manner as debts are recoverable by the Act for the trial of small and mean causes; and such justices before whom the same shall be recovered, shall have power to commit the offender or offenders to goal, if he, she or they shall produce no goods of which the said penalty and damages may be levied, there to remain without bail, until such penalty and damages shall be paid; any law statute, usage or custom, to the contrary notwithstanding.

7.   And be it further enacted by the authority aforesaid, that it shall and may be lawful for every justice assigned to keep the peace in this Province, within his respective county and jurisdiction, upon his own knowledge or view, or upon information received upon oath, either to go in person, or by warrant or warrants directed to any constable or other proper person, to command to their assistance any number of persons as they shall see convenient, to disperse any assembly or meeting of slaves which may disturb the peace or endanger the safety of his Majesty's subjects, and to search all suspected places for arms, ammunition or stolen goods, and to apprehend and secure all such slaves as they shall suspect to be guilty of any crimes or offences whatsoever, and to bring them to speedy trial, according to the directions of this Act; and in case any constable or other person shall refuse to obey or execute any of the warrants of precepts of such justices, or any of them, within their several limits and precincts, or shall refuse to assist the said justices or constables, of any of them, when commanded or required, such person or persons shall forfeit and pay the sum of five pounds, current money, to be recovered by a warrant under the hand and seal of any other justice of the peace, in the same way and manner as is directed by the Act of the trial of small and mean causes.

8.   And be it further enacted by the authority aforesaid, that if any person shall me maimed, wounded or disabled, in pursuing, apprehending, or taking any slave that is runaway or charged with any criminal offence, or in doing any other act, matter or thing, in obedience to or in pursuance of the direction of this Act, he shall receive such reward from the public, as the General Assembly shall think fit; and if any such person shall be killed his heirs, executors or administrators, shall receive the like reward.

9.   And whereas, natural justice forbids that any person, of what condition soever, should be condemned unheard, and the order of civil government requires that for the due and equal administration of justice, some convenient method and form of trial should be established;

Be it therefore enacted by the authority aforesaid, that all crimes and offences which shall be committed by slaves in this Province, and for which capital punishment shall or lawfully may be inflicted, shall be heard, examined, tried, adjudged and finally determined by any two justices assigned to keep the peace, and any number of freeholders not less than three or more than five, in the county where the offences shall be committed, and who lives in the parts adjacent, and can be most conveniently assembled; either of which justices, on complaint made or information received of any such offence committed by a slave, shall commit the offender to the safe custody of the constable of the parish where such offence shall be committed, and shall without delay, by warrant under his hand and seal, call to his assistance and request any one of the nearest justices of the peace to associate with him, and shall, by the same warrant, summon such a number of the neighboring freeholders as aforesaid, to assemble and meet together with the said justices, at a certain day and place, not exceeding three days after the apprehending of such slave or slaves; and the justices and the freeholders being so assembled, shall cause the slave accused or charged, to be brought before them, and shall hear the accusation which shall be brought against, such slave, and his or her defense, and shall proceed to the examination of witnesses and other evidences, and finally to hear and determine the matter brought before them, in the most summary and expeditious manner; and in case the offender shall be convicted of any crime for which by laws the offender ought to suffer death, the said justices shall give judgment, and award and cause execution of their sentence to be done, by inflicting such manner of death, and at such time, as the said justices, by and with the consent of the freeholders, shall direct and which they shall judge will be most effectual to deter others from offending in the like manner.

10.   And be it further enacted by the authority aforesaid, that if any crime or offence not capital, shall be committed by any slave, such slave shall be proceeded against and tried for such offence in the manner herein before directed, by any on justice of the peace and any two freeholders of the county where the offence shall be committed, and can be most conveniently assembled; and the said justice and freeholders shall be assembled, summoned an called together, and shall proceed upon the trial of any slave who shall commit any offence not capital, in the like manner as it shall be convicted before them of any offence not capital, the said on justice, by and with the consent of the said freeholders, shall give judgment for the inflicting any corporal punishment; not extending to the taking away life or member, as he and they in their discretion shall think fit, and shall award and cause execution to be done accordingly.

Provided always that if the said one justice and two freeholders upon examination of any slave charged or accused before them for an offence not capital, shall find the same to be a greater offence, and may deserve death, they shall, with all convenient speed, summons and request the assistance of another justice and one or more freeholders, not exceeding three, which said justice and freeholders newly assembled, shall join with the justice and freeholders first assemble, and shall proceed in the trial, and upon final judgment and execution, if the case shall so require, in manner as is hereinbefore directed for the trial of capital offences.

11. And be it further enacted by the authority aforesaid, that two justices and one freeholder, or one justice and two freeholders, of the said two justices and three freeholders, shall make a quorum, and the conviction or acquittal of any slave or slaves by such a quorum of them shall be final in all capital cases; but on the trial of slaves for offences not capital, it shall and may be sufficient if before sentence or judgment shall be given for inflicting a corporal punishment, not extending to life or member, that one justice and any one of the freeholders shall agree that the slave accused is guilty of the offence with which he shall be charged.

12. And be it further enacted by the authority aforesaid, that so soon as the justice or justices and freeholders shall be assembled as aforesaid, in pursuance of the direction of this Act, the said justices shall administer to each other the following oath.

"I, A B, do solemnly swear, in the presence of Almighty God, that I will truly and impartially try and adjudge the prisoner or prisoners who shall be brought before me, upon is or their trial, and honestly and duly, on my party, put in execution, on this trial, an Act entitled An Act for the better ordering and governing Negroes and other slaves in this Province, according to the best of my skill and knowledge. So help me God."

And the said justice or justices, having taken the aforesaid oath, shall immediately administer the said oath to every freeholder who shall be assembled as aforesaid, and shall forthwith proceed upon the trial of such slave or slaves as shall be brought before them.

13. And for the preventing the concealment of crimes and offences committed by slaves, and for the more effectual discovery and bringing slaves to condign punishment, Be it further enacted by the authority aforesaid, that not only the evidence of all free Indians, without oath, but the evidence of any slave, without oath, shall be allowed and admitted in all causes whatsoever, for or against another slave accused of any crime of offence whatsoever; the weight of which evidence being seriously considered, and compared with all other circumstances attending the case, shall be left to the conscience of the justices and freeholders.

14. And whereas, slaves may be harbored and encouraged to commit offences, and concealed and received by free Negroes, and such free Negroes may escape the punishment due to their crimes, for want of sufficient and legal evidence against them;

Be it therefore further enacted by the authority aforesaid, that the evidence of any free Indian or slave, without oath, shall in like manner be allowed and admitted in all cases against any free Negroes, Indians (free Indians in amity with this government, only excepted,) mulattoe or mustizoe; and of all crimes and offences committed by free Negroes, Indians, (except as before excepted), mulattoes or mustizoes, shall be proceeded in, heard, tried, adjudged and determined by the justices and freeholders appointed by this Act for the trial of slave, in like manner, order and form, as is hereby directed an appointed for the proceedings and trial of crimes and offences committed by slaves; any law statue, usage or custom to the contrary notwithstanding.

15. And be it further enacted and declared by the authority aforesaid, that if any slave in this Province shall commit any crime or offence whatsoever, which, by the laws of England or of this Province now in force, is of has been made felony without the benefit of the clergy, and for which the offender by law ought to suffer death, every such slave, being duly convicted according to the directions of this Act shall suffer death; to be inflicted in such manner as the justices, by and with the advice and consent of the freeholders, who shall give judgment to the conviction of such slave, shall direct and appoint.

16. And whereas, some crimes and offences of an enormous nature and of the most pernicious consequence, may be committed by slaves, as well as other persons, which being peculiar to the condition and situation of this Province, could not fall within the provision of the laws of England;

Be it therefore enacted by the authority aforesaid, That the several crimes and offences hereinafter particularly enumerated, are hereby declared to be felony, without the benefit of the clergy, that is to say: - if any slave, free Negro, mulattoe, Indian or mustizoe, shall willfully and maliciously set fire to, burn or destroy any sack of rice, corn or other grain, of the product, growth or manufacture of this Province, or shall willfully and maliciously set fire to, burn or destroy any tar kiln, barrels of pitch, tar turpentine or rosin, or any other the goods or commodities of the growth, produce or manufacture of this Province, or shall feloniously steal, take or carry away any slave, being the property of another, with intent to carry such slave out of this Province, or shall willfully or maliciously poison or administer any poison to any person, free man, woman, servant or slave, every such slave, free Negro, mulattoe, Indian, (except as before excepted,) and mustizoe, shall suffer death as a felon.

17. And be it further enacted by the authority aforesaid, that any slave who shall be guilty of homicide of any sort, upon any whiter person, except by misadventure, or in defense of his master or other person under whose care and government such slave shall be, shall, upon conviction thereof as aforesaid, suffer death; and every slave who shall raise or attempt to raise an insurrection in this Province, shall endeavor to delude or entice any slave to run away and leave this Province, every such slave and slaves, and his and their accomplices, aiders and abettors, shall, upon conviction as aforesaid, suffer death;

Provided always, that it shall and may be lawful to and for the justices who shall pronounce sentence against such slaves, by and with the advice and consent of the freeholders as aforesaid, if several slaves shall receive sentence at one time, to mitigate and alter the sentence of any slave other than such as shall be convicted of the homicide of a whiter person, who they shall think may deserve mercy, and may inflict such corporal punishment, (other than death,) on any such slave, as they in their discretion shall think fit; anything herein contained to the contrary thereof in any wise notwithstanding;

Provided always, that one or more of the said slaves who shall be convicted of the crimes or offences aforesaid, where several are concerned, shall be executed for example, to deter others from offending in the like kind.

18. And to the end that owners of slaves may not be tempted to conceal the crimes of their slaves to the prejudice of this public, Be it further enacted by the authority aforesaid, that in case any slave shall be put to death in pursuance of the sentence of the justices and freeholders aforesaid, (except slaves guilty of murder, and slaves taken in actual rebellion,) the said justices, or one of them, with the advice and consent of any two of the freeholders, shall, before they award and order their sentence to be executed, apprise and value the said Negroes so to be put to death, at any sum not exceeding two hundred pounds current money, and shall certify such appraisement to the public treasurer of this Province, who is hereby authorized and required to pay the same one moiety thereof, at least, to the owner of such slave or to his order, and the other moiety, or such part thereof as such justices and freeholders shall direct, to the person injured by such offence for which such slave shall suffer death.

19. And be it further enacted by the authority aforesaid, that the said justices, or any of them, are hereby authorized, empowered, and required, to summons and compel all persons whatsoever, to appear and to give evidence upon the trial of any slave; and if any person shall neglect or refuse to appear, or appearing, shall refuse to give evidence, or if any master or other person who has the care and government of any slave, shall prevent or hinder any slave under his charge or government, from appearing or giving evidence in any matter depending before the justices and freeholders aforesaid, the said justices may, and they are hereby fully empowered and required to, bind every such person offending as aforesaid, by recognizance with one or more sufficient sureties, to appear at the next general sessions, to answer such their offences and contempt; and for default of finding sureties, to commit such offender to prison.

20. And be it further enacted by the authority aforesaid, that in case the master or other person having charge or government of any slave who shall be accused of any capital crime, shall conceal or convey away any such slave, so that he cannot be brought to trial and condign punishment, every master or other person so offending, shall forfeit the sum of two hundred and fifty pounds current money, if such slave be accused of a capital crime as aforesaid; but if such slave shall be accused of a crime not capital, then such master or other person shall only forfeit the sum of fifty pounds current money.

21. And be it further enacted by the authority aforesaid, that all and every the constable and constables in the several parishes within this Province where any slave shall be sentenced to suffer death or other punishment, shall cause execution to be done of all the orders, warrants, precepts and judgments of the justices hereby appointed to try such slaves; for the charge and trouble of which the said constable or constables, respectively, shall be paid and the public treasurer of this Province, upon a certificate produced under the hands of the said justice or justices before whom such Negroes or slaves shall be tried; unless in such cases shall appear to the said justices and freeholders to the malicious or groundless prosecutions, in which cases the said charges shall be paid by the prosecutors; for whipping or other corporal punishments not extending to life, the sum of twenty shillings; and for any punishment extending to life, the sum of five pounds current money; and such other charges for keeping and maintaining such slaves, as are allowed to the warden of the work house in Charlestown, for keeping and maintaining such slaves, committed to his custody; for the levying of which charges against the prosecutor, the justice or justices are hereby empowered to issue their warrant.

And that no delay may happen in causing execution to be done upon such offending slave or slaves, the constable who shall be directed to cause execution to be done, shall be, and is hereby, empowered to press one or more slave or slaves, in or near the place where such whipping or corporal punishment shall be inflicted, to whip or inflict such other corporal punishment upon the offender or offenders; and such slave or slave so pressed, shall be obedient to and observe the orders and direction of the constable in and about the premises, upon pain of being punished by the said constable, by whipping on the bare back, not exceeding twenty lashes, which punishment the said constable is hereby authorized and empowered to inflict; and the constable shall, if he presses a Negro, pay the said Negro five shillings out of his fee for doing the said execution.

22. And be it further enacted by the authority aforesaid, that if any person in this Province shall, on the Lord's day, commonly called Sunday, employ any slave in any work or labour, (works of absolute necessity and the necessary occasions of the family one excepted,) every person in such case offending, shall forfeit the sum of five pounds, current money, for every slave they shall so work or labour.

23. And be it further enacted by the authority aforesaid, that it shall not be lawful for any slave, unless in the presence of some white person, to carry or make use of fire arms, or any offensive weapons whatsoever, unless such Negro or slave shall have a ticket or license, in writing, from his master, mistress or overseer, to hunt and kill game, cattle, or mischievous birds, or beasts of prey, and that such license be renewed once every month, or unless there be some white person of the age of sixteen years or upwards, in the company of such slave, when he is hunting or shooting or that such slave be actually carrying his master's arms to or from his master's plantation, by a special ticket for that purpose, or unless such slave be found in the day time actually keeping off rice birds, or other birds, within the plantation to which such slave belongs, lodging the same gun at night within the dwelling house of his master, mistress or white overseer; and provided also, that no Negro or other slave shall have liberty to carry any gun, cutlass, pistol or other weapon, abroad from home, at any time between Saturday evening after sun-set, and Monday morning before sun-rise, notwithstanding a license or ticket for so doing.

And in case any person shall find any slave using or carrying fire arms, or other offensive weapons, contrary to the true intention of this Act, every such person may lawfully seize and take away such fire arms or offensive weapons.

But before the property of such goods shall be vested in the person who shall seize the same, such person shall, within forty-eight hours next after such seizure, go before the next justice of the peace, and shall make oath of the manner of the taking; and if such justice of the peace, after such oath shall be made, or if, upon any other examination, he shall be satisfied that the said fire arms or other offensive weapons shall have been seized according to the direction and agreeable to the true intent and meaning of this Act, the said justice shall, by certificate under his hand and seal, declare them forfeited, and that the property is lawfully vested in the person who seized the same.

Provided always, that no such certificate shall be granted by any justice of the peace, until the owner or owners of such fire arms of other offensive weapons so to be seized as aforesaid, or the overseer or overseers who shall or may have the charge of such slave or slaves from whom such fire arms or other offensive weapons shall be taken or seized, shall be duly summoned, to show cause, if any such they have, why the same should not be condemned as forfeited, or until forty-eight hours after the service of such summons, and oath made of the service of such summons before the said justice.

24.   And be it further enacted by the authority aforesaid, that if any slave shall presume to strike any white person, such slave, upon trial and conviction before the justice or justices and freeholders, aforesaid, according to the directions of this Act, shall, for the first and second offence, suffer such punishment as the said justice and freeholders, or such of them as are empowered to try such offence, shall in their discretion, think fit, not extending to life or limb; and for the third offence, shall suffer death.

But in case any such slave shall grievously wound, maim or bruise any white person, though it by only the first offence, such slave shall suffer death.

Provided always, that such striking, wounding, maiming or bruising, not be done by the command, and in the defense of, the person or property of the owner or other person having the care and government of such slave, in which case the slave shall be wholly excused, and the owner or other person having the care and government of such slave shall be answerable, as far as by law he ought.

25.   And be it further enacted by the authority aforesaid, that it shall and may be lawful for every person in this Province, to take, apprehend and secure any runaway or fugitive slave, and they are hereby directed and required to send such slave to the master or other person having the care or government of such slave, if the person taking up or securing such slave knows, or can, without difficulty, be informed, to whom such slave shall belong;

But if not known or discovered, then such slave shall be sent, carried or delivered into the custody of the warden of the work-house in Charlestown; and the master or other person who has the care or government of such slave, shall pay for the taking up of such slave, whether by a free person or slave, the sum of twenty shillings, current money; and the warden of the work-house, upon receipt of every fugitive or runaway slave, is here by directed and required to keep such slave in safe custody until such slave shall be lawfully discharged, and shall, as soon as conveniently it may be, publish, in the weekly gazette, such slave, with the best descriptions he shall be able to give, first carefully viewing and examining such slave, naked to the waist, for any mark or brand, which he shall also publish to the intent the owner or other person who shall have the care and charge of such slave, may come to the knowledge that such slave is in custody.

And if such slave shall make escape through the negligence of the warden of the work-house, and cannot be taken within three months, the said warden of the work-house shall answer to the owner for the value of such slave, or the damage which the owner shall sustain by reason of such escape, as the cause shall happen.

26.   And be it further enacted by the authority aforesaid, that the said warden of the work-house shall, at the charge of the owner of such slave, provide sufficient food, drink, clothing and covering, for every slave delivered into his custody, and shall keep them to moderate labour, and advertise them in the gazette, in the manner aforesaid; and on failure thereof, shall forfeit all his fees due for such slave; and the said warden is hereby directed and required to cause every such slave delivered into his custody as a runaway, upon receipt of such slave, to be whipped on the bare back, not exceeding twenty lashes; and on failure thereof, shall forfeit all his fees due for such slave.

27.   And be it further enacted by the authority aforesaid, that any person who shall take up any runaway slave, and shall deliver such slave either to the master or other person having the care or charge of such slave, or to the warden of the work-house, shall be entitled to receive from the owner or warden of the work-house, upon the delivery, fifteen pence, current money, per mile, for every mils such slave shall have been brought of sent, to be computed from the place where such slave was apprehended.

And if such slave shall be delivered into the custody of the warden aforesaid, the person delivering such slave shall give an account of his name, place of abode, and the time and place when and where such slave was apprehended; which account the said warden shall enter down in a book to be kept for that purpose, and shall give a receipt for any such slave which shall be delivered, as aforesaid, into his custody.

And the said warden is hereby fully authorized and empowered to demand and receive from the owner or other persons having the charge or care of any such slave, for Negroes committed from the month of October to March, including, for finding necessaries, clothing and covering, to be the property of the master, any sum not exceeding six pounds, and the several sums following and no other sum, fee or reward, on any pretence whatsoever, (that is to say,) for apprehending each slave, paid to the person who delivered such slave in custody, twenty shillings, current money; for mileage, paid to the same person, fifteen pence, like money; for a sufficient quantity of provision for each day, for each slave, three shillings and nine pence, like money; for advertising and publishing every slave, as directed by this Act, five shillings, like money, for exclusive of the charge of printing; for receiving such slave, five shillings, and for delivering of him, five shillings, like money; for poundage on money advance, one shilling in the pound, like money.

And the said warden shall and may lawfully detain any slave in custody until the fees and expenses aforesaid be fully paid and satisfied; and in case the owner of such slave, or his overseer, manager, agent, attorney, or trustee, shall neglect or refuse to pay and satisfy the said fees and expenses, for the space of thirty days after the same shall be demanded by notice, in writing, served on the owner of such slave, or (if the owner is absent from this Province,) upon his overseer, agent, manager, attorney or trustee, the said warden shall and may expose any such slave to sale, at public outcry, and after deducting the fees and expenses aforesaid, and the charges of such sale, shall upon demand, return the over-plus money arising by such sale, to any person who has a right to demand and receive the same.

28.   And forasmuch as for want of knowing or finding the owner of any fugitive slave to be delivered to him, as aforesaid, the said warden may not be obliged to keep such slave in his custody, and find and provide provisions for such slave, over and beyond a reasonable time,

Be it therefore further enacted by the authority aforesaid, that if the owner or owners of such fugitive slave shall not, within the space of eighteen months from the time of commitment, make his, her or their claim or claims, or it shall not be otherwise made known to the said warden, within the time aforesaid, to whom such committed slave shall belong, it shall and may be lawful for the said warden to sell such slave at public outcry, in Charlestown, he the said warden first advertising such sale six weeks successively in the public gazette, together with the reason of the sale of such slave, and out of the money arising by such sale, to pay, deduct or retain to himself what shall be then due for money by him disbursed on receipt of such fugitive slave, and for his fees and provisions, together with the reasonable charges arising by such sale, and the overplus money, (if any there shall be,) shall be rendered and paid by the said warden to the public treasurer for the time being, in trust, nevertheless, for the use of the owner or owners of such slave, provided the same be claimed by him, her or them within one year and a day after such sale, or in default of such claim, within the time aforesaid, to the use of the public of this Province to be applied as the General Assembly shall direct.

29.   And be it further enacted by the authority aforesaid, that if any free Negro, mulatto or mustizo, or any slave, shall harbour, conceal or entertain any slave that shall run away or shall be charged or accused with any criminal matter, every free Negro, mulatto and mustizo, and every slave, who shall harbour, conceal or entertain any such slave, being duly convicted thereof, according to the directions of this Act, if a slave, shall suffer such

corporal punishment, not extending to life or limb, as the justice or justices who shall try such slave shall, in his or their discretion, think fit;

And if a free Negro, mulatto or mustizo, shall forfeit the sum of ten pounds, current money, for the first day, and twenty shillings for every day after, to the use of the owner of owners of such slave so to be harboured, concealed or entertained, as aforesaid, to be recovered by warrant, under the hand and seal of any one of his Majesty's justices of the peace, in and for the county where such slave shall be so harboured, concealed or entertained, in like manner as debts are directed to be recovered by the Act for trial of small and mean causes;

And that in case such forfeitures cannot be levied, or such free Negroes, mulattos or mustizoes shall not pay the same, together with the charges attending the prosecution, such free Negro, mulatto or mustizo shall be ordered by the said justice to be sold at public outcry, and the money arising by such sale shall, in the first place, be paid and applied for and towards the forfeiture due, made payable to the owner or owners, and the charges attending the prosecution and sale, and the overplus, (if any,) shall be paid by the said justice into the hands of the public treasurer, to be afterwards paid and applied in such manner as by the General Assembly of this Province shall be directed and appointed.

30.   And be it further enacted by the authority aforesaid, that no slave who shall dwell, reside, inhabit or be usually employed in Charlestown, shall presume to buy, sell, deal, traffic, barter, exchange or use commerce for any goods, wares, provisions, grain, victuals, or commodities, of any sort or kind whatsoever, (except as hereinafter particularly excepted and provided, and under such provisos, conditions, restrictions and limitations as are herein particularly directed, limited and appointed) on pain that all such goods, wares, provisions, grain, victuals or commodities, which by any slave shall be so bought, sold, dealt, trafficked or bartered for, exchanged or used in commerce, shall be sized and forfeited, and shall be sued for and recovered before any one justice assigned to keep the peace in Charlestown, and shall be applied and disposed of, one half to him or them who shall seize, inform and sue for the same, and the other half to the commissioners of the poor of the parish of St. Philips, Charlestown; and moreover, that the said justice shall order every slave who shall be convicted of such offence, to be publicly whipped on the bare back, not exceeding twenty lashes;

Provided always that it shall and may be lawful for any slave who lives or is usually employed in Charlestown, after such license and ticket as hereinafter is directed shall be obtained, to buy or sell fruit, fish and garden stuff, and to be employed as porters, carters or fishermen, and to purchase anything for the use of their masters, owners or other person who shall have the charge and government of such slave, in open market, under such regulations as are or shall be appointed by law concerning the market of Charlestown, or in any open shop kept by a white person.

31.   And be it further enacted by the authority aforesaid, that no slave or slaves whatsoever, belonging to Charlestown, shall be permitted to buy any thing to sell again, or to sell any thing upon their own account, in Charlestown; and it shall and may be lawful for any person or persons whosoever to seize and take away all and all manner of goods, wares or merchandize, that shall be found in the possession of any such slave or slaves in Charlestown, which they have bought to sell again, or which they shall offer to sale upon their own accounts, in Charlestown, one half of which shall be to the use of the poor of the said parish, and the other to the informer, and shall be adjudged and condemned by any justice of the peace in the said parish.

32.   And be it further enacted by the authority aforesaid, that if any keeper of a tavern or punch house, or retailer of strong liquors, shall give, sell utter or deliver to any slave, any beer, ale, cider, wine, run, brandy, or other spirituous liquors, or strong liquor whatsoever, without the license or consent of the owner, or such other person who shall have the care or government of such slave, ever person so offending shall forfeit the sum of five pounds, current money, for the first offence, and for the second offence, ten pounds; and shall be bound in recognizance in the sum of one hundred pounds, current money, with one or more sufficient sureties, before any of the justices of the court of general sessions, not to offend in the like kind, and to be of good behaviour, for one year; and for want of such sufficient sureties, to be committed to prison without bail or mainprize, for any term not exceeding three months.

33.   And whereas, several owners of slaves do suffer their slaves to go and work where they please, upon conditions of paying to their owners certain sums of money agreed upon between the owner and the slave; which practice has occasioned such slaves to pilfer and steal, to raise money for their owners, as well as to maintain themselves in drunkenness and evil courses; for prevention for which practices for the future,

Be it enacted by the authority aforesaid, that no owner, master or mistress of any slave, after the passing of this Act, shall permit or suffer any of his, her or their slaves to go and work out of their respective houses of families, without a ticket in writing, under pain of forfeiting the sum of ten pounds, current money, for every such offence, to be paid the one half to the church-wardens of the parish, for the use of the poor of the parish in which the offence is committed, and the other half to him or them that will inform and sue for the same, to be recovered in the same way as debts are by the Act for the trail of small and mean causes.

And every person employing any slave without a ticket from the owner of such slave, shall forfeit to the informer five pounds, current money, for each day he so employees such slave, over and above the wages agreed to be paid such slave for his work; provided that the said penalty of five pounds per diem, shall not extend to any person whose property in such slave is disputable; and provided, that nothing herein contained shall hinder any person or persons from hiring out by the year, week, or day, or any other time, any Negroes or slaves, to be under the care and direction of his or their owner, master or employer, and that the master is to receive the whole of the earnings of such slave or slaves, and that the employer have a certificate or note, in writing, of the time or terms of such slave's employment, from the owner, attorney or overseer of every such slave, severally and respectively.

And whereas, several owners of slaves have permitted them to *keep canoes, and to breed and raise horses, neat cattle and hogs, and to traffic and barter* in several parts of this Province, for the particular and peculiar benefit of such slaves, by which means they have not only and opportunity of receiving and concealing stolen goods, but to *plot and confederate together,* and form *conspiracies dangerous to the peace and safety of the whole Province;*

Be it therefore enacted by the authority aforesaid, That it shall not be lawful for any slave so to buy, sell, trade, traffic, deal, or barter for any goods or commodities, (except as before excepted,) nor shall any slave be permitted to keep any boat, perriauger or canoe, or to raise and breed, for the use and benefit of such slave, any horses, mares, neat cattle, sheep or hogs, under pain of forfeiting all the goods and commodities which shall be so bought, sold traded, trafficked, dealt or bartered for, by any slave, and of all the boats, perriaugers, or canoes, cattle, sheep or hogs, which any slave shall keep, raise or breed for the peculiar use, benefit and profit of such slave; and it shall and may be lawful for any person of persons whatsoever, to seize and take away from any slave, all such goods, commodities, boats perriaugers, canoes, horses, mares, neat cattle, sheep or hogs, and to deliver the same into the hands of any one of his Majesty's justices of the peace, nearest to the place where the seizure shall be made;

And such justice shall take the oath of such person who shall make any such seizure, concerning the manner of seizing and taking the same, and if the said justice shall be satisfied that such seizure hath been made according to the directions of this Act, he shall pronounce and declare the goods so seized, to be forfeited, and shall order the same to be sold at public outcry; and the monies arising by such sale shall be disposed of and applied as is hereinafter directed; provided, that if any goods shall be seized which come to the possession of any slave by theft, finding or otherwise, without the knowledge, privity, consent or connivance of the person who have a right to the property or lawful custody of any such goods, all such goods shall be restored, on such person's making an oath before any justice as aforesaid, who is hereby empowered to administer such oath, to the effect or in the following words:

"I, X, do sincerely swear, that I have a just and lawful right or title to certain goods seized and taken by Y, out of the possession of a slave named S; and I do sincerely swear and declare, that I did not, directly or indirectly, permit or suffer the said slave, or any other slave whatsoever, to use, keep or employ the said goods for the use, benefit or profit of any slave whatsoever, or to sell, barter or give away the same; but that the same goods were in the possession of the said slave by theft, finding or otherwise, or to be kept bona fide for my use, or for the use of Z, a free person, and not for the use or benefit of any slave whatsoever. So help me God."

That oath shall be taken mutates mutandis, as the case shall happen; provided also, that it shall be lawful for any person, being the owner of having the care or government of any slave who resides or is usually employed in any part of this Province, without the limits of Charlestown, to elsewhere, within this Province, the goods or commodities with which such slave shall be instructed, be particularly and distinctly set down and specified, and signed by the owner or other person having the charge and government of such slave, or by some other person by his, her or their order and direction.

35. Provided also, and be it enacted by the authority aforesaid, that this Act shall not extend or be constructed to extend to debar and of the inhabitants of Charlestown from sending any of their slaves resided therein, to sell in open market, any sort of provisions whatever, which the owner of such slave shall have received and brought from his or her state in the country, to be sold at the first hand;

Nor shall such slaves be debarred from buying any kind of provisions for the use and consumption of their masters and mistresses of their families, and for which such slave or slaves shall have a license or permit from the master of mistress, or some other person under whose care such slave shall be; anything in this, or any other Act, to the contrary notwithstanding.

36. And for that as it is absolutely necessary to the safety of this Province, that all due care be taken to restrain the wanderings and meetings of Negroes and other slaves, at all times, and more especially on Saturday nights, Sundays, and other holidays, and their using and carrying wooden swords, and other mischievous and dangerous weapons, or using or keeping of drums, horns, or other loud instruments, which may call together or give sign or notice to one another of their wicked designs and purposes; and that all masters, overseers and others may be enjoined, diligently and carefully to prevent the same,

Be it enacted by the authority aforesaid, that it shall be lawful for all masters, overseers and other persons whosoever, to apprehend and take up any Negro or other slave that shall be found out of the plantation of his or their master or owner, at any time, especially on Saturday nights, Sundays or other holiday, not being on lawful business, and with a letter from their master, or a ticket, or not having a white person with them; and the said Negro or other slave or slaves, met or found out of the plantation of his or their master or mistress, though with a letter or ticket, if he or they be armed with such offensive weapons aforesaid, him or them to disarm, take up and whip.

And whatsoever master, owner or overseer shall permit or suffer his or their Negro or other slave or slaves, at any time hereafter, to beat drums, blow horns, or use any other loud instruments or whosoever shall suffer and countenance any public meeting or feastings of strange Negroes or slaves in their plantations, shall forfeit ten pounds, current money, for every such offence, upon conviction or proof as aforesaid; provided, an information or other suit be commenced within one month after forfeiture thereof for the same.

37. And whereas, cruelty is not only highly unbecoming those who pro-fess themselves Christians, but is odious in the eyes of all men who have any sense of virtue of humanity; therefore, to restrain and prevent barbar-ity being exercised towards slaves,

Be it enacted by the authority aforesaid, that if any person of persons whosoever, shall willfully murder his own slave, or the slave of any other person, every such person, shall, upon conviction thereof, forfeit and pay the sum of seven hundred pounds, current money, and shall be rendered, and is hereby declared altogether and forever incapable of holding, exercis-ing, enjoying or receiving the profits of any office, place or employment, civil or military, within this Province.

And in case any such person shall not be able to pay the penalty and forfeitures hereby inflicted an imposed, every such person shall be sent to any of the frontier garrisons of this Province, or committed to the work house in Charlestown, there to remain for the space of seven years, and to serve or to be kept at hard labor.

And in case the slave murdered shall be the property of any other per-son, than the offender, the pay usually allowed by the public to the soldiers of such garrison, or the profits of the labor of the offender, if committed to the work house in Charlestown, shall be paid to the owner of the slave murdered.

And if any person shall, on sudden heat or passion, or by undue correc-tion, kill his own slave, or the slave of any other person, he shall forfeit the sum of three hundred and fifty pounds, current money.

And in case any person or persons shall willfully cut out the tongue, put out the eye, castrate, or cruelly scald, burn, or deprive any slave of any limb or member, or shall inflict any other cruel punishment, other than by whipping or beating with a horse-whip, cow-skin, switch or small stick, or by putting irons on, or confining or imprisoning such slave, every such person shall, for every such offence, forfeit the sum of one hundred pounds, current money.

38. And be it further enacted by the authority aforesaid, that in case any person in this Province, who shall be owner, or shall have the care, government or charge of any slave or slaves, shall deny, neglect or refuse to allow such slave or slaves, under his or her charge, sufficient clothing, covering or food, it shall and may be lawful for any person or persons, on behalf of such slave or slaves, to make complaint to the next neighboring justice, in the parish where such slave or slaves live or are usually employed;

And if there shall be no justice in the parish, then to the next justice in the nearest parish; and the said justice shall summons the party against whom such complaint shall be made, and shall enquire of, hear and determine the same; and if the said justice shall find the said complaint to be true, or that such person will not exculpate or clear himself from the charge, by his or her own oath, which such person shall be at liberty to do, in all cases where positive proof is not given of the offence, such justice shall and may make such orders upon the same, for the relief of such slave or slaves, as he in his discretion shall think fit, and shall and may set and impose a fine or penalty on any person who shall offend in the premises, in any sum not exceeding twenty pounds, current money, for each offense, to be levied by warrant of distress and sale of the offender's good, returning the over-plus, if any shall be; which penalty shall be paid to the churchwardens of the parish where the offence shall be committed, for the use of the poor of the said parish.

39.   And whereas, by reason of the extend and distance of plantations in this Province, the inhabitants are far removed from each other, and many cruelties may be committed on slaves, because no white person may be present to give evidence to the same, unless some method be provided for the better discovery of such offences; and as slaves are under the government, so they ought to be under the protection, of masters and managers of plantations;

Be it therefore further enacted by the authority aforesaid, that if any slave shall suffer in live, limb or member, or shall be maimed, beaten or abused, contrary to the directions and true intent and meaning of this Act, when no white person shall be present, or being present, shall neglect or refuse to give evidence, or be examined upon oath, concerning the same, in every such case, the owner or other person who shall have the care and government of such slave, and in whose possession or power such slave shall be, shall be deemed, taken, reputed and adjudged to be guilty or such offence, and shall be proceeded against accordingly, without further proof, unless such owner or other person as aforesaid, can make the contrary appear by good and sufficient evidence, or shall be his own oath, clear and exculpate himself; which oath, every court where such offence shall be tried, is hereby empowered to administer, and to acquit the offender accordingly, if clear proof of the offence be now made by two witnesses at least; any law, usage or custom to the contrary notwithstanding.

40. And whereas, many of the slaves in this Province wear clothes much above the condition of slaves, for the procuring whereof they use sinister and evil methods;

For the prevention, therefore, of such practices for the future, Be it enacted by the authority aforesaid, that no owner or proprietor of any Negro slave, or other slave, (except livery men and boys,) shall permit or suffer such Negro or other slave, to have or wear any sort of apparel whatsoever, finer, other, or greater value than Negro cloth, duffels, kerseys, osnabrigs, blue linen, check linen or coarse garlic, or calicoes, checked cottons, or Scotch plaids, under the pain of forfeiting all and every such apparel and garment, that any person shall permit or suffer his Negro or other slave to have or wear, finer, other or of greater value than Negro cloth, duffels, coarse kerseys, osnabrigs, blue linen, check linen or coarse garlix or calicoes, checked cottons or Scotch plaids, as aforesaid; and all and every constable and other persons are hereby authorized, empowered, and required, when as often as they shall find any such Negro slave, or other slave, having or wearing any sort of garment or apparel whatsoever, finer, other or of greater value than Negro cloth, duffels, coarse kerseys, osnabrigs, blue linen, check linen, or coarse garlix, or calicoes, checked cottons or Scottish plaids, as aforesaid, to seize and take away the same, to his or their own use, benefit and behoof; any law, usage or custom to the contrary notwithstanding.

Provided always, that if any owner of any such slave or slaves, shall think the garment or apparel of his said slave not liable to forfeiture, or to be taken away by virtue of this Act, he may not apply to any neighboring justice of the peace, who is hereby authorized and empowered to determine any difference or dispute that shall happen thereupon, according to the true intent and meaning of this Act.

41. And whereas, an ill custom has prevailed in this Province, of firing guns in the night time; for the prevention thereof for the future,

Be it enacted by the authority aforesaid, that if any person shall fire or shoot off any gun or pistol in the night time, after dark and before daylight, without necessity, every such person shall forfeit the sum of forty shillings, current money, for each gun so fired as aforesaid, to be recovered by warrant from any one justice of the peace for the county where the offence is committed, according to the direction of the Act for the trial of small and mean causes, and shall be paid to the church-wardens for the parish where the offence shall be committed, for the use of the poor of the said parish.

42. And be it further enacted by the authority aforesaid, that no slave or slaves shall be permitted to rent or hire any house, room, store or planta-tion, on his or her own account, or to be used or occupied by any slave or slaves; and any person or persons who shall let or hire and house, room, store or plantation, to any slave or slaves, or to any free person, to be occu-pied by any slave or slave, every such person so offending shall forfeit and pay to the informer the sum of twenty pounds, current money, to be recov-ered as in the Act for the trial of small and mean causes.

43. And whereas, it may be attended with ill consequences to permit a great number of slaves to travel together in the high roads without some white person in company with them;

Be it therefore enacted by the authority aforesaid, that no men slaves exceeding seven in number, shall hereafter be permitted to travel together in any high road in this Province, without some white person with them; and it shall and may be lawful for any person or persons, who shall see any men slaves exceeding seven in number, without some white person with them as aforesaid, traveling or assembled together in any high road, to apprehend all and every such slaves, and shall and may whip them, not exceeding twenty lashes on the bare back.

And whereas, many owners of slaves, and others who have the care, management and overseeing of slaves, so confine them so closely to hard labor, that they have not sufficient time for natural rest;

Be it therefore enacted by the authority aforesaid, that if any owner of slaves, or other person who shall have the care, management or overseeing of any slaves, shall work or put to labor any such slave or slaves, *more than fifteen hours* in for and twenty hours, from the twenty-fifth day of March to the twenty-fifth day of September, or more than fourteen hours in for and twenty hours, from the twenty-fifth day of September to the twenty-fifth day of March, every such person shall forfeit any sum not exceeding twenty pounds, nor under five pounds, current money, for every time he, she or they shall offend herein, at the discretion of the justice before whom such complaint shall be made.

45. And whereas, the having of slaves taught to write, or suffering them to be employed in writing, may be attended with great inconveniences;

Be it therefore enacted by the authority aforesaid, that all and every person and persons whatsoever, who shall hereinafter teach or cause any slave or slaves to be taught, to write, or shall use or employ any slave as a scribe in any manner of writing whatsoever, hereafter taught to write, every such person and persons, shall, for every such offense, forfeit the sum of one hundred pounds current money.

46. And whereas, plantations settled with slaves without any white person thereon, may be harbours for runaways and fugitive slaves;

Be it therefore enacted by the authority aforesaid, that no person or persons hereafter shall keep any slaves on any plantation or settlement, without having a white person on such plantation or settlement, under pain of forfeiting the sum of ten pounds current money, for every month which any such person shall so keep any slaves on any plantation or settlement, without a white person as aforesaid.

47. And whereas, many disobedient and evil minded Negroes and other slaves, being the property of his Majesty's subjects of this Province, have lately deserted the service of their owners, and have fled to St. Augustine and other places in Florida, in hopes of being there received and protected; and whereas, many other slaves have attempted to follow the same evil and pernicious example, which, (unless timely prevented,) may tend to the very great loss and prejudice of the inhabitants of this Province;

Be it therefore enacted by the authority aforesaid, that from and after the passing of this act, any white person or persons, free Indian or Indians, who shall, on the south side of Savannah river, take and secure, and shall from thence bring to the work house in Charlestown, any Negroes or other slaves, which within the space of six months have deserted, or who shall hereafter desert, from the services of their owners or employers, every such whit person or persons, free Indian or Indians, on evidence of the said slaves being taken as aforesaid, and the same certified by any two justices of the peace in this Province, shall be paid by the public treasurer of this Province the several rates and sums following, as the case shall appear to be;

Provided always, that nothing in this clause contained shall extend to such slaves as shall desert from any plantation situate within thirty miles of the said Savannah river, unless such slaves last mentioned shall be found on the south side of Altamahaw River;

That is to say, for each grown man slave brought alive, the sum of fifty pounds; for every grown woman or boy slave above the age of twelve years brought alive, the sum of twenty five pounds;

For every Negro child under the age of twelve years, brought alive, the sum of five pounds; for every scalp of a grown Negro slave with the two ears, twenty pounds; and for every Negro grown slave, found on the south side of St. John's river, and brought alive as aforesaid, the sum of one hundred pounds;

And for every scalp of a grown Negro slave with the two ears, taken on the south side of St. John's river, the sum of fifty pounds.

48. And be it further enacted by the authority aforesaid, that the expense of taking and securing all slaves brought alive as aforesaid, shall be at the charge of the respective owners; and no such slave or slaves taken on the south side of Savannah river, and brought to the work houses of Charlestown, as aforesaid, shall be delivered out of the custody of the warden of the said workhouse, without a certificate to him first produced from the public treasurer of this Province, that the money by him, disbursed, for the taking and securing the said slave or slaves, is fully satisfied to the treasurer, besides the following fees, which the said treasurer is hereby required to allow, pay and charge for the trouble necessary to be taken concerning the place and manner of apprehending the said slaves, viz, to the two justices who shall examine, take and certify the said evidence, for each slave brought alive, the sum of forty shillings; and to the treasurer for his trouble in executing this Act, for each slave brought alive as aforesaid, the sum of twenty shillings; and to the warden of the work house, the sum of three shillings and nine pence per diem, for his maintaining the same while in custody.

And on the commitment of any slave of slaves to the custody of the said warden, where the public treasurer shall, by virtue of this Act, expend any money for apprehending the same, the said warden is hereby required to advertise in the public gazette of this Province for the space of three months, the best description he can form of all and every the said slaves, with the place and manner of their being taken; and in case the owner of employer of the said slave or slaves, shall neglect within that time, to redeem the said slave or slaves, by fully satisfying the public treasurer the changes he shall be at, in such manner and proportion as by this Act is directed, then, and in every such case, the said public treasurer shall be at liberty to dispose of every such slave or slaves to the best bidder at public auction, which sale shall be deemed good and effectual, to all intents and purposes, to such person or persons as shall purchase the same; and the produce of every such slave or slaves, shall first go towards satisfying the expense of the said public treasurer and warden of the work house, for the taking, securing and keeping the said slave or slaves, as aforesaid; and then the surplus, (if any,) shall be paid to the respective owner or owners.

49. And be it further enacted by the authority aforesaid, that from and after the passing of this Act, where any slave or slaves shall be tried and condemned to be executed for deserting, out of this Province, every such slave or slaves shall, before their execution, be valued by the tryers of the same; and in every such case the owner or owners of every such slave, shall be paid by the public of this Province, the full sum and rates at which such executed slave or slaves shall be valued as aforesaid, without being a charge to any particular owner or owners; any law, usage or custom to the contrary notwithstanding.

50. And be it further enacted by the authority aforesaid, that all charge of taking and bringing in slaves as aforesaid, shall be defrayed and paid by the public.

51. And be it further enacted by the authority aforesaid, that if any constable or other person, directed to required to do or perform any matter or think, required, commanded, or enjoined by this Act, who shall know or be credibly informed of any offence which shall be committed against this Act, within his parish, precinct or limits, and shall not give information thereof to some justice of the peace, and endeavor the conviction of the offenders according to his duty, but such constable or other person as aforesaid, or any person lawfully called in aid of the constable or such other person as aforesaid, shall willfully and willingly omit the performance of his duty in the execution of this Act, and shall be thereof convicted, he shall forfeit for every such offence, the sum of twenty pounds current money.

And in case any justice of the peace, warden of the work house, or freeholder, shall willfully or willingly omit the performance of his duty in the execution of this act, every such justice of the peace and warden of the work house, shall forfeit the sum of forty pounds current money; and every such freeholder shall forfeit the sum of fifteen pounds current money; which several penalties shall be recovered and disposed of as hereinafter is directed;

And moreover, the judges and justice of the court of general sessions of the peace, oyer and terminer, assize and assize and general gaol delivery, are hereby commanded and required to give offenders against this Act in charge in open court; and all grand juries, justices of the peace, constables, and other officers, are hereby required to make due and true presentment of such of the said offences as come to their knowledge.

52.   And be it further enacted by the authority aforesaid, that if any person shall be at any time sued for putting in execution any of the powers contained in this Act, such person shall and may plead the general issue and give the special matter and this Act in evidence;

And if the plaintiff be nonsuit, or a verdict pass for the defendant, or if the plaintiff discontinue his action, or enter a noli [sic] prosequi, or if upon demurrer judgment be given for the defendant, every such defendant shall have his full double costs.

53.   And be it further enacted by the authority aforesaid, that this Act, and all clauses therein contained, shall be constructed most largely and beneficially for the promoting and carrying into execution this Act, and for the encouragement and justification of all persons to be employed in the execution thereof; and that no record, warrant, process or commitment to be made by virtue of this Act, or the proceedings thereupon, shall be reversed, avoided, or any way impeached, by reason of any default in form.

54.   And be it further enacted by the authority aforesaid, that all fines, penalties and forfeitures imposed or inflicted by this Act, which are not hereby particularly disposed of, or the manner of recovery directed, shall, if not exceeding the value of twenty pounds current money, be recovered, levied and distrained for, by warrant from any one justice of the peace, in the country or precinct where such offence shall be committed, according to the Act for the trial of small and mean causes;

And in case such fine, penalty or forfeiture shall exceed the value of twenty pounds, current money, the same shall be recovered by action of debt, bill, plaint or information, in any court of record in this Province, wherein no privilege, protection, essoign, wager of law, or non vult ulterius prosequi, or any more than one imparlance, shall be admitted or allowed; and all the said fines, penalties and forfeitures, which shall be recovered by this Act, and are not before particularly disposed of, shall be applied and disposed of, half to his majesty, his heirs and successors, to be applied by the

General Assembly for the use of this Province, and the other half to him or them who will sue or inform the same.

55.   And be it further enacted by the authority aforesaid, that his Majesty's part of the fines, penalties and forfeitures which shall be recovered by the virtue of this Act, shall be paid into the hands of the justices, or in the court where the same shall be recovered, who shall make a memorial and record of the payment of the same, and shall, without delay, send a transcript of such memorial or record to the public treasurer of this Province, from the said courts or justices who shall receive his Majesty's part of such fines and forfeitures; which memorial shall be a charge on the judges or justices respectively to whom the same shall be paid; and the public treasurer of this Province for the time being, shall and may, and he is hereby authorized and empowered to, levy and recover the same by warrant of distress, and sale of the goods and chattels of the said judges or justices respectively, who shall be charged with the same, in case they or any of them shall neglect or refuse to make such memorial or record as aforesaid, or send such transcript thereof, as before directed, or shall neglect or refuse to pay the same over to the treasurer within twenty days after the receipt of the same;

Provided always, that no person shall be prosecuted for any fine, forfeiture or penalty imposed by this Act, unless such prosecution shall be commenced within six months after the offense shall be committed.

56.   And whereas, several Negroes did lately rise in rebellion, and did commit many barbarous murders at Stono and other parts adjacent thereto; and whereas, in suppressing the said rebels, several of them were killed and others taken alive and executed; and as the exigence and danger the inhabitants at that time were in an exposed to, would not admit of the formality of a legal trial of such rebellious Negroes, but for their own security the said inhabitants were obliged to put such Negroes to immediate death; to prevent, therefore, any person or persons being questioned for any matter or thing done in the suppression or execution of the said rebellious Negroes, as also any litigious suit, action or prosecution that may be brought, sued or prosecuted or commenced against such person or persons for or concerning the same;

Be it enacted by the authority aforesaid, that all and every act, matter and thing, had, done, committed and executed, in and about the suppressing and putting all and every the said Negro and Negroes to death, is and are hereby declared lawful, to all intents and purposes whatsoever, as fully and amply as if such rebellious Negroes had undergone a formal trial and condemnation, notwithstanding any want of form or omission whatever in the trial of such Negroes; and any law, usage or custom to the contrary thereof in any wise notwithstanding.

57.   And be it further enacted by the authority aforesaid, that this Act shall be deemed a public Act, and shall be taken notice of without pleading the same before all judges, justices, magistrates and courts within this province.

58.   And be it further enacted by the authority aforesaid, that this Act shall continue in force for the space of three years, and from thence to the end of the next session of the General Assembly, and no longer.

Signed C. Pinckney, Speaker

In the Council Chamber, Commons House of Assembly of Carolina, the 10th day of May, 1740.

Assented to by William Bull. Lieutenant Governor and Commander-in-chief.

Source: "Act for the better ordering and governing of Negroes and other Slaves in this Province" (May 1740), http://www.duhaime.org/LawMuseum/LawArticle -1499/1740-Slave-Code-of-South-Carolina-Articles-25-28.aspx

The New York Conspiracy (1741)

The slaves Quack and Cuffee were tried and convicted on charges of burglary and arson. Justice Daniel Horsmanden was convinced they were implicated in a conspiracy to torch New York City as part of an insurrection conspiracy, but rested content with executing them as criminals. The selection from the trial transcript reproduced here includes Horsmanden's speech at their sentencing, as well as the "confessions" that Quack and Cuffee made at their execution site, probably in the hope that they would be reprieved at the last minute. They were not.

Then the jury were charged, and a constable was sworn to attend them as usual; and they withdrew; and being soon returned, found the prisoners guilty of both indictments. The prisoners were asked, what they had to offer in arrest of judgment, why they should not receive sentence of death? and they offering nothing but repetitions of protestations of their innocence; the third justice **Justice Horsmanden** proceeded to sentence, as followeth:

Quack and Cuffee, the criminals at the bar,

"You both now stand convicted of one of the most horrid and detestable pieces of villainy, that ever satan instilled into the heart of human creatures to put in practice; ye, and the rest of your colour, though you are called slaves in this country; yet you are all far, very far, from the condition of other slaves in other countries; nay, your lot is superior to that of thousands of white people. You are furnished with all the necessaries of life, meat, drink, and clothing, without care, in a much better manner than you could provide for yourselves, were you at liberty; as the miserable condition of many free people here of your complexion might abundantly convince you. What then could prompt you to undertake so vile, so wicked, so monstrous, so execrable and hellish a scheme, as to murder and destroy your own masters and benefactors? nay, to destroy root and branch, all the white people of this place, and to lay the whole town in ashes.

"I know not which is the more astonishing, the extreme folly, or wickedness, of so base and shocking a conspiracy; for as to any view of liberty or government you could propose to yourselves, upon the success of burning the city, robbing, butchering, and destroying the inhabitants; what could it be expected to end in, in the account of any rational and considerate person among you, but your own destruction? And as the wickedness of it, you might well have reflected, you that have sense, that there is a God above, who has always a clear view of all your actions, who sees into the utmost recesses of the heart, and knoweth all your thoughts; shall he not, do ye think, for all this bring you into judgment, at that final and great day of account, the day of judgment, when the most secret treachery will be disclosed, and laid open to the view, and everyone will be rewarded according to their deeds, and their use of that degree of reason which God Almighty has entrusted them with.

"Ye that were for destroying us without mercy, ye abject wretches, the outcasts of the nations of the earth, are treated here with tenderness and humanity; and, I wish I could not say, with too great indulgence also; for you have grown wanton with excess of liberty, and your idleness has proved your ruin, having given you the opportunities of forming this villainous and detestable conspiracy; a scheme compounded of the blackest and foulest vices, treachery, blood-thirstiness, and ingratitude. But be not deceived, God Almighty only can and will proportion punishments to men's offences; ye that have shewn no mercy here, and have been for destroying all about ye, and involving them in one general massacre and ruin, what hopes can ye have of mercy in the other world? For shall not the judge of all the earth do right? Let me in compassion advise ye then; there are but a few moments between ye and eternity; ye ought therefore seriously to lay to heart these things; earnestly and sorrowfully to bewail your monstrous and crying sins, in this your extremity; and if ye would reasonably entertain any hopes of mercy at the hands of God, ye must shew mercy here yourselves, and make what amends ye can before ye leave us, for the mischief you have already done, by preventing any more being done. Do not flatter yourselves, for the same measure which you give us here, will be measured to you again in the other world; ye must confess your whole guilt, as to the offences of which ye stand convicted, and for which ye will presently receive judgment; ye must discover the whole scene of iniquity which has been contrived in this monstrous confederacy, the chief authors and actors, and all and every the parties concerned, aiding and assisting therein, that by your means a full stop may be put to this horrible and devilish undertaking. And these are the only means left ye to shew mercy; and the only reasonable ground ye can go upon, to entertain any hopes of mercy at the hands of God, before whose judgment seat ye are so soon to appear.

"Ye cannot be so stupid, surely, as to imagine, that when ye leave this world, when your souls put off these bodies of clay, ye shall become like the beasts that perish, that your spirits shall only vanish into the soft air and cease to be. No, your souls are immortal, they will live forever, either to be eternally happy, or eternally miserable in the other world, where you are now going.

"If ye sincerely and in earnest repent you of your abominable sins, and implore the divine assistance at this critical juncture, in working out the great and momentous article of the salvation of your souls; upon your making all the amends, and giving all the satisfaction which is in each of your powers, by a full and complete discovery of the conspiracy, and of the several persons concerned in it, as I have observed to ye before, then and only upon these conditions can ye reasonably expect mercy at the hands of God Almighty for your poor, wretched and miserable souls.

"Here ye must have justice, for the justice of human laws has at length overtaken ye, and we ought to be very thankful, and esteem it a most merciful and wondrous act of Providence, that your treacheries and villainies have been discovered; that your plot and contrivances, your hidden works of darkness have been brought to light, and stopped in their career; that in the same net which you have hid so privly for others your own feet are taken: that the same mischief which you have contrived for others, and have in part executed, is at length fallen upon your own pates, whereby the sentence which I am now to pronounce will be justified against ye; which is,

"That you and each of you be carried from hence to the place from whence you came, and from thence to the place of execution, where you and each of you shall be chained to a stake, and burnt to death; and the lord have mercy upon your poor, wretched souls."

Ordered, that the execution of the said Quack and Cuffee be on Saturday the 30th of this instant, between the hours of one and seven o'clock in the afternoon of the same day.

SATURDAY, MAY 30

This day Quack and Cuffee were executed at the stake according to sentence.

The spectators at this execution were very numerous; about three o'clock the criminals were brought to the stake, surrounded with piles of wood ready for setting fire to, which the people were very impatient to have done, their resentment being raised to the utmost pitch against them, and no wonder. The criminals shewed great terror in their countenances, and looked as if they would gladly have discovered all they knew of this accursed scheme, could they have had any encouragement to hope for a reprieve. But as the case was, they might flatter themselves with hopes: they both seemed inclinable to make some confession; the only difficulty between them at last being, who should speak first. Mr. Moore, the deputy secretary, undertook singly to examine them both, endeavoring to persuade them to confess their guilt, and all they knew of the matter, without effect; till at length Mr. Roosevelt came up to him, and said he would undertake Quack, whilst Mr. Moore examined Cuffee; but before they could proceed to the purpose, each of them was obliged to flatter his respective criminal that his fellow sufferer had begun, which stratagem prevailed: Mr. Roosevelt stuck to Quack altogether, and Mr. Moore took Cuff's confession, and sometimes also minutes of what each said; and afterwards upon drawing up their confessions in form from their minutes, they therefore intermixed what came from each.

Quack's confession at the stake. He said,

1. "That Hughson was the first contriver of the whole plot, and promoter of it; which was to burn the houses of the town; Cuffee said, to kill the people.
2. "That Hughson brought in first Caesar (Vaarck's); then Prince (Auboyneau's); Cuffee (Philipse's); and others, amongst whom were old Kip's negro; Robin (Chambers's); Cuffee (Gomez's); Jack (Codweis's) and another short negro, that cooks for him.
3. "That he Quack did fire the fort, that it was by a lighted stick taken out of the servants hall, about eight o'clock at night, that he went up the back stairs with it and so through Barbara's room, and put it near the gutter, betwixt the shingles, and the roof of the house.
4. "That on a Sunday afternoon, a month before the firing of the fort, over a bowl of punch, the confederates at Hughson's (amongst whom were the confederates above named, Albany, and Tickle, alias Will, Jack and Cook (Comfort's); old Butchell; Caesar, and Guy (Horsfield's); Tom (Van Rants's); Caesar (Peck's); Worcester, and others) voted him Quack, as having a wife in the fort, to be the person who should fire the fort, Sandy, and Jack (Codweis's); Caesar, and Guy (Horsfield's); were to assist him in it.
5. "That Hughson desired the negroes to bring to his house, what they could get from the fire, and Hughson was to bring down country people in his boat to further the business, and would bring in other negroes.
6. "That forty or fifty to his knowledge were concerned, but their names he could not recollect (the mob pressing and interrupting).
7. "That Cuffee (Gomez's); and Caesar (Peck's), fired Van Zant's storehouse.
8. "That Mary Burton had spoke the truth, and could name many more.

9. "Fortune (Wilkins's) and Sandy, had done the same; and Sandy could name the Spaniards, and say much more, which Cuffee particularly confirmed.

10. "Being asked what view Hughson had in acting in this manner? He answered, to make himself rich.

11. "That after the fire was over, Quack was at Hughson's house, Jack (Comfort's), a leading man, Hughson, wife and daughter present, and said, the job was done, meaning the fire; that he went frequently to Hughson's house, and met there Tickle and Albany.

12. "Quack said his wife was no ways concerned, for he never would trust her with it: and that Denby knew nothing about the matter.

13. "Jamaica (Ellis's) not concerned that he knew of, but was frequently at Hughson's with his fiddle.

14. "Said he was not sworn by Hughson, but other were." McDonald (the witness against Quack upon the trial) at the stake desired Mr. Pinhorne to ask Quack, whether he had wronged him in what he had said of him at court? He answered no; it was true he did pass him at the fort gate, about eleven o'clock that morning.

Cuffee's confession at the stake. - He said,

1. "That Hughson was the first contriver of all, and pressed him to it: that he Cuffee was one of the first concerned.

2. "The fire was intended to begin at Comfort's shingles, and so through the town.

3. "Old Kip's Negro; Robin (Chambers's); Jack (Comfort's); and Cuffee (Gomez's); were of the conspirators: Albany and Tickle were concerned.

4. "That he was sworn, and Caesar and Prince also by Hughson.

5. "That Cuffee (Gomez's) and Caesar (Peck's); burnt Van Zant's store-house.

6. "That Sandy set fire to Mr. Machado's house; Niblet's Negro wench can tell it; and Becker's Bess' knows it.

7. "That he set fire to the storehouse as sworn against him, that when his master went to the Coffee-House, he ran out of the other door, and went the back way into the storehouse, having lighted charcoal

in his pocket between two oyster shells, he put the fire between the ropes and the boards, and leaving it on fire, went home.

8. "That Hughson's people were to raise a mob to favour the design.

9. "That the evidence that Peterson, did see him (was true); that Fortune did see him the night before.

10. "That Fortune knew and was as deeply concerned as he; and Sandy was concerned, and knew the Spaniards.

11. "There was about fifty concerned; and that all were concerned that a constable who stood by had seen all at Hughson's house."

After the confessions were minuted down (which were taken in the midst of great noise and confusion) Mr. Moore desired the sheriff to delay the execution until the governor be acquainted therewith, and his pleasure known touching their reprieve; which, could it have been effected, it was thought might have been means of producing great discoveries; but from the disposition observed in the spectators, it was much to be apprehended, there would have been great difficulty, if not danger in an attempt to take the criminals back. All this was represented to his honour; and before Mr. Moore could return from him to the place of execution, he met the sheriff upon the common, who declared his opinion, that the carrying the negroes back would be impracticable; and if that was his honour's order it could not be attempted without a strong guard, which could not be got time enough; and his honour's directions for the reprieve being conditional and discretionary, for these reasons the execution proceeded.

Source: A Journal of the Proceedings in the Detection of the Conspiracy Formed by Some White People in Conjunction with Negros and Other Slaves (New York: James Parker, printer, 1744), 93–100.

> *By July 1741, the excessive executions and deportations of defendants accused of conspiring to burn New York City had spread to the other British colonies on the North Atlantic seaboard. An unknown correspondent from Massachusetts wrote to Cadwallader Colden in that month to express his or her dismay at what appeared to be indiscriminate persecution. Colden (1688–1776), a philosopher and botanist who would twice serve as colonial governor of New York, had already voiced reservations about the probity of the trials.*

Sir,

I am a stranger to you & to New York, & so much beg pardon for the mistakes I may be guilty of in the subsequent attempt; The Design whereof is to endeavor the putting an end to the bloody Tragedy that has been, & I suppose still is acting amongst you in regard to the poor Negros (sic) and the Whites too. [News of the "horrible executions"] puts me in mind of our New England Witchcraft in the year 1692 Which if I don't mistake new York justly reproached us for, & mocked at our Credulity about . . .

It is true I have heard something of your Forts being burnt, but that might be by Lightning from heaven, by Accident, by some malicious person or persons of our own color. What other Feats have been performed to petrify your hearts against the poor blacks & some of your neighbors the whites, I can't tell; But 2 things seem impossible to me almost in *rerum natura* [in nature], That whites should join with the Blacks, or that the Blacks (among whom there are no doubt some rational persons) should attempt the Destruction of a City when it is impossible they should escape the just & direful Vengeance of the Countries round about, which would immediately & unavoidably pour in upon them & destroy them.

Possibly there have been some murmuring amongst the Negroes & a mad fellow or 2 has threatened & designed Revenge, for the Cruelty & inhumanity they have met with, which is too rife in the English Plantations . . . And f that be all it is a pity there have been such severe animadversions. And if nothing will put an end hereto till some of higher degree & better circumstances & Characters are accused (which finished our Salem Witchcraft) the sooner the better, lest all the poor People of the Government perish in the merciless flames of an Imaginary Plot.

In the meantime excuse me & don't be offended, if out of Friendship to my poor Countrymen & compassion to the Negros (who are flesh & blood as well as we & ought to be treated with Humanity) I entreat you not to go on to Massacre & destroy your own Estates by making Bonfires of the Negros & perhaps thereby loading yourselves with greater Guild than theirs. For we have too much reason to fear that the Divine Vengeance does & will pursue us for our ill treatment of the bodies & souls of our poor slaves, and therefore let Justice be done to your own people.

Source: Undated and anonymous letter to Cadwallader Colden, in "Letters and Papers of Cadwallader Colden," *New-York Historical Society Publications* 67 (1934), 270–272.

The Prosser Conspiracy (1800)

Acknowledging that Gabriel Prosser's conspiracy to revolt was motivated by democratic or "Jacobin" ideals of liberty and equality, this commentator, writing in the midst of the postconspiracy hangings, argues that insurrections are inevitable so long as the hypocrisy of slavery in a nation that values freedom endures.

It is very certain from all that has been discovered, that this dreadful conspiracy originates with some vile French Jacobins, aided and abetted by some of our own profligate and abandoned democrats. Liberty and equality have brought the evil upon us. A doctrine which, however intelligible, and admissible, in a land of freemen, is not only unintelligible and inadmissible, but dangerous and extremely wicked in this country, where every white man is a master, and every black man is a slave. This doctrine . . . cannot fail of producing either a general insurrection, or a general emancipation. It has been most imprudently propagated at many of our tables, while our servants have been standing behind our chairs, for several years past . . . .What else then could we expect than what has happened?

That man must be a fool, my friend, who thinks that there can be any compromise between liberty and slavery.

The question now is a plain one—shall we abolish slavery or shall we emancipate? There is no middle course to it. We must do one thing or t'other.

If we continue it—we must restrict it. We must re-enact all those rigorous laws which experience has proved a necessity to keep it within bounds. In a word, if we will keep a ferocious monster in our country, we must keep him in chains. What man in his senses would keep a lion or tyger [sic] loose in the streets? Slavery is a monster—the most horrible of all monsters—tyranny excepted. The thing in human shape that submits to the former is little better than a beast—the thing in human shape that submits to the latter is the worse of bests. Democracy therefore, in Virginia, is like virtue in hell. The Ethiopean [sic] can never be washed white. The slaveholder can never be a Democrat. He who affects to be a Democrat and is, at the same time, an owner of slaves, is a devil incarnate. He tells a damnable and diabolical lie in the face of day, which his own conscience revolts at the moment he utters it, and which he knows every man of truth of common sense, of common honesty, must turn from with horror.

The love of liberty in the breast of a slave-holder, is like a diminutive, distant and hardly visible star in the center of a black cloud in a dark night, serving only to render the scene more distant, and, as [John] Milton says, "to make darkness visible!" [A phrase from *Paradise Lost*.] Every slave holder who has been loud in the cause of liberty, has proved the justness of this simile, by emancipating his slaves in the hour of death, when his grim master would no longer permit him to deceive himself or others.

Source: Fredericksburg Virginia Herald, September 23, 1800.

The German Coast Revolt (1811)

This short notice, originally appearing in the Louisiana Courier *but quickly reprinted in two dozen newspapers across the nation, records shock at the number of slaves killed in the aftermath of Charles Deslondes's uprising. That it originated in a Southern rather than Northern paper only underscores the unnecessary violence with which the revolt was squelched.*

New Orleans, Jan. 24

An accurate enumeration was taken on Thursday last, of the negroes killed and missing, from Mr. Fortier's to Mr. Andry's, and is as follows, viz,

Killed and executed,	66
Missing,	17
Sent to N. Orleans for trial,	16
	—
	99

From this statement, the loss is not so great as we first calculated it to be. Those reported missing are supposed generally to be dead in the woods, as many bodies have been seen by the patrols.

We are sorry to hear that a ferocious sanguinary disposition marked the character of some of the inhabitants. Civilized man ought to remember well his standing, and never let himself sink down to the level of a savage: our laws are summary enough, and let them govern.

Source: Connecticut Herald, March 5, 1811.

Negro Fort Resistance (1816)

Two newspaper accounts chronicle the destruction of Negro Fort.

"Extract of a letter from an officer who was present at the destruction of the Negro Fort in East Florida"

The fifth hot shot passed through their magazine, and a dreadful explosion ensued. Some of the Negroes and Choctaws were found a considerable distance from the fort, all torn to pieces! Nearly every soul in this den of robbers perished. The number of men, women, and children numbered in all to about 300. The chief of the Choctaws was found alive, but very much bruised and burnt. The chief of the Negroes (whom they called Sergeant Major), was also found alive, but quite blind. These two the Indians scalped and shot.

The only loss sustained on our side was midshipman Luffborough, and three sailors who were sent on shore for the purpose of procuring water, and were killed and scalped by the Indians. This happened before our troops arrived. The officers attached to this command were, colonel Clinch, major Mulenburg, captain Taylor, lieutenants McGavock, Wilson, Randolph, and Dr. Buck. Our only regret, notwithstanding our complete success, is, that *Nicholls* and *Woodbine*, the British agents who planted this *virtuous* community, were not included in the explosion.

Source: Daily National Intelligencer, September 2, 1816.

"Extract of a letter from a gentleman in New-Orleans to another in Philadelphia"

You will have heard of the blowing up of the Negro Fort (alias British establishment) at Appalachicola [*sic*]. The following is a correct statement, it may in substance be relied on.

Sailing master Loonis, the commander of one gun boat, and sailing master Basset, the commander of another, received orders to convoy two schooners loaded with provisions, etc. up the river Appalachicola [sic], to a division of our army under col. Clinch, operating against the unfriendly Creek Indians —The commanders of the gun boats were particularly instructed not to commit hostilities upon the Spanish government, and not to molest the negro fort, unless they attempted to prevent their passing.

On the arrival of the gun boats at Appalachicola [sic] bay, Mr. Loonis received a letter from col. Clinch, by an Indian, requesting him to wait until he could come down with a small command to aid him in case the fort should interfere, and requesting him to stop all boats from descending the river. On making its appearance, Loonis sent a boat from the gun boat to stop it; but they fired into our boat and it was returned. Mr. Loonis afterward sent midshipman Lusborough to get some water, on reaching the shore, more than fifty Negroes and Indians rose from their hiding place, and fired a volley of musketry into the boat. Lusborough and two seamen were killed, one made his escape by swimming to a sandbar, and the two others taken prisoners—they tarred them all over and burnt them alive—the boats then proceeded up within a mile and a half of the fort, and the fort then opened their 24 pounders upon them: the gun boat commanded by Basset fired 9 cold shot, to ascertain the exact distance, put in a red hot one, which entered their magazine and blew up the fort—300 Negroes and Indians were all killed except 27—and those wounded except 4—in the fort was 3000 stand of British musketry; 500 barrels and 300 kegs powder, a great deal of provisions and British uniform flints, etc. 4 24 pounders, 4 six pounders, 1 four pounder field piece, with ammunition wagons [sic], etc. and a five inch howitzer.—So much for this British establishment. I wish Nichkolls [sic] and Woodbine had been in the fort when it blew up.

The Spaniards now seem to insinuate it was an interference with their territory, although they officially told general Jackson, they were not accountable for anything the British did there, it was an Indian territory. The fort was commanded by a negro, who was taken alive, though since dead: he confessed he fought under British colours, they were up in the fort—orders were, to let no white man approach the fort, or ascend the river, without the private signal of the British.

Source: The American Beacon and Commercial Diary, November 4, 1816.

The Vesey Conspiracy (1822)

In the opening pages of the published proceedings of Denmark Vesey's trial, an account is offered of his religious sensibilities and his method of recruiting fellow conspirators. What especially comes across is the anger that white authorities felt about Vesey's message that slave insurrection is biblically justified.

At the head of this conspiracy stood Denmark Vesey, a free negro; with him the idea undoubtedly originated. For several years before he disclosed his intentions to any one, he appears to have been constantly and assiduously engaged in endeavoring to embitter the minds of the colored population against the white. He rendered himself perfectly familiar with all those parts of the Scriptures, which he thought he could pervert to his purpose; and would readily quote them, to prove that slavery was contrary to the laws of God; that slaves were bound to attempt their emancipation, however shocking and bloody might be the consequences, and that such efforts would not only be pleasing to the Almighty, but were absolutely enjoined, and their success predicted in the Scriptures. His favorite texts when he addressed his own color were, Zechariah, chapter 14th, verses 1, 2 and 3, and Joshua, chapter 4th, verse 21; and in all his conversations he identified their situation with that of the Israelites. The number of inflammatory pamphlets on slavery brought into Charleston from some of our sister states, within the last four years, (and once from Sierra Leone) and distributed amongst the colored population of the city, for which there was a great facility, in consequence of the unrestricted intercourse allowed to persons of color between the different States in the Union; and the speeches in Congress of those opposed to the admission of Missouri into the Union, perhaps garbled and misrepresented, furnished him with ample means for inflaming the minds of the colored population of this state; and by distorting certain parts of those speeches, or selecting from them particular passages, he persuaded but too many that Congress had actually declared them free, and that they were held in bondage contrary to the laws of the land. Even whilst walking through the streets in company with another, he was not idle; for if his companion bowed to a white person he would rebuke him, and observe that all men were born equal, and that he was surprised that anyone would degrade himself by such conduct; that he would never cringe to the whites, nor ought anyone who had the feelings of a man. When answered, We are slaves, he would sarcastically and indignantly reply, "You deserve to remain slaves;" and if he were further asked, What can we do, he would remark, "Go and buy a spelling book and read the fable of Hercules and the Waggoner;" which he would then repeat, and apply it to their situation. He also sought every opportunity of entering into conversation with white persons when they could be overheard by negroes near by, especially in grog-shops; during which conversation he would artfully introduce some bold remark on slavery; and sometimes, when from the character he was conversing with he found he might be still bolder, he would go so far, that had not his declarations in such situations been clearly proved, they would scarcely have been credited. He continued this course, until sometime after the commencement of the last winter; by which time he had not only obtained incredible influence amongst persons of color, but many feared him more than their owners, and one of them declared, even more than his God.

At this period he sounded Rolla and Ned, two slaves of his Excellency Thomas Bennett, and finding them ready to acquiesce in his schemes, he made the same proposals to Jack, belonging to Mrs. Purcell, and Peter, belonging to Mr. Poyas, who also consented with equal promptness. These men were his first four associates; three of whom, viz: Rolla, Ned and Peter, immediately became his most active agents. Some time after Christmas he was also joined by Gullah Jack, belonging to Mr. Pritchard, and subsequently by Monday, belonging to Mr. Gell; who soon proved themselves to be as fit men for his purpose, and as active as Rolla, Ned and Peter. These constituted his five principal officers, by whose means, aided by some others whom he employed to go about and travel the country adjacent to Charleston, and amongst the latter of whom the principal agents were Lot Forrester and Frank Ferguson, he engaged great numbers to join in the intended insurrection. He also at his house held nocturnal meetings, for the purpose of interchanging opinions, maturing the plan, collecting and giving information, &c.; at which meetings numbers of the insurgents, both from country and town attended; and where collections were made for the purpose of providing arms, ammunition, &c. and for defraying such expenses as might be indispensibly necessary. He also attended meetings at other places appointed by him; at one place in particular on Charleston Neck, about two miles and a half from the city.

Besides his five principal officers already mentioned, he had other recruiting agents, though on a smaller scale, amongst whom were William Palmer, Wm. Garner, Charles Drayton and Peirault Strohecker. In order to induce the colored population to join them, every principle which could operate upon the mind of man was artfully employed: Religion, Hope, Fear, Deception, were resorted to as occasion required. All were told, and many believed, that God approved of their designs; those whose fears would have restrained them, were forced to yield by threats of death; those whose prudence and foresight induced them to pause, were cheered with the assurance that assistance from St. Domingo and Africa were at hand; whilst those upon whom none of these principles operated, were excited from despair on being informed, that the whites, perceiving they were becoming too numerous, had resolved to create a false alarm of fire, and as they came out in the dead of the night to kill them, in order to thin their numbers. And strange as it may appear, yet vast numbers of the Africans firmly believed that Gullah Jack was a sorcerer; that he could neither be killed nor taken; and that whilst they retained the charms which he had distributed they would themselves be invulnerable. Add to all this, their belief that Congress had emancipated them, and we may readily credit the declaration of Monday Gell and Perault, that they never spoke to any person of color on the subject, or knew of any one who had been spoken to by the other leaders, who had withheld his assent.

Vesey being a free man encountered none of those obstacles which would have been in the way of a slave; his time was at his own disposal, and he could go wherever he pleased, without interruption; qualifications and advantages absolutely necessary for the Chief in a Conspiracy, and which enabled him to travel so much about the country as he did.

On perusing the testimony, the declaration of one or two of the witnesses that this plot had been in agitation for four years will strike the observation of every one; but it must not be supposed therefrom, that recruiting or enlisting had been progressing for that time; or that, for that time there existed any direct proposal from Vesey or any one else for such a measure. Such was not the case. No active measures were taken until near last Christmas. In speaking of this attempt being in agitation for four years, allusion was had to Vesey's conduct and language during that time; and to the dissatisfaction which appeared since, to exist amongst the coloured population. This was about the time that the African congregation, (so called from its being composed wholly of persons of colour and almost entirely of blacks,) was formed, and their Church built in Hampstead; of which Vesey had been a member, and of which his principal associates, Gullah Jack, Monday, Ned and Peter, were also members; and the two last, were class leaders. It was also about this time, that class meetings of the coloured people had become so common as they now are; each class having a coloured preacher or leader as they were termed, named by the Minister of the Church to which he belonged; at which meetings, held usually at night in some retired building, avowedly for religious instruction and worship, no white person attended. That inflammatory and insurrectionary doctrines, without any direct proposal for such an attempt, were inculcated at these meetings or some of them, was positively proved; and further, that they were to be used as places of rendezvous and rallying points, for communicating to all, the exact night and hour, on which the first blow was to be struck. The great impropriety of allowing meetings of any kind to be held solely by slaves, and at such times and places, must forcibly strike every reflecting mind. The African congregation above mentioned was not only composed altogether of coloured persons, but their Ministers were also coloured; and were stated to have been regularly ordained Bishops and Ministers of the Gospel. The influence which such men and class leaders must necessarily acquire over the minds of the ignorant blacks is evident; and if a disposition exists in them to obtain for their own colour and themselves, the freedom and privileges enjoyed by the whites, by enlisting into their cause perverted religion and fanaticism, that desperation is kindled in their hearers, the consequences of which are but too well known. Is it to be wondered at that, under all the foregoing circumstances, an attempt to create an insurrection should be contemplated!

Vesey perceiving that so far every thing had answered his most sanguine expectations, himself in possession of vast influence over his own colour, and their minds poisoned and embittered against the white population, began about Christmas 1821, to probe those whom he had selected as leaders; and found as he expected a ready acquiescence in his measures by all of them except Monday Gell, who wavered for some time before he joined. In the selection of his leaders, Vesey shewed great penetration and sound judgment. Rolla was plausible, and possessed uncommon self-possession; bold and ardent, he was not to be deterred from his purpose by danger.

Ned's appearance indicated, that he was a man of firm nerves, and desperate courage. Peter was intrepid and resolute, true to his engagements, and cautious in observing secrecy where it was necessary; he was not to be daunted nor impeded by difficulties, and though confident of success, was careful in providing against any obstacles or casualties which might arise, and intent upon discovering every means which might be in their power if thought of before hand. Gullah Jack was regarded as a Sorcerer, and as such feared by the natives of Africa, who believe in witchcraft. He was not only considered invulnerable, but that he could make others so by his charms; and that he could and certainly would provide all his followers with arms. He was artful, cruel, bloody; his disposition in short was diabolical. His influence amongst the Africans was inconceivable. Monday was firm, resolute, discreet and intelligent.

With these men as his principal officers, amongst whom Peter and Monday was certainly the most active, Vesey began to seduce others at the commencement of the present year. Peter and Monday (and probably the other leaders) kept lists of those who had joined their company or band. As Monday did not join until the business of enlisting had considerably progressed, and proceeded very prudently himself, he had but few on his list, according to his own confession only forty-two; but Peter who had consented as soon as spoken to, and was bold and active in his exertions, had six hundred names on his list; whom he had engaged in Charleston, from that division of the city in which he resided, which was South-Bay. Peter also had in his possession another list of names, or as the witness afterwards explained himself, a memorandum of the whole number engaged, and who amounted as the witness was told to nine thousand, partly from the country and partly from the city. It is true that the witness who made these assertions did not see the lists himself; but he, heard it from one who was in daily communication with Peter, and who was then endeavouring, and succeeded in inducing the witness to join; and as Peter wrote a good hand and was active throughout the whole affair, it is impossible to doubt but that he had such lists; but whether the numbers mentioned were really engaged or not, there is no mode of ascertaining; and it is more than probable that they were greatly exaggerated, and perhaps designedly so. That Peter was engaged in enlisting, was positively proved; but so scrupulously and resolutely to the last did he observe his pledge of secrecy to his associates, *that of the whole number arrested and tried, not one of them belonged to Peter's company.* Monday acknowledged that he had kept a list, but had he not become state's evidence, but had died without disclosing as Peter did, as well might we have doubted that *he kept a list.* In the course of the trials it was also stated, that Vesey had a variety of papers and books relating to this transaction, *which he burnt when the discovery of the intended attempt was made.* Monday also burnt his list, *and probably so did Peter at the same time.*

As these leaders only communicated to each other the numbers, and not the names of those whom they had engaged, and who constituted their company; and as with the exception of Monday, none of them betrayed their associates; the companies of Vesey, Peter, Ned, Rolla and Gullah Jack have escaped detection and punishment; with the exception *of a few of Gullah Jack's band,* who were discovered in consequence of one of his men betraying such of his companions as he knew, together with his leader.

In enlisting men the great caution observed by the leaders was remarkable. Few if any domestic servants were spoken to, as *they* were distrusted; and all who were consulted were told, that death would certainly await them if they informed; and Peter whilst he urged one of his agents to speak to others and solicit them to join, at the same time gave him this charge, "but take care and don't mention it to those waiting men who receive presents of old coats, &c. from their masters, or they'll betray us; *I will speak to them.*" The enlistments appear to have been principally confined to Negroes hired or working out, such as Carters, Draymen, Sawyers, Porters, Labourers, Stevidores, Mechanics, those employed in lumber yards, and in short to those who had certain allotted hours at their own disposal, and to the neighbouring country negroes. When the proposal was made to any one to join, such arguments of threats were made use of as would ensure success, and which the leaders had been cautious to prepare before hand, and suit to the different tempers and dispositions they would have to deal with.

As Vesey, from whom all orders emanated, and perhaps to whom only all important information was conveyed, died without confessing any thing, any opinion formed as to the numbers actually engaged in the plot, must be altogether conjectural; but enough has been disclosed to satisfy every reasonable mind, that considerable numbers were concerned. Indeed the plan of attack, which embraced so many points to be assailed at the same instant, affords sufficient evidence of the fact.

The extent of country around Charleston which was embraced in this attempt, has not been so precisely ascertained as to be traced on a map with as much certainty as a division line between two states; but enough has been discovered, to induce a belief, that it extended to the North of Charleston many miles towards Santee, and unquestionably into St. John's Parish; to the South to James' and John's Islands; and to the West beyond Bacon's Bridge over Ashley River. That all who inhabited this extent of country were engaged in the plot, will not be pretended; it was not necessary or perhaps adviseable [sic]; for at the season of the year in which the attempt was to be made, all the planters and their families are compelled to be absent from their plantations. If therefore a small number on a plantation or in the neighbourhood were engaged in the plot, and acquainted with the precise night and hour of its execution, it would be an easy matter for them in the course of the preceding day, or within a few hours of their taking their own departure, to induce many others whose minds were already poisoned to proceed with them.

Source: Lionel H. Kennedy and Thomas Parker, *An Official Report of the Trials of Sundry Negroes, Charged with an Attempt to Raise an Insurrection in the State of South-Carolina* (Charleston, SC: James R. Schenck, 1822), 1–26.

> *Vesey remained silent as the judge at his trial condemned him, although observers reported that they saw a single tear roll down his face. He was hanged on July 2, 1822, at Blake's Lands, a desolate area outside the city.*

Denmark Vesey—the Court, on mature consideration, have pronounced you GUILTY—You have enjoyed the advantage of able Counsel, and were also heard in your own defense, in which you endeavored, with great art and plausibility, to impress a belief of your innocence. After the most patient deliberation, however, the Court were not only satisfied of your guilt, but that you were the author, and original instigator of this diabolical plot. Your professed design was to trample on all laws, human and divine; to riot in blood, outrage, rapine and conflagration, and to introduce anarchy and confusion in their most horrid forms. Your life has become, therefore, a just and necessary sacrifice, at the shrine of indignant Justice. It is difficult to imagine what *infatuation* could have prompted you to attempt an enterprise so wild and visionary. You were a free man; were comparatively wealthy; and enjoyed every comfort, compatible with your situation. You had, therefore, much to risk, and little to gain. From your age and experience, you *ought* to have known, that success was impracticable.

A moment's reflection must have convinced you, that the ruin of *your* race, would have been the probable result, and that years would have rolled away, before they could have recovered that confidence, which, they once enjoyed in this community. The only reparation in your power, is a full disclosure of the truth. In addition to treason, you have committed the grossest impiety, in attempting to pervert the sacred words of God into a sanction for crimes of the blackest hue. It is evident, that you are totally insensible of the divine influence of that Gospel, "all whose paths are peace." It was to reconcile us to our destinies on earth, and to enable us to discharge with fidelity, all the duties of life, that those holy precepts were imparted by Heaven to fallen man.

If you had searched them with sincerity, you would have discovered instructions, immediately applicable to the deluded victims of your artful wiles—"*Servants (says Saint Paul) obey in all things your masters, according to the flesh, not with eye-service, as men-pleasures, but in singleness of heart, fearing God.*" And again "*Servants (says Saint Peter) be subject to your masters with all fear, not only to the good and gentle, but also to the forward.*"

On such texts comment is unnecessary.

Your "lamp of life" is nearly extinguished, your race is run; and you must shortly pass "from time to eternity." Let me then conjure you to devote the remnant of your existence in solemn preparation for the awful doom that awaits you. Your situation is deplorable, but not destitute of spiritual consolation. To that Almighty Being alone, whose Holy Ordinances, you have trampled in the dust, can you now look for mercy, and although "your sins be as scarlet," the tears of sincere penitence may obtain forgiveness at the "Throne of Grace." You cannot have forgotten the history of the malefactor on the Cross, who, like yourself, was the wretched and deluded victim of offended justice. His conscience was awakened in the pangs of dissolution, and yet there is reason to believe, that his spirit was received into the realms of bliss. May *you* imitate his example, and may *your* last moments prove like his!

Source: Lionel H. Kennedy and Thomas Parker, *An Official Report of the Trials of Sundry Negroes, Charged with an Attempt to Raise an Insurrection in the State of South-Carolina* (Charleston, SC: James R. Schenck, 1822), 177–178.

Nat Turner's Revolt (1831)

The most remarkable document in the literature of slave revolts and conspiracies to revolt is the Confessions of Nat Turner. *Compiled by a Virginia lawyer named Thomas Ruffin Gray from a series of interviews he had with Turner, the pamphlet, published shortly after Turner's execution, sold between 40,000 and 50,000 copies. There is no doubt that the opinions of editor Gray are reflected in the document. But there is also no doubt that some, and perhaps much, of Turner's voice is also captured in it. The* Confessions *is reprinted here in its entirety.*

Agreeable to his own appointment, on the evening he was committed to prison, with permission of the jailer, I visited NAT on Tuesday the 1st November, when, without being questioned at all, commenced his narrative in the following words:

SIR, You have asked me to give a history of the motives which induced me to undertake the late insurrection, as you call it. To do so I must go back to the days of my infancy, and even before I was born. I was thirty-one years of age the 2d of October last, and born the property of Benj [amin] Turner, of this county. In my childhood a circumstance occurred which made an indelible impression on my mind, and laid the ground work of that enthusiasm, which has terminated so fatally to many, both white and black, and for which I am about to atone at the gallows. It is here necessary to relate this circumstance—trifling as it may seem, it was the commencement of that belief which has grown with time, and even now, sir, in this dungeon, helpless and forsaken as I am, I cannot divest myself of. Being at play with other children, when three or four years old, I was telling them something, which my mother overhearing, said it had happened before I was I born—I stuck to my story, however, and related somethings which went, in her opinion, to confirm it—others being called on were greatly astonished, knowing that these things had happened, and caused them to say in my hearing, I surely would be a prophet, as the Lord had shewn me things that had happened before my birth. And my father and mother strengthened me in this my first impression, saying in my presence, I was intended for some great purpose, which they had always thought from certain marks on my head and breast— [a parcel of excrescences which I believe are not at all uncommon, particularly among negroes, as I have seen several with the same. In this case he has either cut them off or they have nearly disappeared]— My grandmother, who was very religious, and to whom I was much attached—my master, who belonged to the church, and other religious persons who visited the house, and whom I often saw at prayers, noticing the singularity of my manners, I suppose, and my uncommon intelligence for a child, remarked I had too much sense to be raised, and if I was, I would never be of any service to any one as a slave—To a mind like mine, restless, inquisitive and observant of everything that was passing, it is easy to suppose that religion was the subject to which it would be directed, and although this subject principally occupied my thoughts— there was nothing that I saw or heard of to which my attention was not directed—The manner in which I learned to read and write, not only had great influence on my own mind, as I acquired it with the most perfect ease, so much so, that I have no recollection whatever of learning the alphabet—but to the astonishment of the family, one day, when a book was shewn me to keep me from crying, I began spelling the names of differ- ent objects—this was a source of wonder to all in the neighborhood, par- ticularly the blacks—and this learning was constantly improved at all opportunities—when I got large enough to go to work, while employed, I was reflecting on many things that would present themselves to my imagination, and whenever an opportunity occurred of looking at a book, when the school children were getting their lessons, I would find many things that the fertility of my own imagination had depicted to me before; all my time, not devoted to my master's service, was spent either in prayer, or in making experiments in casting different things in moulds made of earth, in attempting to make paper, gunpowder, and many other experi- ments, that although I could not perfect, yet convinced me of its practi- cability if I had the means. I was not addicted to stealing in my youth, nor have ever been—Yet such was the confidence of the negroes in the neighborhood, even at this early period of my life, in my superior judgment, that they would often carry me with them when they were going on any roguery, to plan for them. Growing up among them, with this confidence in my superior judgment, and when this, in their opinions, was perfected by Divine inspiration, from the circumstances already alluded to in my infancy, and which belief was ever afterwards zealously inculcated by the austerity of my life and manners, which became the subject of remark by white and black. Having soon discovered to be great, I must appear so, and therefore studiously avoided mixing in society, and wrapped myself in mystery, devoting my time to fasting and prayer—By this time, having arrived to man's estate, and hearing the scriptures commented on at meetings, I was struck with that particular passage which says: "Seek ye the kingdom of Heaven and all things shall be added unto you." I reflected much on this passage, and prayed daily for light on this subject— As I was praying one day at my plough, the spirit spoke to me, saying "Seek ye the kingdom of Heaven and all things shall be added unto you." *Question*—what do you mean by the Spirit. *Ans.* The Spirit that spoke to the prophets in former days—and I was greatly astonished, and for two years prayed continually, whenever my duty would permit—and then again I had the same revelation, which fully confirmed me in the impression that I was ordained for some great purpose in the hands of the Almighty. Several years rolled round, in which many events occurred to strengthen me in this my belief. At this time I reverted in my mind to the remarks made of me in my childhood, and the things that had been shewn me— and as it had been said of me in my childhood by those by whom I had been taught to pray, both white and black, and in whom I had the greatest confidence, that I had too much sense to be raised, and if I was, I would never be of any use to any one as a slave. Now finding I had arrived to man's estate, and was a slave, and these revelations being made known to me, I began to direct my attention to this great object, to fulfil the purpose for which, by this time, I felt assured I was intended. Knowing the influence I had obtained over the minds of my fellow servants, (not by the means of conjuring and such like tricks—for to them I always spoke of such things with contempt) but by the communion of the Spirit whose revelations I often communicated to them, and they believed and said my wisdom came from God. I now began to prepare them for my purpose, by telling them something was about to happen that would terminate in fulfilling the great promise that had been made to me—About this time I was placed under an overseer, from whom I ran away and after remaining in the woods thirty days, I returned, to the astonishment of the negroes on the plantation, who thought I had made my escape to some other part of the country, as my father had done before. But the reason of my return was, that the Spirit appeared to me and said I had my wishes directed to the things of this world, and not to the kingdom of Heaven, and that

I should return to the service of my earthly master—"For he who knoweth his Master's will, and doeth it not, shall be beaten with many stripes, and thus, have I chastened you." And the negroes found fault, and murmured [sic] against me, saying that if they had my sense they would not serve any master in the world. And about this time I had a vision—and I saw white spirits and black spirits engaged in battle, and the sun was darkened—the thunder rolled in the Heavens, and blood flowed in streams—and I heard a voice saying, "Such is your luck, such you are called to see, and let it come rough or smooth, you must surely bare it." I now withdrew myself as much as my situation would permit, from the intercourse of my fellow servants, for the avowed purpose of serving the Spirit more fully—and it appeared to me, and reminded me of the things it had already shown me, and that it would then reveal to me the knowledge of the elements, the revolution of the planets, the operation of tides, and changes of the seasons. After this revelation in the year 1825, and the knowledge of the elements being made known to me, I sought more than ever to obtain true holiness before the great day of judgment should appear, and then I began to receive the true knowledge of faith. And from the first steps of righteousness until the last, was I made perfect; and the Holy Ghost was with me, and said, "Behold me as I stand in the Heavens"—and I looked and saw the forms of men in different attitudes—and there were lights in the sky to which the children of darkness gave other names than what they really were—for they were the lights of the Saviour's hands, stretched forth from east to west, even as they were extended on the cross on Calvary for the redemption of sinners. And I wondered greatly at these miracles, and prayed to be informed of a certainty of the meaning thereof—and shortly afterwards, while laboring in the field, I discovered drops of blood on the corn as though it were dew from heaven—and I communicated it to many, both white and black, in the neighborhood—and I then found on the leaves in the woods hieroglyphic characters, and numbers, with the forms of men in different attitudes, portrayed in blood, and representing the figures I had seen before in the heavens. And now the Holy Ghost had revealed itself to me, and made plain the miracles it had shown me— For as the blood of Christ had been shed on this earth, and had ascended to heaven for the salvation of sinners, and was now returning to earth again in the form of dew—and as the leaves on the trees bore the impression of the figures I had seen in the heavens, it was plain to me that the

Saviour was about to lay down the yoke he had borne for the sins of men, and the great day of judgment was at band. About this time I told these things to a white man, (Etheldred T. Brantley) on whom it had a wonderful effect—and he ceased from his wickedness, and was attacked immediately with a cutaneous eruption, and blood oozed from the pores of his skin, and after praying and fasting nine days, he was healed, and the Spirit appeared to me again, and said, as the Saviour had been baptised so should we be also—and when the white people would not let us be baptised by the church, we went down into the water together, in the sight of many who reviled us, and were baptised by the Spirit—After this I rejoiced greatly, and gave thanks to God. And on the 12th of May, 1828, I heard a loud noise in the heavens, and the Spirit instantly appeared to me and said the Serpent was loosened, and Christ had laid down the yoke he had borne for the sins of men, and that I should take it on and fight against the Serpent, for the time was fast approaching when the first should be last and the last should be first. *Ques.* Do you not find yourself mistaken now? *Ans.* Was not Christ crucified. And by signs in the heavens that it would make known to me when I should commence the great work—and until the first sign appeared, I should conceal it from the knowledge of men—And on the appearance of the sign, (the eclipse of the sun last February) I should arise and prepare myself, and slay my enemies with their own weapons. And immediately on the sign appearing in the heavens, the seal was removed from my lips, and I communicated the great work laid out for me to do, to four in whom I had the greatest confidence, (Henry, Hark, Nelson, and Sam)—It was intended by us to have begun the work of death on the 4th July last—Many were the plans formed and rejected by us, and it affected my mind to such a degree, that I fell sick, and the time passed without our coming to any determination how to commence—Still forming new schemes and rejecting them, when the sign appeared again, which determined me not to wait longer.

Since the commencement of 1830, I had been living with Mr. Joseph Travis, who was to me a kind master, and placed the greatest confidence in me; in fact, I had no cause to complain of his treatment to me. On Saturday evening, the 20th of August, it was agreed between Henry, Hark and myself, to prepare a dinner the next day for the men we expected, and then to concert a plan, as we had not yet determined on any. Hark, on the following morning, brought a pig, and Henry brandy, and being joined by Sam, Nelson, Will and Jack, they prepared in the woods a dinner, where,

about three o'clock, I joined them. Q. Why were you so backward in joining them. A. The same reason that had caused me not to mix with them
for years before.

I saluted them on coming up, and asked Will how came he there, he
answered, his life was worth no more than others, and his liberty as dear
to him. I asked him if he thought to obtain it? He said he would, or lose
his life. This was enough to put him in full confidence. Jack, I knew, was
only a tool in the hands of Hark, it was quickly agreed we should commence at home (Mr. J. Travis') on that night, and until we had armed
and equipped ourselves, and gathered sufficient force, neither age nor sex
was to be spared, (which was invariably adhered to.) We remained at the
feast until about two hours in the night, when we went to the house and
found Austin; they all went to the cider press and drank, except myself.
On returning to the house, Hark went to the door with an axe, for the purpose of breaking it open, as we knew we were strong enough to murder the
family, if they were awaked by the noise; but reflecting that it might create
an alarm in the neighborhood, we determined to enter the house secretly,
and murder them whilst sleeping. Hark got a ladder and set it against the
chimney, on which I ascended, and hoisting a window, entered and came
down stairs, unbarred the door, and removed the guns from their places.
It was then observed that I must spill the first blood. On which, armed
with a hatchet, and accompanied by Will, I entered my master's chamber,
it being dark, I could not give a death blow, the hatchet glanced from his
head, he sprang from the bed and called his wife, it was his last word, Will
laid him dead, with a blow of his axe, and Mrs. Travis shared the same fate,
as she lay in bed. The murder of this family, five in number, was the work
of a moment, not one of them awoke; there was a little infant sleeping in a
cradle, that was forgotten, until we had left the house and gone some distance, when Henry and Will returned and killed it; we got here, four guns
that would shoot, and several old muskets, with a pound or two of powder.
We remained some time at the barn, where we paraded; I formed them in a
line as soldiers, and after carrying them through all the manoeuvres I was
master of, marched them off to Mr. Salathul Francis', about six hundred
yards distant. Sam and Will went to the door and knocked. Mr. Francis
asked who was there, Sam replied, it was him, and he had a letter for
him, on which he got up and came to the door, they immediately seized
him, and dragging him out a little from the door, he was dispatched by

repeated blows on the head; there was no other white person in the family. We started from there for Mrs. Reese's, maintaining the most perfect silence on our march, where finding the door unlocked, we entered, and murdered Mrs. Reese in her bed, while sleeping; her son awoke, but it was only to sleep the sleep of death, he had only time to say who is that, and he was no more. From Mrs. Reese's we went to Mrs. Turner's, a mile distant, which we reached about sunrise, on Monday morning. Henry, Austin, and Sam, went to the still, where, finding Mr. Peebles, Austin shot him, and the rest of us went to the house; as we approached, the family discovered us, and shut the door. Vain hope! Will, with one stroke of his axe, opened it, and we entered and found Mrs. Turner and Mrs. Newsome in the middle of a room, almost frightened to death. Will immediately killed Mrs. Turner, with one blow of his axe. I took Mrs. Newsome by the hand, and with the sword I had when I was apprehended, I struck her several blows over the head, but not being able to kill her, as the sword was dull. Will turning around and discovering it, despatched her also. A general destruction of property and search for money and ammunition, always succeeded the murders. By this time my company amounted to fifteen, and nine men mounted, who started for Mrs. Whitehead's, (the other six were to go through a byway to Mr. Bryant's and rejoin us at Mrs. Whitehead's,) as we approached the house we discovered Mr. Richard Whitehead standing in the cotton patch, near the lane fence; we called him over into the lane, and Will, the executioner, was near at hand, with his fatal axe, to send him to an untimely grave. As we pushed on to the house, I discovered some one run round the garden, and thinking it was some of the white family, I pursued them, but finding it was a servant girl belonging to the house, I returned to commence the work of death, but they whom I left, had not been idle; all the family were already murdered, but Mrs. Whitehead and her daughter Margaret. As I came round to the door I saw Will pulling Mrs. Whitehead out of the house, and at the step he nearly severed her head from her body, with his broad axe. Miss Margaret, when I discovered her, had concealed herself in the corner, formed by the projection of the cellar cap from the house; on my approach she fled, but was soon overtaken, and after repeated blows with a sword, I killed her by a blow on the head, with a fence rail. By this time, the six who had gone by Mr. Bryant's, rejoined us, and informed me they had done the work of death assigned them. We again divided, part going to Mr. Richard Porter's, and from thence to Nathaniel Francis', the others to Mr. Howell Harris', and Mr. T. Doyles. On my reaching Mr. Porter's, he had escaped with his family. I understood there, that the alarm had already spread, and I immediately returned to bring up those sent to Mr. Doyles, and Mr. Howell Harris'; the party I left going on to Mr. Francis', having told them I would join them in that neighborhood. I met these sent to Mr. Doyles' and Mr. Harris' returning, having met Mr. Doyle on the road and killed him; and learning from some who joined them, that Mr. Harris was from home, I immediately pursued the course taken by the party gone on before; but knowing they would complete the work of death and pillage, at Mr. Francis' before I could there, I went to Mr. Peter Edwards', expecting to find them there, but they had been here also. I then went to Mr. John T. Barrow's, they had been here and murdered him. I pursued on their track to Capt. Newit Harris', where I found the greater part mounted, and ready to start; the men now amounting to about forty, shouted and hurraed as I rode up, some were in the yard, loading their guns, others drinking. They said Captain Harris and his family had escaped, the property in the house they destroyed, robbing him of money and other valuables. I ordered them to mount and march instantly, this was about nine or ten o'clock, Monday morning. I proceeded to Mr. Levi Waller's, two or three miles distant. I took my station in the rear, and as it 'twas my object to carry terror and devastation wherever we went, I placed fifteen or twenty of the best armed and most to be relied on, in front, who generally approached the houses as fast as their horses could run; this was for two purposes, to prevent their escape and strike terror to the inhabitants—on this account I never got to the houses, after leaving Mrs. Whitehead's, until the murders were committed, except in one case. I sometimes got in sight in time to see the work of death completed, viewed the mangled bodies as they lay, in silent satisfaction, and immediately started in quest of other victims—Having murdered Mrs. Waller and ten children, we started for Mr. William Williams'—having killed him and two little boys that were there; while engaged in this, Mrs. Williams fled and got some distance from the house, but she was pursued, overtaken, and compelled to get up behind one of the company, who brought her back, and after showing her the mangled body of her lifeless husband, she was told to get down and lay by his side, where she was shot dead. I then started for Mr. Jacob Williams, where the family were murdered—Here we found a young man named Drury, who had come on business with Mr. Williams—he was pursued, overtaken and shot. Mrs. Vaughan was the next place we visited—and after murdering the family here, I determined on starting for Jerusalem—Our number amounted now to fifty or sixty, all mounted and armed with guns, axes, swords and clubs— On reaching Mr. James W. Parkers' gate, immediately on the road leading to Jerusalem, and about three miles distant, it was proposed to me to call there, but I objected, as I knew he was gone to Jerusalem, and my object was to reach there as soon as possible; but some of the men having relations at Mr. Parker's it was agreed that they might call and get his people. I remained at the gate on the road, with seven or eight; the others going across the field to the house, about half a mile off. After waiting some time for them, I became impatient, and started to the house for them, and on our return we were met by a party of white men, who had pursued our blood-stained track, and who had fired on those at the gate, and dispersed them, which I knew nothing of, not having been at that time rejoined by any of them—Immediately on discovering the whites, I ordered my men to halt and form, as they appeared to be alarmed—The white men, eighteen in number, approached us in about one hundred yards, when one of them fired, (this was against the positive orders of Captain Alexander P. Peete, who commanded, and who had directed the men to reserve their fire until within thirty paces) And I discovered about half of them retreating, I then ordered my men to fire and rush on them; the few remaining stood their ground until we approached within fifty yards, when they fired and retreated. We pursued and overtook some of them who we thought we left dead; (they were not killed) after pursuing them about two hundred yards, and rising a little hill, I discovered they were met by another party, and had halted, and were re-loading their guns, (this was a small party from Jerusalem who knew the negroes were in the field, and had just tied their horses to await their return to the road, knowing that Mr. Parker and family were in Jerusalem, but knew nothing of the party that had gone in with Captain Peete; on hearing the firing they immediately rushed to the spot and arrived just in time to arrest the progress of these barbarous villains, and save the lives of their friends and fellow citizens.) Thinking that those who retreated first, and the party who fired on us at fifty or sixty yards distant, had all only fallen back to meet others with ammunition. As I saw them re-loading their guns, and more coming up than I saw at first, and several of my bravest men being wounded, the others became panic struck and squandered over the field;

the white men pursued and fired on us several times. Hark had his horse shot under him, and I caught another for him as it was running by me; five or six of my men were wounded, but none left on the field; finding myself defeated here I instantly determined to go through a private way, and cross the Nottoway river at the Cypress Bridge, three miles below Jerusalem, and attack that place in the rear, as I expected they would look for me on the other road, and I had a great desire to get there to procure arms and ammunition. After going a short distance in this private way, accompanied by about twenty men, I overtook two or three who told me the others were dispersed in every direction. After trying in vain to collect a sufficient force to proceed to Jerusalem, I determined to return, as I was sure they would make back to their old neighborhood, where they would rejoin me, make new recruits, and come down again. On my way back, I called at Mrs. Thomas's, Mrs. Spencer's, and several other places, the white families having fled, we found no more victims to gratify our thirst for blood, we stopped at Majr. Ridley's quarter for the night, and being joined by four of his men, with the recruits made since my defeat, we mustered now about forty strong. After placing out sentinels, I laid down to sleep, but was quickly roused by a great racket; starting up, I found some mounted, and others in great confusion; one of the sentinels having given the alarm that we were about to be attacked, I ordered some to ride round and reconnoitre, and on their return the others being more alarmed, not knowing who they were, fled in different ways, so that I was reduced to about twenty again; with this I determined to attempt to recruit, and proceed on to rally in the neighborhood, I had left. Dr. Blunt's was the nearest house, which we reached just before day; on riding up the yard, Hark fired a gun. We expected Dr. Blunt and his family were at Maj. Ridley's, as I knew there was a company of men there; the gun was fired to ascertain if any of the family were at home; we were immediately fired upon and retreated, leaving several of my men. I do not know what became of them, as I never saw them afterwards. Pursuing our course back and coming in sight of Captain Harris', where we had been the day before, we discovered a party of white men at the house, on which all deserted me but two, (Jacob and Nat,) we concealed ourselves in the woods until near night, when I sent them in search of Henry, Sam, Nelson, and Hark, and directed them to rally all they could, at the place we had had our dinner the Sunday before, where they would find me, and I accordingly returned there as soon as it was dark and remained until Wednesday evening, when discovering white men riding around the place as though they were looking for someone, and none of my men joining me, I concluded Jacob and Nat had been taken, and compelled to betray me. On this I gave up all hope for the present; and on Thursday night after having supplied myself with provisions from Mr. Travis's, I scratched a hole under a pile of fence rails in a field, where I concealed myself for six weeks, never leaving my hiding place but for a few minutes in the dead of night to get water which was very near; thinking by this time I could venture out, I began to go about in the night and eaves drop the houses in the neighborhood; pursuing this course for about a fortnight and gathering little or no intelligence, afraid of speaking to any human being, and returning every morning to my cave before the dawn of day. I know not how long I might have led this life, if accident had not betrayed me, a dog in the neighborhood passing by my hiding place one night while I was out, was attracted by some meat I had in my cave, and crawled in and stole it, and was coming out just as I returned. A few nights after, two negroes having started to go hunting with the same dog, and passed that way, the dog came again to the place, and having just gone out to walk about, discovered me and barked, on which thinking myself discovered, I spoke to them to beg concealment. On making myself known they fled from me. Knowing then they would betray me, I immediately left my hiding place, and was pursued almost incessantly until I was taken a fortnight afterwards by Mr. Benjamin Phipps, in a little hole I had dug out with my sword, for the purpose of concealment, under the top of a fallen tree. On Mr. Phipps' discovering the place of my concealment, he cocked his gun and aimed at me. I requested him not to shoot and I would give up, upon which he demanded my sword. I delivered it to him, and he brought me to prison. During the time I was pursued, I had many hair breadth escapes, which your time will not permit you to relate. I am here loaded with chains, and willing to suffer the fate that awaits me.

I here proceeded to make some inquiries of him after assuring him of the certain death that awaited him, and that concealment would only bring destruction on the innocent as well as guilty, of his own color, if he knew of any extensive or concerted plan. His answer was, I do not. When I questioned him as to the insurrection in North Carolina happening about the same time, he denied any knowledge of it; and when I looked him in the face as though I would search his inmost thoughts, he replied, "I see sir, you doubt my word; but can you not think the same ideas, and strange appearances about this time in the heaven's might prompt others, as well as myself, to this undertaking." I now had much conversation with and asked him many questions, having forborne to do so previously, except in the cases noted in parenthesis; but during his statement, I had, unnoticed by him, taken notes as to some particular circumstances, and having the advantage of his statement before me in writing, on the evening of the third day that I had been with him, I began a cross examination, and found his statement corroborated by every circumstance coming within my own knowledge or the confessions of others whom had been either killed or executed, and whom he had not seen nor had any knowledge since 22d of August last, he expressed himself fully satisfied as to the impracticability of his attempt. It has been said he was ignorant and cowardly, and that his object was to murder and rob for the purpose of obtaining money to make his escape. It is notorious, that he was never known to have a dollar in his life; to swear an oath, or drink a drop of spirits. As to his ignorance, he certainly never had the advantages of education, but he can read and write, (it was taught him by his parents,) and for natural intelligence and quickness of apprehension, is surpassed by few men I have ever seen. As to his being a coward, his reason as given for not resisting Mr. Phipps, shews the decision of his character. When he saw Mr. Phipps present his gun, he said he knew it was impossible for him to escape as the woods were full of men; he therefore thought it was better to surrender, and trust to fortune for his escape. He is a complete fanatic, or plays his part most admirably. On other subjects he possesses an uncommon share of intelligence, with a mind capable of attaining anything; but warped and perverted by the influence of early impressions. He is below the ordinary stature, though strong and active, having the true negro face, every feature of which is strongly marked. I shall not attempt to describe the effect of his narrative, as told and commented on by himself, in the condemned hole of the prison. The calm, deliberate composure with which he spoke of his late deeds and intentions, the expression of his fiend-like face when excited by enthusiasm, still bearing the stains of the blood of helpless innocence about him; clothed with rags and covered with chains; yet daring to raise his manacled hands to heaven, with a spirit soaring above the attributes of man; I looked on him and my blood curdled in my veins.

I will not shock the feelings of humanity, nor wound afresh the bosoms of the disconsolate sufferers in this unparalleled and inhuman massacre, by detailing the deeds of their fiend-like barbarity. There were two or three who were in the power of these wretches, had they known it, and who escaped in the most providential manner. There were two whom they thought they left dead on the field at Mr. Parker's, but who were only stunned by the blows of their guns, as they did not take time to re-load when they charged on them. The escape of a little girl who went to school at Mr. Waller's, and where the children were collecting for that purpose excited general sympathy. As their teacher had not arrived, they were at play in the yard, and seeing the negroes approach, ran up on a dirt chimney (such as are common to log houses,) and remained there unnoticed during the massacre of the eleven that were killed at this place. She remained on her hiding place till just before the arrival of a party, who were in pursuit of the murderers, when she came down and fled to a swamp, where, a mere child as she was, with the horrors of the late scene before her, she lay concealed until the next day, when seeing a party go up to the house, she came up, and on being asked how she escaped, replied with the utmost simplicity, "The Lord helped her." She was taken up behind a gentleman of the party, and returned to the arms of her weeping mother Miss Whitehead concealed herself between the bed and the mat that supported it, while they murdered her sister in the same room, without discovering her. She was afterwards carried off, and concealed for protection by a slave of the family, who gave evidence against several of them on their trial. Mrs. Nathaniel Francis, while concealed in a closet heard their blows, and the shrieks of the victims of these ruthless savages; they then entered the closet where she was concealed, and went out without discovering her. While in this hiding place, she heard two of her women in a quarrel about the division of her clothes. Mr. John T. Baron, discovering them approaching his house, told his wife to make her escape, and scorning to fly, fell fighting on his own threshold. After firing his rifle, he discharged his gun at them, and then broke it over the villain who first approached him, but he was overpowered, and slain. His bravery, however, saved from the hands of these monsters, his lovely and amiable wife, who will long lament a husband so deserving of her love. As directed by him, she attempted to escape through the garden, when she was caught and held by one of her servant girls, but another coming to her rescue, she fled to the woods, and concealed herself. Few indeed, were those who escaped their work of death. But fortunate for society, the hand of retributive justice has overtaken them; and not one that was known to be concerned has escaped.

Source: The Confessions of Nat Turner, the Leader of the Late Insurrection in Southampton, Virginia, as fully and voluntarily made to Thomas R. Gray (Baltimore: Lucas & Deaver, printers, 1831), 7–20.

In this stirring editorial that appeared in his The Liberator, *longtime abolitionist William Lloyd Garrison both predicts that the Turner uprising is the beginning of the end of slavery and insists that there was no causal link between the violence of the insurrection and Garrison's own advocacy of emancipation. The real cause, Garrison argues, is the brutal way in which slaves are treated.*

What we have so long predicted—at the peril of being stigmatized as an alarmist and declaimer—has commenced its fulfilment. The first oppression, leaving not one stone upon another, has been made. The first drops of blood, which are but the prelude to a deluge from the gathering clouds, have fallen. The first flash of the lightning, which is to smite and consume, has been felt. The first wailings of a bereavement, which is to clothe the earth in sackcloth, have broken upon our ears . . .

You have seen, it is to be feared, but the beginning of sorrows. All the blood which has been shed will be required at your hands. At your hands alone? No—but at the hands of the people of New-England and of all the free states. The crime of oppression is national. The south is only the agent in this guilty traffic . . .

Ye accuse the pacific friends of emancipation of instigating the slaves to revolt. Take back the charge as a foul slander. The slaves need no incentives at our hands. They will find them in their stripes—in their emaciated bodies—in their ceaseless toil—in their ignorant minds—in every field, in every valley, on every hilltop and mountain, wherever you and your fathers have fought for liberty—in your speeches, your conversations, your celebrations, your pamphlets, your newspapers—voices in the air, sounds from across the ocean, invitations to resistance above, below, around them! What more do they need? Surrounded by such influences, and smarting under their newly made wounds, is it wonderful [that is, surprising] that they should rise to contend—as other "heroes" have contended—for their lost rights? It is *not* wonderful . . .

For ourselves, we are horror-struck at the late tidings. We have exerted our utmost efforts to avert the calamity. We have warned our countrymen of the danger of persisting in their unrighteous conduct. We have preached to the slaves the pacific precepts of Jesus Christ. We have appealed to Christians, philanthropists and patriots, for their assistance to accomplish the great work of national redemption through the agency of moral power—of public opinion—of individual duty. How have we been received? We have been threatened, proscribed, vilified and imprisoned—a laughing-stock and a reproach. Do we falter, in view of these things? Let time answer. If we have been hitherto urgent, and bold, and denunciatory in our efforts—hereafter we shall grow vehement and active with the increase of danger. We shall cry, in trumpet tones, night and day, Woe to this guilty land, unless she speedily repent of her evil doings! The blood of millions of her sons cries aloud for redress! IMMEDIATE EMANCIPATION can alone save her from the vengeance of Heaven, and cancel the debt of ages!

Source: The Liberator, September 3, 1831.

The Cheneyville Conspiracy (1837)

Solomon Northup, whose memoir Twelve Years a Slave *famously chronicled his life as a Louisiana slave, recalls hearing about the Cheneyville conspiracy while he was in captivity, and meeting its chief planner and traitor, Lew Cheney.*

The year before my arrival in the country there was a concerted movement among a number of slaves on Bayou Boeuf, that terminated tragically indeed. It was, I presume, a matter of newspaper notoriety at the time, but all the knowledge I have of it, has been derived from the relation of those living at that period in the immediate vicinity of the excitement. It has become a subject of general and unfailing interest in every slave-hut on the bayou, and will doubtless go down to succeeding generations as their chief tradition. Lew Cheney, with whom I became acquainted—a shrewd, cunning negro, more intelligent than the generality of his race, but unscrupulous and full of treachery—conceived the project of organizing a company sufficiently strong to fight their way against all opposition, to the neighboring territory of Mexico.

A remote spot, far within the depths of the swamp back of Hawkins' plantation, was selected as the rallying point. Lew flitted from one plantation to another, in the dead of night, preaching a crusade to Mexico, and like, Peter the hermit, creating a furor of excitement wherever he appeared. At length a large number of runaways were assembled; stolen mules, and corn gathered from the fields, and bacon filched from smokehouses, had been conveyed into the woods. The expedition was about ready to proceed, when their hiding place was discovered. Lew Cheney, becoming convinced of the ultimate failure of his project, in order to curry favor with his master, and avoid the consequences which he foresaw would follow, deliberately determined to sacrifice all his companions. Departing secretly from the encampment, he proclaimed among the planters the number collected in the swamp, and, instead of stating truly the object they had in view, asserted their intention was to emerge from their seclusion the first favorable opportunity, and murder every white person along the bayou.

Such an announcement, exaggerated as it passed from mouth to mouth, filled the whole country with terror. The fugitives were surrounded and taken prisoners, carried in chains to Alexandria, and hung by the populace. Not only those, but many who were suspected, though entirely innocent, were taken from the field and from the cabin, and without the shadow of process or form of trial, hurried to the scaffold. The planters on Bayou Boeuf finally rebelled against such reckless destruction of property, but it was not until a regiment of soldiers had arrived from some fort on the Texas frontier, demolished the gallows, and opened the doors of the Alexandria prison, that the indiscriminate slaughter was stayed. Lew Cheney escaped, and was even rewarded for his treachery. He is still living, but his name is despised and execrated by all his race throughout the parishes of Rapides and Avoyelles.

Source: Solomon Northup, *Twelve Years a Slave* (New York: Miller, Orton, & Mulligan, 1855), 246–248.

The *Creole* Revolt (1841)

News of the rebellion aboard the Creole was greeted with anger and alarm by the South. This article, which first appeared in the New Orleans Bee, furiously castigates the British for offering the ships slave cargo safe harbor and freedom.

MUTINY AND MURDER

The Brig Creole, Captain Ensor, of Richmond, bound for New Orleans with a cargo of tobacco, one hundred and thirty-five slaves and four or five passengers, was on the 7th ult. taken possession of by the slaves who rose and mutinied—killing and wounding several white persons. it appears that on the 7th ult., at 8 p.m., the brig was hove to in the belief that she was approaching Abaco. The next day after the passengers and crew not on duty had retired, at about half past 9 o'clock p.m. the slaves mutinied and murdered a passenger named Hewell, owner of a portion of the slaves, by stabbing him with a bowie knife. They wounded the captain and one of the hands dangerously, the chief mate and another of the hands severely. But little defense could be made, as the victims were totally unprepared for an attack ... There is reason to believe that the whole plot was arranged before they left Richmond ...

Forced to obey, the crew set sale and arrived at Nassau on the 9th ult. on arriving, the American Consul had the Captain and two of the men immediately taken on shore & their wounds dressed, while every attention was paid to the wounded on board ... Nineteen slaves were identified as having participated in the mutiny and murder. They were placed in confinement until further orders, the Governor refusing to have them sent to America under the circumstances. The remainder were liberated by her Majesty's authorities, on the ground that the slaves must be considered and treated as passengers, having the right to land in boats from the shore whenever they thought proper.

The refusal of the British authorities to deliver the wretches implicated in this atrocious attack, to the jurisdiction of the country in which they are held as slaves, adds another item to the black catalogue of outrages upon American rights, committed by the English government. It will, we trust, form an important feature in the deliberations of Congress on the subject of the grievances which American property and American citizens have suffered through the arrogance and despotism of the minions of the British crown. The trite adage that there is a point beyond which forbearance ceased to become a virtue, was never more applicable than to the tame and spiritless manner in which our diplomatic intercourses with Great Britain, in regard to her haughty assumptions of power over the flag and property of this confederacy has been conducted. Better a dozen wars with all their attendant horrors, than the everlasting reproach of pusillanimously submitting to encroachment and tyranny which become more odious and exacting in proportion to the humility with which they are endured.

Source: Woodville Republican, December 11, 1841.

The Second Creek Conspiracy (1861)

No public records of the failed slave conspiracy at Second Creek, Mississippi, were ever made. The following letter from John McFarland, a New Orleans business-man, captures some of the horrific details of its aftermath. McFarland repeats information given to him by a friend, one Dr. Smith, who had just returned from Natchez, Mississippi, and witnessed executions.

[Dr. Smith] relates that three days ago he saw with his own eyes at the race track near [Natchez]. Eight Negroes swung off one plank and hung, and two whipped to death dying under the lash. Twenty others were hung two weeks or so ago. The people thought they were going to "rise" to murder the whites and get their mistresses for wives. Took up negroes as usual and extorted confessions by whipping, resulting in the above tragedy. The negroes implicated and hung were carriage drivers, fancy boys—confidential servants &c—no field hands, contented with their lot, at all . . .

All testimony was extracted from the negroes by whipping. There may possibly have been some grounds for this, but not to the extent of the punishment and I think all resulted from allowing these fancy slaves too much liberty and making pets of them. A negro is a curious being—he will not allow you to treat him as you would desire to do and his happiest condition is when he lives under strictly enforced laws and kept busy.

Source: "John McFarland to 'My Dear Sir,'" October 25, 1861, in Lizzie McFarland Blackmore Collection, Box 1, Folder 11, Letterbook, 235–238, Mississippi Department of Archives and History. Reprinted in Winthrop D. Jordan, *Tumult and Silence at Second Creek: An Inquiry into a Civil War Slave Conspiracy*, rev. ed. (Baton Rouge: Louisiana State University Press, 1995), 341.

ANALYTICAL ESSAYS

PERSPECTIVES: THE STONO REVOLT

The Stono revolt, the largest one in the North American colonies, broke out on a Sunday in early September 1739. Named after the place where it began, a warehouse next to South Carolina's Stono River, the insurrection was led by an African-born slave with military experience whom the surviving records refer to as "Jemmy" or "Cato." The rebels headed south, bound for Spanish Florida, where authorities had promised freedom to any slave in the British colonies who managed to cross the border. Along the way, Cato and his followers, eventually numbering between 60 and 100 men, burned plantation homes, killed whites, and picked up new recruits.

By sheer coincidence, South Carolina's acting governor, William Bull, nearly ran into the slave army as he was returning to Charles Town (Charleston) after presiding at a trial. He dispatched a warning to the local militia that the slaves, chanting what some future commentators believe were African war songs, were on the move. The militia caught up with them by the Edisto River. Volleys were fired from both sides before the slaves were scattered. Many of them were killed as soon as they were cornered, and some appear to have been tortured before they died. Following the rebellion, the South Carolina General Assembly passed a Comprehensive Negro Act (May 1740), which mandated severe limitations on the movement of slaves.

The conventional interpretation of the Stono uprising is that it was the result of a conspiracy masterminded by Cato and other warriors from the Angola and Konga regions of Africa who, defeated in battle with other African tribes, had been captured and sold to white slavers. Proud and intensely independent, the African-born slaves resolved to fight their way to Spanish Florida, killing whites, collecting weapons, and adding to their ranks along the way. The first stage of the revolt began when about 20 of the conspirators gathered at the Stono River Bridge store to steal weapons. They discovered two white men in the warehouse and murdered them before absconding with as many guns as the store held. The fact that the slaves were heard chanting war songs when confronted later in the day by the militiamen, as well as the brief gun battle that ensued, further suggests that they were rebelling. This interpretation is shared by most historians who write about the Stono revolt.[1]

But there is an alternative interpretation of what happened on that Sunday night in 1739, defended recently by historian Peter Charles Hoffer. Hoffer does not dispute the conventional account of the events that transpired after the band of slaves left the warehouse, but he does offer a different explanation of how the revolt started. According to him, the genesis of the insurrection was a simple burglary that went bad.

In the marshy Low Country where the Stono rebellion occurred, local whites were required by law to maintain the drainage ditches dug on either side of major roadways, and slaves were predictably given the wearisome task. But this meant that the public work had to be done on Sundays, the only day of the week that many slaves could call their own. Hoffer suggests that slaves deeply resented this extra work and that the ones who had been selected to do it on the weekend of the insurrection angrily broke into the warehouse not to steal weapons so much as to reward themselves with food and liquor.

Once at the warehouse, however, they were startled to discover the two white men who, perhaps, were sleeping off a drinking bout of their own. The slaves killed the two men either spontaneously out of surprised panic or with the calculated recognition of the punishment that awaited them if their burglary came to light. But with the two murders, the slaves sealed their legal doom; blacks who murdered whites were guaranteed a short trial and speedy execution. So, figuring that they now had nothing to lose, the slaves determined to fight their way to Florida and freedom. What began as a break-in quickly became an insurrection. As Hoffer puts it,

> The trigger for the escalating violence of that night was not an ideology of freedom ... The work crew's plan—to break into a store and obtain what they thought was their due for a hard day's labor—would evolve as the night wore on into something most of them had not planned. Efforts to

escape the scene of accidental mayhem [the store] would lead to more mayhem. The uproar, abetted by some slaves' efforts to gain aid from neighboring plantation slaves, would recruit a body of men who had not been part of the work crew, and these men's motives would differ from the diggers.[2]

Hoffer believes that this explanation of the Stono revolt is preferable to the conventional one because had the insurrection been the culmination of a conspiracy, word would almost certainly have leaked out, as in so many other cases of slave conspiracy. But of course this is speculation on his part. At least one other conspiracy, Nat Turner's 1831 one, escaped betrayal by fellow slaves or discovery by whites.

Given the fact that the insurrectionists were shot on sight rather than tried, there are no transcripts or written records of confessions to lend support either to Hoffer's revisionist account of the Stono uprising or to the conventional one. Both are plausible possibilities that must remain open given the absence of further documentation. Even oral tradition about the revolt passed on from one generation to the next is silent on the motives of Cato and his men. In the 1830s, one of Cato's descendants, George Cato, was interviewed. When asked about the causes for the rebellion, he responded: "How it all start? Dat what I ask but nobody ever tell me how 100 slaves between de Combahee and Edisto rivers come to meet in de woods not far from de Stono River on September 9, 1739."[3]

Notes

1. See, for example, the four contemporary essays on the Stono rebellion collected in Mark M. Smith (ed.), *Stono: Documenting and Interpreting a Southern Slave Revolt* (Columbia: University of South Carolina Press, 2005), 59–123.

2. Peter Charles Hoffer, *Cry Liberty: The Great Stono River Slave Rebellion of 1739* (New York: Oxford University Press, 2012), 76.

3. " 'As it come down to me': Black Memories of Stono in the 1930s," in Mark M. Smith (ed.), *Stono*, 56.

COUNTERFACTUAL ESSAY: GABRIEL PROSSER'S REVOLT

Richmond, August 30, 1800. Gabriel Prosser, a hired-out slave, was poised to lead a rebellion against servitude by taking Richmond, the capital of Virginia. He had plotted the insurrection for weeks, enlisting slaves from both his own Henrico County as well as adjacent ones. Prosser's plan of attack was three pronged. One column of slaves would set fire to factories down by the James River as a distraction; while attention was focused on the fire, a second column would march to the city's penitentiary, where Governor James Monroe had stored gunpowder; simultaneously, a third column, led by Prosser himself, would take the capitol building and seize its arsenal of weapons.

Inspired by the recent French Revolution and the successful slave revolt in Saint Dominque (Haiti), Prosser intended to march under a flag inscribed "Death or Liberty!" He instructed his fellow rebels to spare Quakers and French men and women they may encounter, the first because they opposed slavery, the second because they were representatives of a republic that, at least in Prosser's mind, took its endorsement of liberty, equality, and fraternity seriously. But slave owners, especially harsh ones, were open game. Prosser, in fact, intended to kill his own master.

It is not at all clear what Prosser's ultimate goal was; he seems to have thought no further than imagining himself dining with white merchants the evening of a successful insurrection. Perhaps he intended to establish a free republic in Richmond, or perhaps he dreamt of leading his band of rebels to Saint Dominique. But regardless of specific goals, he and those who followed him were determined to be free.

Then, on the very night that Prosser intended to lead his men to Richmond, fate intervened. A colossal rain storm hit Richmond and its outlying areas, quickly causing swamps and creeks to flood and preventing access to the capital city. Soaking and frustrated, Prosser and the few fellow rebels who had managed to make it to the gathering place returned to their plantations. Prosser began planning another march on Richmond, but before he could launch it, a slave by the name of Pharaoh informed on him. An alarmed James Monroe, governor of Virginia, immediately called up over 600 state militiamen. In the space of a month, Prosser and his lieutenants were rounded up, quickly tried, and executed.

But what if the downpour had not occurred? What if the full company of men from Henrico, Caroline, and Hanover had made it to the rallying spot, located not far from the land of the planter who owned Prosser, and had actually marched on Richmond? Could they have taken the city?

In the year that Prosser intended to take Richmond, the city's black population was double that of whites. Many of Richmond's slaves were in the city because they had been hired out by their planter masters, and they had acquired a taste for freedom. One-third of Richmond's blacks were free and doubtlessly anxious to remain so. It is thus entirely plausible that if Prosser had managed to get his men to the city, they would have been joined by a sizeable percentage of Richmond's blacks.

Even with only makeshift weapons, Prosser's men, provided the fiery diversion down at the docks sent white men scurrying to contain the blaze, clearly outnumbered the handful of guards at the powder magazine. Prosser also hoped that the black doorkeeper at the capitol building would give his third column easy access to the arsenal stored there. With firearms in their hands (although it is likely that many of the slaves had never held a gun in their lives and would not have known how to reload), Prosser's rebels might have succeeded in terrorizing Richmond's citizens and, more importantly, capturing no less a prisoner than James Monroe.

If the slaves had taken the city, could they have held it? For a while, at any rate. If the second and third columns were successful, the slaves would have had weapons enough to spare and leading citizens of the city would have been either killed or imprisoned. Moreover, given that the international slave trade would not be outlawed for another eight years, it is likely that some of Prosser's rebels were African warriors, kidnapped by tribal enemies and sold into captivity. If so, they would have been trained in the art of war and could have given the rest of Prosser's men a quick tutelage in how to fight.

It is also the case that even with the governor in jail, the state militia would have mustered to put down the rebellion. Doubtlessly white civilians, infuriated at the presumption of Prosser and his men, would have joined the fight. In all likelihood, the city would have eventually been recaptured, but perhaps only at great cost to both white residents and militia. Prosser and his men would have set up blockades at strategic road points, and knowing that they had everything to lose if the city was recaptured, they would have probably fought furiously, especially if guided by African warriors.

Had Prosser managed to capture Richmond, even if he lost it after a few weeks or months, the entire nation would have been galvanized by alarm. Slave revolts and conspiracies to revolt had never succeeded up to 1800, and little white blood had yet been shed in them. But taking a capital city would have sent shock waves through both South and North, and could have fundamentally changed the way Southerners regarded their slaves. Most slave owners were convinced that their own slaves were peaceful, grateful servants, even if those same owners looked upon slaves belonging to others as unpredictable savages. Seizing Richmond would have badly shaken white trust and confidence in the peculiar institution—so much so that the Virginia Assembly might have debated, as it did after Nat Turner's 1831 revolt, the wisdom of hanging on to slavery.

Moreover, the capture of a state governor would have likewise rocked the nation. No white man had ever been kidnapped in a slave revolt, although a few had been killed, and especially not a high-ranking official. Would Prosser and his army have used Monroe as a bargaining chip? Would they have demanded safe passage to Saint Domonique in return for the governor? Or would they, once surrounded by militiamen, have murdered Monroe, thereby changing the course of the American presidency in the early Republic? Of course, we can only speculate. But what we can be reasonably confident in saying is that if Gabriel Prosser had succeeded in achieving what he set out to do, Southerners would have forever after looked differently at slaves. No longer could they have thought of blacks as inferior in will, intelligence, or strength.

TURNING POINT: NAT TURNER'S REVOLT

We do not know, and probably will never know, just how many slave revolts and conspiracies took place in the colonial and antebellum periods. Chances are good that many of them went undocumented, either because the slaves involved were quickly killed without benefit of trial or because slave owners were reluctant to publicize such discontent for fear that it would inspire other slaves to insurrect.

But it can safely be said that every one of the conspiracies and revolts we do know about, including the ones explored in this book, were "turning points" in at least two ways. First, they raised the collective anxiety level among whites in slaveholding cultures. There was a tendency on the part of whites who owned slaves to hold ambivalent attitudes about human bondage. One was that slaves in general were untrustworthy, savage, and unpredictable; hence, the anxiety. But this evaluation applied mainly to the slaves owned by others. The other conviction was that the slaves they owned themselves were gentle, docile, and loyal, a defense mechanism against the chronic anxiety. Yet with every new conspiracy or revolt that came to light, more slaveholders were shown that even their own slaves were capable of disloyalty.

The second "turning point" that followed nearly every revolt or conspiracy was a tightening up of colonial or state laws that controlled the behavior of blacks. Restrictions on their freedom of movement and assembly; prohibitions on teaching slaves to read, write, or worship without the presence of whites; and ever-stiffer penalties for behavior that whites deemed unacceptable were the price paid for rebellion.

Having said this, however, it is also the case that one slave uprising stands out from the rest: the one launched in 1831 by Nat Turner. It especially horrified Southerners as well as many Northerners. It led to the predictable tightening of slave laws, but also to an unprecedented legislative debate about ending slavery. Moreover, Turner's revolt strengthened the Southern conviction that Northern abolitionists were inciting slaves to revolt. Finally, the South's public defense of slavery changed tones.

Nat Turner's rebellion, which occurred in Southampton County, Virginia, was launched by a 30-year-old slave who had the reputation of being a religious visionary. Literate and clearly intelligent, Nat believed that he was called by God to avenge generations of slaves. He launched his crusade on the night of August 22, 1831. He and his followers eventually killed some 60 white men, women, and children before being routed by state militia. Turner escaped and hid for two months before being apprehended. He was tried and hanged in quick order. It is estimated that some 100 slaves lost their lives, either by trial or by vigilantes, in the wake of the rebellion.

One reason the Turner rebellion so raised the anxiety level of white Southerners who already had a state-of-siege mentality is that it was widely publicized with graphic descriptions of the murders. A down-on-his-luck attorney by the name of Thomas Ruffin Gray saw a money-making opportunity in interviewing Turner and publishing the slave's remarks in a pamphlet. Upward of 50,000 copies in multiple editions were sold of Turner's *Confessions*, snapped up by fascinated but horrified Southerners and Northerners alike.

Following the insurrection, Virginia followed the custom of tightening its slave laws to impose new restrictions on slaves and free blacks. Slaves were prohibited from preaching, an obvious backlash against Turner's religious charisma and from purchasing liquor—many of Turner's fellow rebels, although not himself, fortified themselves during their killing spree with alcohol. Free blacks were forbidden to learn reading or writing, to serve on juries, and from practicing certain trades. Additionally, a State Colonization Society was organized to investigate the feasibility of deporting free blacks, by force if necessary, either to other states or to a foreign destination such as Liberia. In the wake of the Turner insurrection, other slaveholding states likewise passed new restrictions on the behavior of slaves.

But in Virginia, the Turner rebellion also prompted a candid discussion about ending slavery, born not so much out of concern for the welfare of slaves as the desire to remove the source of chronic white anxiety. Just two months after Nat Turner's execution, the Virginia House of Delegates met to consider emancipating slaves. No less a figure than one of Thomas Jefferson's grandchildren was in favor of doing so, as were many delegates from the mountainous western regions of Virginia, where slavery was minimal. But Virginian legislators eventually voted down all the emancipatory bills, and slavery endured.

A further consequence of Nat Turner's revolt that constitutes a major turning point was the overt accusation of Virginian notables that "outside agitators" from the North were responsible for the insurrection. Virginia governor John Floyd explicitly accused Northern abolitionists of stirring up slaves with incendiary rhetoric about the evils of slavery. He insisted that white clergy and laypersons had preached freedom to slaves who, because they were less intelligent than whites and easily influenced, were inspired to acts of rebellion that were doomed to fail. It is likely that Floyd was referring in part to the antislavery crusade of William Lloyd Garrison's *The Liberator*, which began publication just months before the insurrection.

Finally, in keeping with the general Southern attitude that slaves were inferior humans, and as a response to Northern antislavery charges that slaves were mistreated by their masters, a new Southern justification for slavery began to emerge. Prior to the Turner revolt, many Southerners had openly acknowledged that human bondage was an evil, but defended it, albeit often reluctantly, as an economic necessity for the South. After the revolt, defenses of slavery shifted to a paternalistic insistence that slavery was in fact a benevolent institution because blacks, if free, would be unable to look after themselves. This new narrative painted white masters as generous father-figures who fed, clothed, and sheltered child-like slaves. It is difficult to ascertain if Southern slaveholders actually believed this new justification of slavery, but it remained the prevalent defense right up to the Civil War.

PRIMARY DOCUMENT ESSAY: THE CONDEMNATION OF DENMARK VESEY
The Vesey Conspiracy

Vesey remained silent as the judge at his trial condemned him, although observers reported that they saw a single tear roll down his face. He was hanged on July 2, 1822, at Blake's Lands, a desolate area outside the city.

Denmark Vesey—the Court, on mature consideration, have pronounced you GUILTY—You have enjoyed the advantage of able Counsel, and were also heard in your own defense, in which you endeavored, with great art and plausibility, to impress a belief of your innocence. After the most patient deliberation, however, the Court were not only satisfied of your guilt, but that you were the author, and original instigator of this diabolical plot. Your professed design was to trample on all laws, human and divine; to riot in blood, outrage, rapine and conflagration, and to introduce anarchy and confusion in their most horrid forms. Your life has become, therefore, a just and necessary sacrifice, at the shrine of indignant Justice. It is difficult to imagine what *infatuation* could have prompted you to attempt an enterprise so wild and visionary. You were a free man; were comparatively wealthy; and enjoyed every comfort, compatible with your situation. You had, therefore, much to risk, and little to gain. From your age and experience, you *ought* to have known, that success was impracticable.

A moment's reflection must have convinced you, that the ruin of *your* race, would have been the probable result, and that years would have rolled away, before they could have recovered that confidence, which, they once enjoyed in this community. The only reparation in your power, is a full disclosure of the truth. In addition to treason, you have committed the grossest impiety, in attempting to pervert the sacred words of God into a sanction for crimes of the blackest hue. It is evident, that you are totally insensible of the divine influence of that Gospel, "all whose paths are peace." It was to reconcile us to our destinies on earth, and to enable us to discharge with fidelity, all the duties of life, that those holy precepts were imparted by Heaven to fallen man.

If you had searched them with sincerity, you would have discovered instructions, immediately applicable to the deluded victims of your artful wiles—"*Servants (says Saint Paul) obey in all things your masters, according to the flesh, not with eye-service, as men-pleasures, but in singleness of heart, fearing God.*" And again "*Servants (says Saint Peter) be subject to your masters with all fear, not only to the good and gentle, but also to the forward.*"

On such texts comment is unnecessary.

Your "lamp of life" is nearly extinguished, your race is run; and you must shortly pass "from time to eternity." Let me then conjure you to devote the remnant of your existence in solemn preparation for the awful doom that awaits you. Your situation is deplorable, but not destitute of spiritual consolation. To that Almighty Being alone, whose Holy Ordinances, you have trampled in the dust, can you now look for mercy, and although "your sins be as scarlet," the tears of sincere penitence may obtain forgiveness at the "Throne of Grace." You cannot have forgotten the history of the malefactor on the Cross, who, like yourself, was the wretched and deluded victim of offended justice. His conscience was awakened in the pangs of dissolution, and yet there is reason to believe, that his spirit was received into the realms of bliss. May *you* imitate his example, and may *your* last moments prove like his!

Source: Kennedy, Lionel H. and Thomas Parker, *An Official Report of the Trials of Sundry Negroes, Charged with an Attempt to Raise an Insurrection in the State of South-Carolina* (Charleston, SC: James R. Schenck, 1822), 177–178.

Denmark Vesey was a freedman who plotted a slave insurrection in which he intended his followers to take Charleston, South Carolina; kill as many whites as possible; and set sail for the republic of Saint Dominique. The plan was discovered, and Denmark, along with over 30 others, was captured, tried, and sentenced to death. Several dozen more slaves were either deported or released.

Denmark spent the first 32 years of his life as a slave. He belonged to a slave ship captain named Vesey, who retired and settled down in Charleston. Denmark was a skilled carpenter who was frequently hired out by his master to other whites who needed his services. They paid the captain Denmark's wages, who then allowed Denmark to keep a small portion for himself.

In 1799, Denmark used some of his wages to buy a winning lottery ticket. He immediately purchased his freedom and used the rest of the prize to set up a successful carpentry business. He appears to have had several children from a number of wives. But the wives were all slaves, and so were his children, a fact that increasingly frustrated him. As he would later say, his desire for his children to be free was a prime motive for the insurrection he planned.

In 1818, Vesey cofounded a parish of the African Methodist Episcopal (AME) church in Charleston. Although the all-black parish was watched carefully by authorities, who distrusted gatherings of free or enslaved blacks, and despite a few raids and imprisonments, including that of the church's minister, Denmark was able to hold night discussion groups in which he taught that the biblical account of Moses leading the Hebrews into freedom was a prophetic sign that slavery was displeasing to God.

In both the church meetings and private conversation, Denmark planned the insurrection over a period of two years, beginning in 1820. He and his lieutenants carefully selected the slaves with whom they shared the plan, always warning them to keep silent about the plot on pain of death. Denmark set the date of the insurrection for July 14, probably, given his admiration for the slave rebellion in Saint Dominique, to coincide with Bastille Day. But before the date arrived, the plan was leaked by a couple of slaves who had been invited to join, and after a few days of hesitation, the white authorities finally took the possibility of an insurrection seriously. Arrests followed, although Denmark was not one of the first to be captured and jailed. His trial, in which he was allowed to represent himself and even to question witnesses, was held in late June. But his conviction was a forgone conclusion, and he was hanged on July 2. Vesey apparently remained silent as the sentence of death was pronounced at the end of his trial, although reporters reported that they saw a single tear roll down his cheek.

The words of the judge who sentenced Vesey to death offer a revealing glimpse into the presuppositions of white officials—and others—in the antebellum South when it came to slavery.

In the first place, the judge was obviously surprised that Denmark had performed well as his own counsel, and he rather begrudgingly complimented the defendant for endeavoring, "with great art and plausibility, to impress a belief of your innocence." Although Denmark was clearly a literate and intelligent man, his judge was amazed that a freed slave would be capable of rationally defending himself.

In the second place, the document reveals just how horrified the judge and, indeed, all of white Charleston were at the possibility of an insurrection. In purple prose, the judge referred to it as a "diabolical plot" that intended to "trample on all laws, human and divine; to riot in blood, outrage, rapine, and conflagration, and to introduce anarchy and confusion in their most horrid forms."

The judge went on to express genuine surprise that a free slave, who was "comparatively wealthy," would have risked all on an "infatuation" of insurrection. Surely, the judge chided, Denmark must have known that "success was impracticable." It is not clear if the judge knew the defendant's reasons for plotting a rebellion, but if he did, he brushed them aside. To his way of thinking, a free slave in Charleston had everything he could have possibly wanted. It was clear that, from his perspective, Denmark, ungrateful for the benefits given him as one of the city's freedman, had been carried away by blind ambition.

But perhaps the most astounding feature of the document was the presiding judge's accusation that Denmark had "pervert[ed] the sacred words of God into a sanction for crimes of the blackest hue." He referred, of course, to Denmark's reading scripture as an indictment of slavery. The Bible, the judge continued, was imparted to humankind in order to "reconcile us to our destinies on earth" and to encourage us to discharge our duties with "fidelity." His insinuation was transparent. Some people—blacks—were destined by God to be slaves, while others—whites—were destined to be their masters. For good measure, the judge cited St. Paul's instructions to servants to obey their masters (Ephesians 6:5) as a counter to Denmark's interpretation of scripture.

Apparently inspired by his own appeal to religious rhetoric, the judge concluded his remarks to Denmark by expressing the fervent hope that the condemned rebel would acknowledge his sins "as red as scarlet" and reconcile with God before his execution. "You cannot have forgotten the history of the malefactor on the Cross," the judge intoned, "who, like yourself, was the wretched and deluded victim of offended justice." And he concluded with the earnest plea that Denmark, during his final moments, would come to imitate the thief's contrition.

A twenty-first-century reader of this extraordinary document is tempted to suspect that the judge was speaking cynically; surely he could not have actually believed that the Bible justified slavery, that a freed slave would be happy while his children were in bondage, or that any black person, free or enslaved, had the wherewithal to conduct himself or herself with "great art and plausibility" in a courtroom. But such an interpretation would be mistaken, for the judge, like the vast majority of his fellow Southerners—and a good percentage of Northerners, for that matter—was perfectly serious. His response helps explain why Southerners were often bewildered and felt a sense of betrayal, in addition to panic at the thought of "anarchy and confusion in their most horrid forms," when they discovered a plot on the part of blacks to revolt. To their minds, it seemed like callous ingratitude.

ANNOTATED BIBLIOGRAPHY

Aptheker, Herbert. *American Negro Slave Revolts*, 50th anniversary ed. New York: International Publishers, 1993. A pioneering history of slave conspiracies and revolts. Sometimes criticized for its leftist perspective and overreliance on newspaper accounts, the book nonetheless remains a classic.

Bontemps, Arna. *Black Thunder*. Boston, MA: Beacon Press, 2003. A novel about Gabriel Prosser's 1800 conspiracy, originally published in 1936. Bontemps argues that many of Prosser's followers believed the plot to take Richmond failed because of Gabriel's lack of religion.

Brown, Roger Lyle. "Last Stand for Freedom in Florida: The Story of Negro Fort," in Y. N. Kly (ed.), *The Invisible War: The African American Anti-Slavery Resistance from the Stono Rebellion through the Seminole Wars*. Atlanta, GA: Clarity Press, 2006: 24–45.

Covington, James. "The Negro Fort." *Gulf Coast Historical Review* 5 (1990): 78–91. Origins and destruction of Negro Fort.

Davis, Thomas J. *A Rumor of Revolt: The "Great Negro Plot" in Colonial New York.* Amherst: University of Massachusetts Press, 1990. Narrative history of the 1741 conspiracy. Davis, unlike some historians, argues for the reality of the plot.

Delaney, Martin R. *Blake, or the Huts of America*. Boston, MA: Beacon Press, 1970. Published in serial form in 1861–1862, a novel about a black rebel who foments revolt in the Southern states and eventually founds a black republic in Cuba.

Dillon, Merton L. *Benjamin Lundy and the Struggle for Negro Freedom*. Urbana: University of Illinois Press, 1966. Biography of the abolitionist editor of

The Genius of Universal Emancipation who was physically beaten for defending a slave revolt aboard the ship *Decatur*.

Dorman, James H. "The Persistent Specter: Slave Rebellion in Territorial Louisiana." *Louisiana History* 18 (1977): 389–404. Anxiety and paranoia in slave-holding communities, especially after the German Coast revolt.

Egerton, Douglas R. *Gabriel's Rebellion: The Virginia Slave Conspiracies of 1800 and 1802*. Chapel Hill: University of North Carolina Press, 1993. The bulk of the book deals with Prosser's conspiracy, with four additional chapters about a later and minor conspiracy in Halifax, Virginia.

Egerton, Douglas R. *He Shall Go Out Free: The Lives of Denmark Vesey*, rev. ed. Lanham, MD: Rowman & Littlefield, 2004. The best study of Vesey's conspiracy to revolt.

French, Scott. *The Rebellious Slave: Nat Turner in American Memory*. Boston, MA: Houghton Mifflin, 2004. A good study of the various ways in which the Turner rebellion has been remembered. French also argues that the revolt was part of a larger conspiracy.

Genovese, Eugene D. *From Rebellion to Revolution: Afro-American Slave Revolts in the Making of the Modern World*. Baton Rouge: Louisiana State University Press, 2006. Originally published in 1976, Genovese argues that slave conspiracies and revolts were driven by the ideals of eighteenth-century revolutionary movements.

Genovese, Eugene D. *Roll, Jordan, Roll: The World the Slaves Made*. New York: Vintage, 1976. Magisterial study of slave life in the antebellum South. Especially pertinent is Book IV's discussion of slave revolts and resistance.

Greenberg, Kenneth S. (ed.). *Nat Turner: A Slave Rebellion in History and Memory*. New York: Oxford University Press, 2004. Excellent collection of essays on the rebellion, covering topics as diverse as the reliability of Turner's "Confessions" and the symbolic significance of mutilating the corpses of rebels.

Greenberg, Kenneth S. (ed.) *The Confessions of Nat Turner and Related Documents*. Boston, MA: Bedford/St. Martin's, 1996. Convenient collection that includes Turner's "Confessions" as well as contemporary newspaper accounts of the rebellion, trial records, and private letters. Very good "Introduction" by the editor.

Hendrick, George and Willene Hendrick. *The Creole Mutiny: A Tale of Revolt Aboard a Slave Ship*. Chicago, IL: Ivan R. Dee, 2008. A narrative history of the 1841 ship revolt and its aftermath. Suffers from a lack of source documentation.

Hendrick, George and Willene Hendrick (eds). *Two Slave Rebellions at Sea.* St. James, NY: Brandywine Press, 2000. Reproduces, with "Introduction," two nineteenth-century short stories inspired by revolts aboard slave ships: Frederick Douglass's "The Heroic Slave" and Herman Melville's "Benito Cereno."

Higginson, Thomas Wentworth. *Black Rebellion: Five Slave Revolts.* New York: Da Capo Press, 1998. An edition of a leading nineteenth-century abolitionist's description of slave revolts, including Gabriel Prosser's, Denmark Vesey's, and Nat Turner's. Not historically reliable, but offers a glimpse into the mind of a period opponent of slavery.

Hoffer, Peter Charles. *Cry Liberty: The Great Stono River Slave Rebellion of 1739.* New York: Oxford University Press, 2012. Revisionist history that argues that the Stono rebellion may have been sparked by a burglary gone bad.

Hoffer, Peter Charles. *The Great New York Conspiracy of 1741: Slavery, Crime, and Colonial Law.* Lawrence: University Press of Kansas, 2003. A lawyer by training, Hoffer focuses on the legal case against the accused conspirators.

Johnston, James Hugo. "The Participation of White Men in Virginia Negro Insurrections." *Journal of Negro History* 16 (April 1931), 158–167. Explores both rumored and real black-white involvement in revolts and conspiracy to revolt.

Jones, Howard. "The Peculiar Institution and National Honor: The Case of the Creole Slave Revolt." *Civil War History* 21 (1975), 28–50. Focuses on American fury at British refusal to respect human "property" aboard the *Creole*.

Jordan, Winthrop D. *Tumult and Silence at Second Creek: An Inquiry into a Civil War Slave Conspiracy*, rev. ed. Baton Rouge: Louisiana State University, 1995. The only account of an 1861 conspiracy triggered by the outbreak of civil war. Sometimes criticized as being too speculative.

Kennedy, Lionel H. and Thomas Parker. *An Official Report of the Trials of Sundry Negroes Charged with an Attempt to Raise an Insurrection in the State of South-Carolina.* Charleston, SC: James R. Schenck, 1822. An account, complete with trial transcripts, of Denmark Vesey's conspiracy.

Lepore, Jill. *New York Burning: Liberty, Slavery, and Conspiracy in Eighteenth-Century Manhattan.* New York: Alfred A. Knopf, 2005. A social history of the 1841 conspiracy that argues for no fewer than four other in colonial New York.

Lofton, John. *Denmark Vesey's Revolt: The Slave Plot That Lit a Fuse to Fort Sumter.* Kent, OH: Kent State University Press, 1983. Despite the hyperbolic subtitle, a good account of the conspiracy that illuminates South Carolina culture in the early nineteenth century.

Nicholls, Michael L. *Whispers of Rebellion: Narrating Gabriel's Conspiracy.* Charlottesville: University of Virginia Press, 2013. Argues that Prosser's rebellion was less Enlightenment-values driven than conventionally supposed.

Northup, Solomon. *Twelve Years a Slave.* Baton Rouge: Louisiana State University Press, 1996. Reprint of the 1853 memoir of an ex-slave. Northup briefly discusses the Cheneyville conspiracy.

Pearson, Edward A. (ed.). *Designs against Charleston: The Trial Record of the Denmark Vesey Slave Conspiracy of 1822.* Although severely criticized for "unrelenting Carelessness," Pearson's book is still worth a cautious consultation.

Porter, Kenneth W. *The Black Seminoles: History of a Freedom-Seeking People.* Revised and edited by Alcione M. Amos and Thomas P. Senter. Gainesville: University Press of Florida, 1996. Useful resource for the events surrounding Negro Fort and the First Seminole War.

Rasmussen, Daniel. *American Uprising: The Untold Story of America's Largest Slave Revolt.* New York: Harper Perennial, 2011. Narrative history of the German Coast rebellion.

Robertson, David. *Denmark Vesey.* New York: Vintage, 1999. Narrative history of Vesey's conspiracy and trial. Chapters 8 and 9 focus on historical memory of Vesey as a black leader.

Rodriguez, Junius P. " 'Always En Garde': The Effects of Slave Insurrection upon the Louisiana Mentality, 1811–1815." *Louisiana History* 33 (1992), 39–416. The German Coast rebellion and its aftermath.

Rodriguez, Junius P. "Complicity and Deceit: Lewis Cheney's Plot and Its Blood Consequences," in Michael A. Bellesiles (ed.), *Lethal Imagination: Violence and Brutality in American History.* New York: New York University Press, 1999, 139–147.

Rodriguez, Junius P. (ed.). *Encyclopedia of Slave Resistance and Rebellion.* 2 Vols. Westport, CT: Greenwood Press, 2007. Indispensable research tool.

The second volume offers an appendix of primary documents relating to slave conspiracies and revolts.

Sale, Maggie Montesinos. *The Slumbering Volcano: American Slave Ship Revolts and the Production of Rebellious Masculinity*. Durham, NC: Duke University Press, 1997. An analysis of nineteenth-century debates about whether blacks had political rights by examining public receptions to two actual, and two fictional, slave ship revolts.

Schwarz, Philip J. (ed.). *Gabriel's Conspiracy: A Documentary History*. Charlottesville: University of Virginia Press, 2012. Excellent compilation of documents from the trials of Gabriel Prosser and his co-conspirators.

Smith, Mark M. (ed.). *Stono: Documenting and Interpreting a Southern Slave Revolt*. Columbia: University of South Carolina Press, 2005. Collects primary source material about the Stono rebellion as well as four modern interpretive essays.

Stowe, Harriet Beecher. *Dred: A Tale of the Great Dismal Swamp*. New York: Penguin, 2000. Nearly as popular in Stowe's day as her *Uncle Tom's Cabin*, a novel in which Dred is a maroon who incites rebellion. Of particular interest is the ongoing debate between Dred and the character Millie about the morality of slave revolts.

Styron, William. *The Confessions of Nat Turner*. New York: Signet, 1966. Pulitzer Prize–winning novel about the rebellion that seeks to express, through the ruminations of the main character, the horrors of American slavery.

Tragle, Henry Irving (ed.). *The Southampton Slave Revolt of 1831*. New York: Vintage, 1973. A larger collection of source material than Greenberg's, including a wide range of newspaper accounts and the complete record of the trials.

Wasserman, Adam. *A People's History of Florida 1513–1876: How Africans, Seminoles, Women, and Lower Class Whites Shaped the Sunshine State*. CreateSpace, 2009. Good account of Negro Fort.

Wood, Peter H. *Black Majority: Negroes in Colonial South Carolina from 1670 through the Stono Rebellion*. New York: W. W. Norton, 1974. A social history of colonial South Carolina's slave culture. The final chapter deals with Stono uprising.

INDEX

About the Author

Kerry Walters, PhD, is the William Bittinger Professor of Philosophy and professor of peace and justice studies at Gettysburg College. He is the award-winning author of 38 books, including ABC-CLIO's *Lincoln, the Rise of the Republicans, and the Coming of the Civil War: A Reference Guide* and *The Underground Railroad: A Reference Guide.*